395

TWENTY TREMENDOUS YEARS

We are all of us defending . . . a cause,
. . . the cause of freedom and justice;
of the weak against the strong;
law against violence;
mercy and tolerance against brutality and iron-bound tyranny

Winston S. Churchill

December 5th 1942

Edited by Paul Tabori

TWENTY TREMENDOUS YEARS
WORLD WAR II AND AFTER

McBride Books   New York

Published 1962 by
Medill McBride Co., Inc.

Library of Congress Catalog Card
62 — 13539

DESIGNED AND PRINTED IN GREAT BRITAIN
BY JARROLD AND SONS LTD, NORWICH

Introduction

IN THIS GALLERY of politicians and soldiers, of dictators and heroes, of traitors and saints, of film-stars and explorers, the reader will find the mid-twentieth century mirrored faithfully—if not from every angle and in every mood. And if the total shows bias, perhaps this is an acceptable one to those who believe in basic human principles that have carried men from anarchy to at least a semblance of order and dignity.

The first quarter of the book is devoted to war—the greatest, most devastating and terrible war in history. A war that could not be avoided once the free world realized that a dictator could not stop if he wanted to remain a dictator. For Britain and America this was a hard lesson to learn; France and most of Europe learned it too late.

The other three-quarters of this volume covers the search for peace that began half-way through the war and is still very far from its end. For every country that gained its independence, for better or for worse, since 1945, another has been enslaved. If this book can be said to take any sides, it has been on the basic idea that without freedom, no progress and no material achievement is of much avail. It is impossible to be completely objective within this framework. You cannot be neutral about an earthquake or unprejudiced about a plague.

I would like to offer my sincere gratitude to the Imperial War Museum and the *Daily Express* Picture Library for their most valuable assistance; and to Miss Marion Shapiro who gave me most efficient help in research and selection of material.

PAUL TABORI
London, January 1961

Daily Express Photonews wish to make acknowledgement to the following for the use of additional pictures:

Aerofilms Ltd., The Associated Press, Barratt's Photo Press Ltd., Cecil Beaton, *BIPPA*, Boeing Airplane Company, Camera Press, John A. Carruthers, Jr., Central Press Photos Ltd., The *Chicago Sun Times*, Columbia Pictures, *Daily Mail*, Clayton Evans, Fox Photos, Gaumont-British Picture Corporation, General Photographic Agency, *The Guardian*, 'Harlip', Imperial War Museum, International News Photos, Phillip Jackson-Camera Press, Karsh of Ottawa-Camera Press, Keystone Press Agency Ltd., Kosmos Press Bureau (London) Ltd., Lafayette Ltd., *Life* Magazine, Studio Lisa, London Express News & Feature Services, London News Agency, Angus McBean, National Film Archives-British Film Institute, National Film Board Photos, *News Chronicle* Reference Library, *New York Times*, P.A.-Reuter, Paris-Match, Pictorial Press Ltd., Planet News, Photographic News Agencies, Paul Popper Ltd., Press Photo Combine, Press Portrait Bureau, Radio Times Hulton Picture Library, Reynolds/ACME/Combine, Rizzoli Press Service Milan, Houston Roger, *Soviet Weekly*, *Sunday Express*, Sport and General Press Agency, F. A. Swaine, Tass Agency, *The Times*, Topical Press Agency, United Press, United States Navy, Universal Pictorial Press, War Office Photos, Wide World Photos, Maynard Frank Wolfe.

The frontispiece is reproduced from a painting by A. Pán by courtesy of Frost & Reed Ltd., Fine Art Publishers, Bristol and London.

1939
to 1941
Europe
at War

For the second time in the lives of most of us we are at war. Over and over again we have tried to find a peaceful way out of the differences between ourselves and those who are now our enemies. But it has been in vain. We have been forced into a conflict. For we are called, with our allies, to meet the challenge of a principle which, if it were to prevail, would be fatal to any civilized order in the world.

September 3, 1939 KING GEORGE VI

The friendship of the peoples of Germany and the Soviet Union, cemented by blood, has every reason to be lasting and firm.

December 21, 1939 STALIN

France is in need of defeat. Defeat is necessary for her regeneration. Victory would strengthen the political régime which has led to her moral ruin. Anything is preferable to the continuation of so perfidious a régime.

April, 1940 MARSHAL PETAIN

I foresee a British victory but only after a bitter, protracted, monstrously destructive struggle. It will take years.

Late April, 1940 COUNT PAUL TELEKI
(Premier of Hungary)

I have nothing to offer but blood, toil, tears and sweat. . . . We have before us an ordeal of the most grievous kind. . . . You ask, what is our policy? I will say: It is to wage war, by sea, land and air, with all our might and with all the strength that God can give us; to wage war against a monstrous tyranny, never surpassed in the dark, lamentable catalogue of human crime.

May 13, 1940 WINSTON CHURCHILL

Let us therefore brace ourselves to our duty and so bear ourselves that if the British Commonwealth and Empire lasts for a thousand years men will still say, 'This was their finest hour.' June 5, 1940 WINSTON CHURCHILL

When I married my Bert 'e made a nice little 'ome for me. Vawses on the mantelpiece, a gramophone in the corner, everything pretty. When 'e went away to the Army I kept worrying lest the Germans should come and bomb it. Kept on worrying, you know! Then two nights ago they came and bombed it. So now there's nothing more to worry about. See? October, 1940 A SCRUBBING MAID
AT CHARING CROSS HOSPITAL
(Quoted in Sir Philip Gibbs: *The Pageant of the Years*)

Democracy's fight against world conquest is being greatly aided, and must be more greatly aided, by the rearmament of the United States and by sending every ounce and every ton of munitions we can possibly spare to help the defenders who are in the front lines. . . . We must be the great arsenal of democracy. December 29, 1940 F. D. ROOSEVELT

Heaven has not made the world for Britain alone. There is no divine decree that three-quarters of the world should be controlled by one race.

February 24, 1941 HITLER

They said . . .

ON APRIL 20, 1939, Adolf Hitler, the Führer of the German Reich, was fifty. He had told Sir Nevile Henderson that he would rather have war before he was too old.

Britain called it 'Hitler's War'. The Nazi encyclopaedias named it 'the English war against Germany'.

Four months later Hitler and Stalin signed a pact which neither of them intended to keep. And at dawn, on September 1, the German Panzers and bombers struck at Poland. The pattern was set for so many invasions; the first *Blitzkrieg* began.

Der englische Krieg gegen Deutschland

**SOMEONE IS TAKING
SOMEONE FOR A WALK**

On September 3, Neville Chamberlain, his voice trembling with emotion, announced that Britain was at war with Germany. Six hours later France joined us.

Winston Churchill the new First Lord of the Admiralty, goes to war.

The United States, in the third year of Roosevelt's second term, was more interested in Ann Sheridan, the 'Oomph Girl', than in the distant war. The President, however much his heart was on the side of the Allies, had to step warily. Bundists, America-Firsters and Communists all joined forces to keep America neutral—each for their own purpose.

'Athenia' survivors brought ashore at an Irish port

A few hours after Mr. Chamberlain spoke, German U-boats struck in the North Atlantic. The passenger ship Athenia, laden with British and American citizens bound for the United States, was sunk. One hundred and twenty-eight lost their lives.

On the Polish plains the weather favoured the invader. Polish cavalry charged German tanks. In twenty-eight days it was all over with the surrender of Warsaw. Long before that the Russians had started to move. In three days they reached the Hungarian frontier. The fourth partition of Poland had taken place.

In the streets of Warsaw the Wehrmacht turn light artillery on Polish homes

In Britain the evacuation of children from London began; men in bowler hats dug trenches in the parks.

On Monday, September 4, in the first British air raid of the war, the R.A.F. struck at the German bases of Wilhelmshaven

The land war was confined to the East. After the carving-up of Poland came the rape of the Baltic States. The first Jewish ghetto was established at Lublin; Prague quivered under martial law, with hundreds of Czech students shot and deported. Late in November Russia invaded Finland. But the Finns were prepared and winter was their ally: they stood their ground at first and threw back the overwhelming forces.

Under Lord Gort (second from right) the British Expeditionary Force landed in France and the 'phoney war' of 1939–40 began

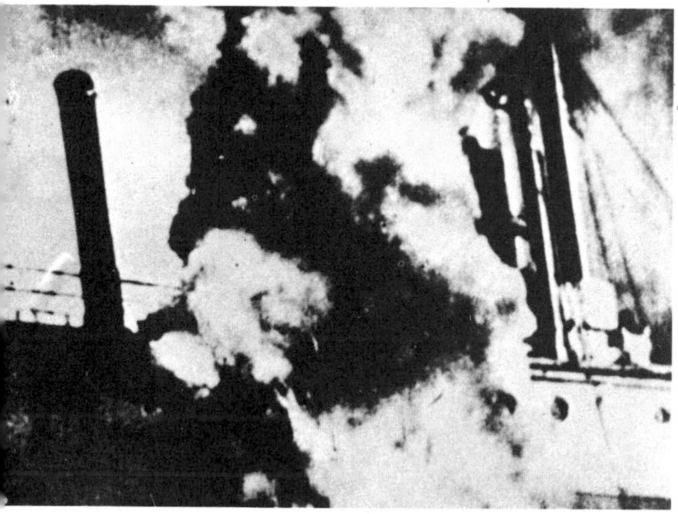

Strike one
The *Royal Oak*—sunk at Scapa Flow by U-W7.

In the West the action was naval. A German U-boat sneaked into Scapa Flow and sank the *Royal Oak*; two unarmed liners were torpedoed. The Royal Navy took its revenge in the Battle of the River Plate which ended in the crippling and scuttling of the pocket battleship *Graf Spee*. Her captain committed suicide for the greater glory of the Fatherland.

Strike two
The *Graf Spee* scuttled off Montevideo after the Battle of the River Plate.

New York: Summer 1939. Americans from all parts of the Union visited a costly peacetime World Fair

London: Christmas 1939. Blackout; a curious atmosphere of waiting for the war to begin

The World Fair in New York still drew millions; the Golden Gate International Exhibition opened in San Francisco. America voted limited aid to Britain and France on a 'cash and carry' basis; Finland was given a loan of $10 million and Roosevelt denounced the Russian attack as a 'wanton flouting of law'. But American ships were still forbidden to enter European waters.

Joe Louis knocked out four challengers. *The Grapes of Wrath* headed the best-seller lists, recalling memories of the barely ended Depression. By the end of the year the world was uneasily poised waiting for Hitler to move again. Germany had the initiative.

Ralph Richardson with Merle Oberon, in 'The Lion has Wings', first of many British war films

15

Turning 'Nelson's eye' on the niceties of Norwegian neutrality, the Royal Navy trapped the German prison-ship 'Altmark' in a fjord and made headlines throughout the free world

THE WINTER OF 1940 was harsh and when butter, bacon and sugar went on the ration, it didn't become any easier. The Thames froze for the first time since 1814.

After ten weeks' resistance, the Mannerheim Line broke and less than a month later the Finns and Russians signed a peace treaty in Moscow. Roosevelt asked for wartime powers and planned to build 150 ships for his Navy at a cost of $250 million. But America was still more interested in J. P. Morgan & Co. becoming a public company or the unmasking of Murder Inc., a business organization of hired killers. Despite Presidential warnings the people felt that war was remote from them personally.

Sumner Welles returned to the United States announcing the failure of a peace mission. The following day the U.S. Army disclosed the development of the Flying Fortress a future major Allied weapon in the liberation

Daladier resigned in France and Paul Reynaud took over. Then came spring—and Neville Chamberlain's sadly 'clouded crystal ball' speech about Hitler having missed the bus. Four days later, in the blustery month of April, the Germans invaded Denmark and Norway using force and trickery in equal measure. The world added a new word to its black vocabulary; Vidkun Quisling became the prototype of traitors and fifth columnists. The first Battle of Narvik began; within five days the British had landed in Norway. It was too little and too late; in less than a month the two Scandinavian countries were overrun, though the Allies gained the Faroes and Iceland as bases.

Hitler and Mussolini met on the Brenner Pass to discuss Italy's entry into the war

The searing trail of war—Namsos, Norway—one of the first of many cities in Western Europe razed by Nazi bombs

The third instalment of the *Blitzkrieg* started with the invasion of the Low Countries and Luxembourg. More than a square mile of Rotterdam was destroyed by the *Luftwaffe* (*above*) and within a week the Dutch Army surrendered. Holland, another European country with a peaceful tradition, fell to the Nazis.

Stukas dive-bombed civilians and retreating soldiers (*below*). All Europe crouched in ditches. The Germans drove on towards the coast and the English Channel.

At Westminster Leopold Amery spoke. To the Prime Minister he said, 'We are fighting today for our life, for our liberty, for our all; we cannot go on being led as we are.' He ended on a Cromwellian note: 'You have sat too long here for any good you have been doing. Depart, I say, and let us have done with you. In the name of God, go.'

A vote of censure was passed on May 10 and Neville Chamberlain resigned. Winston Churchill became Prime Minister. Chamberlain was appointed Lord President of the Council, until, in October, ill-health compelled his resignation. On November 9, he died and was buried in Westminster Abbey.

A British Government was formed which realized that only those who were powerful in the air could hope for victory. Lord Beaverbrook was appointed Minister of Aircraft Production and the industrial power of Britain was applied at full stretch to the task of equipping the R.A.F.

On May 13, the new Prime Minister spoke to the House of Commons, saying 'I have nothing to offer but blood, toil, tears and sweat. . . . You ask what is our policy? It is to wage war. . . . You ask, what is our aim? I can answer in one word, Victory—victory at all costs. . . .'

The little ships, the Royal Navy and the B.E.F., assembled at Dunkirk beach

Elderly gentlemen paraded with rifles

There were plenty of quislings in the West. Marshal Pétain became Vice-Premier in France and the Third Republic began to disintegrate. By May 25, the Germans had surrounded the Belgian Army, large French forces and most of the B.E.F. Calais fell and the Belgians capitulated though their exile Government in Paris repudiated King Leopold.

Then came the epic of the little boats—for a whole week there was a shuttle-service between the East Coast and the teeming beaches of Dunkirk. Over 300,000 British, French and Belgian troops were saved—but all their equipment was lost. The not so merry month of May ended with the Allies in desperate peril.

All Europe was on the march to an unknown destination

The Germans enter Paris—the empty Place de la Concorde echoes the hooves of cavalry

Nor did June bring any relief. Paris was bombed and Churchill made his great fighting speech: 'We shall fight on the beaches, we shall fight in the fields . . . we shall never surrender. . . .' Next day the Battle of France began; on June 10 Italy jumped on the band wagon, declaring war on Britain and France. Churchill flew to Paris, making a dramatic offer for an Anglo-French Union. It was refused. The French armies were retiring across the Marne and the same day when Paris was declared an open city, the Germans entered the capital. Pétain formed a cabinet and announced that his country had asked for armistice terms. For the first time the world heard the name of General De Gaulle when he broadcast from London an appeal for continued French resistance. But whatever resistance there remained, had to go underground.

The tragedy of France ended in Foch's railway carriage at Compiègne where twenty-two years before the Germans had to sign their surrender. Now it was Hitler's turn and he performed a strange little dance of triumph. Pétain choose Laval for his Vice-Premier. The French Government moved to Vichy while De Gaulle was recognized as leader of all free Frenchmen.

General de Gaulle, leader of the Free French

Compiègne: France capitulates

French ships burning after the British attack in North African ports

The surrender of France led to the bitter necessity of the British fighting their former allies: French ships at Oran and Dakar were attacked to prevent them falling into German hands. The Channel Islands were taken by the enemy and Hitler ordered 'Operation Sealion' to be prepared. He was confident that England would capitulate without an invasion.

While the Germans crushed Western Europe, Stalin was gathering the harvest of the Nazi-Soviet Pact in the East. Rumania surrendered two rich provinces; the Baltic States were forced to become part of the U.S.S.R.

In the United States Roosevelt and Wendell Willkie were nominated as Democratic and Republican candidates for the Presidency. In November Roosevelt was elected to his third term, carrying thirty-eight States out of the forty-eight. Slowly and reluctantly America moved towards moral and material support of Britain and the Commonwealth. She built warships, prepared joint defence plans with Canada, passed a Selective Service Bill—for which 16 million Americans registered—and by the end of the year had not only swapped sea and air bases in Newfoundland, the West Indies and British Guiana for fifty destroyers, but, through the system of lend-lease had become the true 'Arsenal of Democracy'.

Wendell Willkie in Britain

After the raid—on the threshold of the Bank of England

Britain stood alone and she was in the front line. The Battle of Britain began on July 10, 1940, with an attack on South Wales docks, on Channel shipping and airfields. The daylight attacks on London started on September 7; on the same night came the first nocturnal blitz. The toll of that first night was 306 killed, 1337 seriously injured; and the death-roll mounted all through the rest of the year. But by the end of August the Germans had lost the decisive struggle and almost 2400 of their planes were destroyed or damaged.

Churchill could proudly say: 'Never in the field of human conflict was so much owed by so many to so few. . . .'

The young pilots of the Spitfires and Hurricanes had frustrated Hitler's plans; the invasion of England, by sea, fixed for September 21, was first postponed and then abandoned.

'Scramble'—R.A.F. pilots run to their fighting planes

FIRST HOUR

SECOND HOUR

THIRD HOUR

FOURTH AND FOLLOWING HOURS

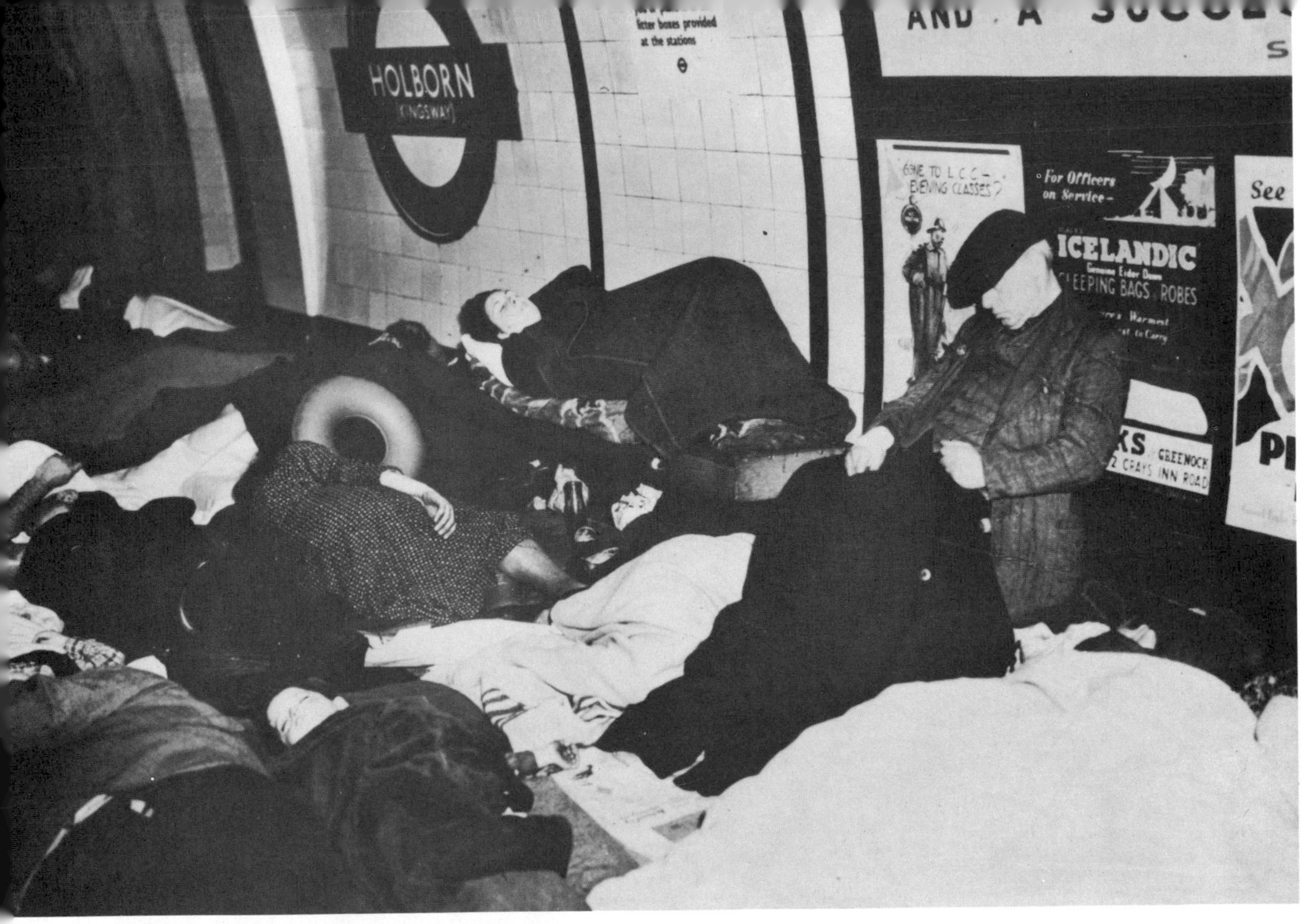

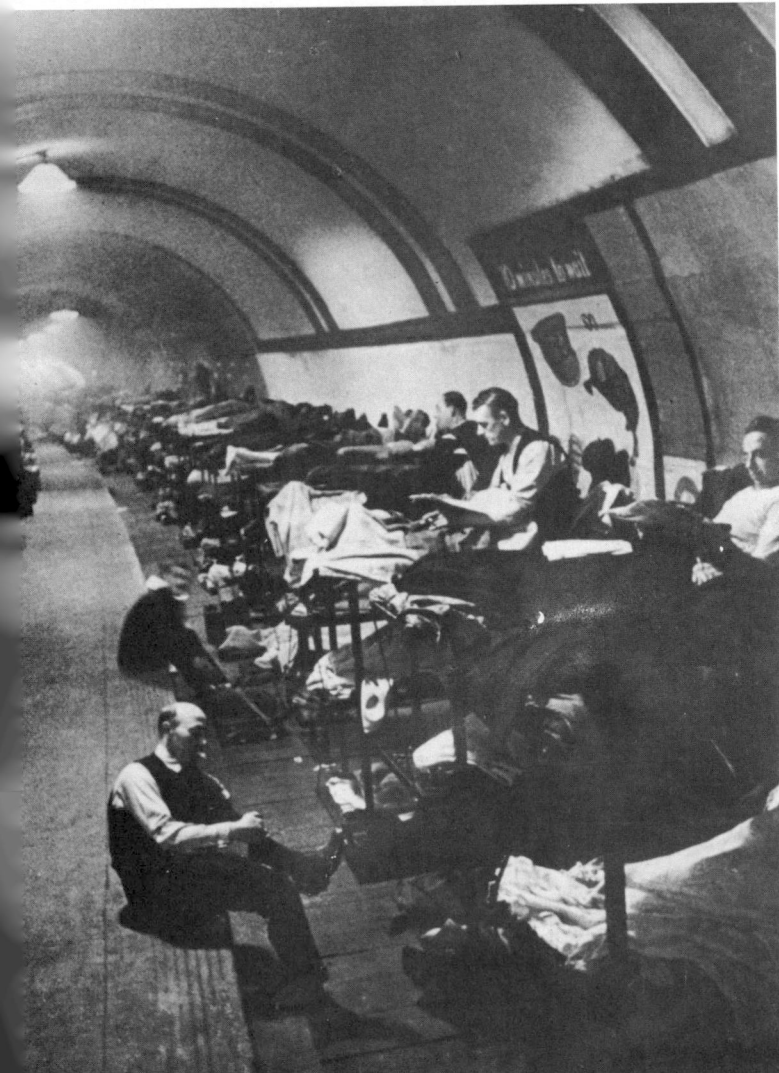

London was quivering under the blows of the *Luftwaffe*: Buckingham Palace, the Guildhall, a whole group of Wren churches, many famous buildings were destroyed or damaged by high explosive and fire. Everybody had a bomb-story to tell; wardens and heavy rescue workers, ambulance drivers and fireguards became the heroes of the Home Front. Wiser than its masters, the people took over the tubes and turned the underground platforms into home-from-home with family compounds, concert parties and cosy squalor.

A thousand people were killed by Nazi bombs in Coventry and the Cathedral was destroyed in a night of frightfulness

Hitler and Franco met secretly and the Caudillo declared that 'Spain will fight at Germany's side'

In the Balkans the Nazi influence grew. King Carol of Rumania abdicated in favour of his son Michael. Germany rewarded Bulgaria's aid with the Dobruja. Antonescu set up an Iron Guard dictatorship in Bucharest. Then came Mussolini's ill-conceived invasion of Greece; the 3rd Alpini Division was trapped in the Pindus gorges and by the end of the year the Greeks had swept the Italians from their country. Yugoslavia and Hungary signed a pact of 'eternal friendship' which was to last less than six months. Germany, Italy and Japan signed a ten-year pact of the 'New Order' in Berlin.

The Royal Navy bombarded Cherbourg and the Fleet Air Arm crippled the Italian Fleet in Taranto Harbour. Hungary also joined the Tripartite Axis Pact; so did Rumania, where German troops were preparing to attack Greece. In Africa the first Western Desert offensive opened and made moderate gains.

War was still far away from America's thoughts. The domestic headlines were occupied with the starting of *PM*, a new style newspaper without advertisements, with the three years sentence on M. L. Annenberg, a Philadelphia publisher, for $1·2 million tax evasion; with the unmasking of Gerhard A. Westrick, the top Nazi agent in the U.S. in his Westchester home; with the death of Senator Ernest Lundeen and twenty-four others in an aeroplane crash and the powder plant explosion at Kenvil, New Jersey, which claimed forty-three victims. There was a twelve-day strike at the Vultee aircraft plant and John L. Lewis, the powerful labour leader, resigned—as he pledged to do if Roosevelt was re-elected. 'The Star-Spangled Banner' was played after each theatrical performance and Kate Smith sang 'God Bless America'. Talullah Bankhead's father died; so did Mrs. W. K. Vanderbilt and Gatti-Casazza, Caruso's friend and Tom Mix, the cowboy star.

The autumn and winter months saw the widening of the blitz. The R.A.F.'s early leaflet raids over Germany now changed into sharp though small-scale attacks—Berlin, Cologne and Düsseldorf being the main targets.

Britain snuggled up in the shelters with a good book. There was Rauschning's *Hitler Speaks*, Howard Spring's *Fame is the Spur*, Graham Greene's *The Power and the Glory*, Fred Kitchen's *Brother to the Ox*, Upton Sinclair's *World's End*—not to mention T. H. White's *The Witch in the Wood*. Chaplin made his first talkie, cocking a snoot at *The Great Dictator*. Hollywood made *The Grapes of Wrath* and *Our Town*. Everybody was singing 'Roll Out The Barrel'.

In December there was a large banner in Piccadilly. It said, defiantly: 'Christmas is 1940 years old and Hitler is only fifty-one. He can't spoil our Christmas.'

Royal Exiles: King George of Greece and King Peter of Yugoslavia

U.S. destroyer—a bundle for Britain

AFRICA PROVIDED THE main news as the year 1941 opened. The British invaded Eritrea and Italian Somaliland; when Benghazi fell, six senior Italian generals and a large part of the Italian forces in Africa were swept into the net. Parachutists landed in Calabria and did considerable damage; Genoa was bombarded by British warships and by the middle of February there was no Italian left on Egyptian, Sudanese or Kenya soil except as a prisoner. In March British Somaliland was regained and the Battle of Cape Matapan crippled the Italian fleet. But by the end of the month the Axis counter-offensive had started.

In occupied Europe life was harsh. The Americans sent food to the French children and Britain let it pass through the blockade.

Hitler and Mussolini met again to make plans for the Balkans. The Italian offensive which opened in Albania in March was halted by the Greeks within a week. Yugoslavia's pro-Axis government signed the Tripartite Pact—but two days later the country revolted. Young King Peter took over at dawn from his uncle, Prince Paul; another four days and diplomatic relations were broken off between Germany and Yugoslavia.

The blitz raged with renewed force. Swansea had one of the heaviest raids in February; Portsmouth, the Merseyside and Clydeside were battered in March and there was a very heavy raid on London. The R.A.F. struck back at Berlin, Hamburg and Düsseldorf. Malta began to earn the glory of the George Cross Island as a target of almost unbroken attacks.

Fall of Tobruk: the Australians took over 35,000 Italian prisoners

Churchill called to the U.S.A.: 'Give us the tools and we will finish the job.' John Winant, as American Ambassador to Britain, smoothed the way to this; Malcolm Macdonald, as High Commissioner in Canada, worked for the closer co-operation of the U.S.A. and the great Dominion.

With the coming of spring the pace of the conflict quickened. In Libya and Cyrenaica the British had to withdraw from Benghazi and the Australians retreated to Tobruk. By the end of April Axis forces had crossed the Egyptian frontier and had captured Sollum though Tobruk held out behind their lines. For many weary weeks the battles see-sawed on the frontier with only limited gains on either side.

Elsewhere in Africa the Imperial Forces had better luck. They occupied Eritrea and freed Addis Ababa; Haile Selassie was the first exiled monarch to return in triumph to his country. By the middle of May the Italian forces in Abyssinia, commanded by the Duke of Aosta, had surrendered.

A dangerous situation was nipped in the bud when Rashid Ali staged a pro-Axis *coup d'état* in Iraq which was supported by Italian and German aircraft. Habbaniyah, the R.A.F. base, was attacked by the Iraqi rebel forces

June 10, 1941: clothes rationing

and they occupied all refineries and oil installations. But at the end of May the revolt collapsed and Rashid Ali fled to Iran. Imperial and Free French Forces entered Syria in June and found little resistance; General Catroux was appointed Commander-in-Chief in the Levant.

There was no spring of gladness in Britain. Income tax rose to ten shillings and post-war credits were introduced; women registered under the Employment Order; with June 1 came clothes rationing. The air-raids continued with little interruption: Coventry was heavily bombed for two nights running, in mid-April an equally heavy raid on London damaged St. Paul's. Liverpool had a whole week of shattering attacks; in another London night of blitz the House of Commons, Westminster Hall, Westminster Abbey and School and the British Museum were hit. The R.A.F. struck back with limited forces: Berlin had the heaviest raid of the war up to date; Hamburg, Cologne, the Ruhr and Rhineland were raided for twenty consecutive nights.

In the Balkans there was nothing but disaster. The Germans destroyed most of Belgrade when their invasion started at dawn, on April 6. Bulgaria joined in the attack. Count Paul Teleki, the Hungarian Premier committed suicide rather than agree to the violation of the solemn pact of friendship he had signed. Within four days the Nazi forces had reached Monastir in Yugoslavia and the Florina Gap in Greece. On April 13 they occupied Belgrade and Yugoslavia capitulated; so did the Greek forces in Epirus and Macedonia. Athens came under martial law; Korizis, the Greek Prime Minister killed himself and three days later Tsouderos, his successor, asked the British troops to leave Greece. By the end of the month the Germans had occupied Athens and it took them only two weeks to capture all the Aegean islands. The invasion of Crete came next; Canea fell within a week and the Greek royal family had to flee again, this time to the safety of Egypt.

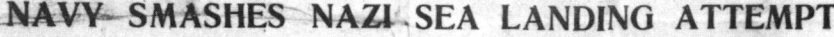

Published in Canea by Creforce

Editorial Office
Fernleaf House
Canea
Telephone 460

THURSDAY
22
MAY 1941
Sunrise 5.18
Sunset 7.52

THE FIRST BRITISH PAPER PUBLISHED IN CRETE

Vol 1   No 3   CANEA, CRETE   Price 2 Drachmas — Free to troops

NAVY SMASHES NAZI SEA LANDING ATTEMPT

BIG CONVOY SUNK LAST NIGHT

THOUSANDS OF GERMAN REINFORCEMENTS DROWNED

German convoys packed with troops and heading for the coast of Crete were intercepted and sunk by the Royal Navy last night. The convoys, heading towards the island in the darkness at full speed, were picked out by searchlights. Whole broadsides were fired at them and ship after ship caught fire and sank. Ammunition vessels exploded. The red glow of burning vessels could be seen clearly from the island.

The Navy continued their hunt throughout the night. Thousands of German troops and great quantities of stores, including guns, ammunition and almost certainly tanks were sent to the bottom.

No German ships reached the Crete shore at all.

VIGOROUS BRITISH COUNTER ATTACKS

Ground attack on Crete from the air with the full force of the Luftwaffe and Nazi parachute troops organisation commenced Tuesday morning. Two days later despite heavy air support of the original attackers we are not only still in possession of the island but have the situation well in hand and Hitler has already lost a large proportion of his crack parachute soldiers he landed in such spectacular style, in the sunny calm of last two days. Both the British and their allies are fighting with a feeling of confidence that they are able to deal with these Germans now that they have come down from their aeroplanes.

AUSTRALIANS PRAISE GREEK ATTACK

SUCCESSFUL ACTION BY COMBINED FORCE

Greek and Cretan troops, fighting side by side with Australians, yesterday gained praise from an Australian Brigadier.

They took part in a counter attack which was completely successful, pushing strong parachute forces out of a position they had managed to seize

After the attack the Brigadier sent in the following despatch:

'Greeks and Cretans did magnificently and our chaps are proud to fight beside them.'

IN GREECE ONCE MORE

Memories, terrible and romantic are jerked throughout the Old Worthy the spectacle of the Greeks and British fighting side by side. History is being repeated, and we appear to be back in those exciting days of the early nineteenth century when Byron led an international crusade to restore Greece to sovereign independence.

Greece was once beloved as the once impregnable Gibraltar of civilisation against the inroads of barbarism. One of the most altruistic of Great Britain's leading phil-Hellenes was the poet Byron. The scenery in these mountains and seas under the face of Helen "launched a thousand ships" for the siege of Troy.

THE EYES OF THE WORLD ARE ON US

The battle of Crete is being watched with the greatest possible interest by the outside world. Messages from Egypt yesterday indicated that the eyes of Great Britain, America and the whole Empire were fixed on our fighting. News of the invasion was flashed home to Newspapers in Australia, New Zealand and the United Kingdom at once.

There is every indication that the Germans will endeavour to press home the attack today but with the situation as solidly in hand as it was last night we can feel confident of the result. We cannot give further detail for obvious security reasons. Conditions in Canea, Retimo and Heraklion are normal.

The blunt fact is that we can hard fighting yesterday we knocked their first plan askew. We can do the same again for their second and any other they like to produce.

Crete News will continue publishing through out this Blitz as long as the printing press remains undamaged. We cannot guarantee as prompt delivery as in earlier times. We print no news from the outside world because all radios were being used yesterday for the battle. Besides for the present in the outside world, the battle for Crete is the news.

Greek Humiliations

The sultans governed the Greeks cleverly through the clergy, but there were intolerable humiliations. Greek boys were compelled to become Moslems and serve as janissaries or household troops at Constantinople and there were always taxes. In the Greek highlands communities called Karmatoles maintained some kind of autonomy.

Thus was set the stage for a struggle that lasted for a dozen years and has never been surpassed for ferocity on both sides. Many volunteers helped the Greeks and in this liven struggle. He helped to unite the Greek factions. He paid soldiers with his own money.

At the end of the first day of Hitler's attack on Crete we were fully holding our own in all sectors. Counter attacks have been launched with strength against main bodies of his troops still holding out.

Parachute troops were dropped around Canea, Maleme, Retimo, and Heraklion in large numbers and gliders and troop carriers landed at various points. At all points they were dropped were the pick of Hitler's parachute troops It is estimated that at least half of the para-

chute troops available for the attack have already been dropped.

Canea town was heavily bombed throughout the day but military damage was negligible. At least four bombers were brought down by AA fire during the day. Our own casualties in yesterday's fighting were light. We have captured considerable quantities of enemy material. The prisoners taken have been obviously perturbed by the fierce resistance they encountered. In some areas considerable numbers of Germans surrendered.

Front page news in Crete

The battle of Suda Bay—German air power caused severe losses to the Royal Navy

The wreckage of Deputy-Führer Hess's plane after his Scottish crash-landing

On the night of May 10–11, 1941, while London was shivering under a hail of fire and high explosive, a lone pilot took off from Augsburg in a fighter-plane with extra fuel tanks. When he landed on a lonely Scottish moor, he had made history. Rudolf Hess, the Deputy-Führer, had flown to Britain on a confused, half-crazy peace mission. He asked for the Duke of Hamilton whom he had never met but whom he foggily imagined to be the head of a 'peace party'.

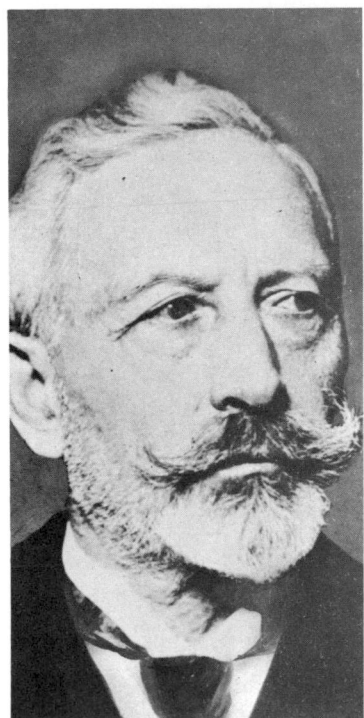

He was both indignant and surprised when he ended up in a well-guarded cell instead of a conference room at 10 Downing Street. Hitler first denied the fact of his 'most stalwart' friend's desertion, then hastily appointed Martin Bormann as his successor.

The battle of the *Bismarck* began on May 24 and lasted four days, four hundred miles west of Brest, until the Royal Navy sunk the great vessel. The ex-Kaiser, dying ten days later at Doorn, may have been thinking of her name-sake the Iron Chancellor whom he had dismissed so curtly.

At Doorn the ex-Kaiser died

Rudolf Hess—visitor from the Reich

Hitler would have had just as little use for the famous Chancellor's advice. His military advisers invoked in vain the all-too-real spectre of war on two fronts: at dawn on June 22 Germany invaded the U.S.S.R., adding another broken treaty to her already full collection. Hess had come to Britain in order to plead for an anti-Communist line-up. Stalin, repeatedly warned by Churchill and others of Germany's hostile intentions, refused to believe them. And so the Nazi blitz hurtled forward across the broad immensity of European Russia. By the end of June they had crossed the River Bug, taken Brest-Litovsk, Vilna, Kaunas and Lwow. The Red State Committee of Defence, headed by Stalin and consisting of Molotov, Voroshilov, Malenkov and Beria was facing a merciless onslaught.

In the U.S. the government seized the *Normandie* with twelve other Vichy ships.

On the day of the German attack on Russia Churchill had broadcast: 'Any State who fights Nazism will have our aid. . . . It follows therefore that we shall give whatever help we can to Russia.'

Germans cross the Berezina; Russian defences are breached

We will never parley, we will never negotiate with Hitler or any of his gang. We shall fight him by land, we shall fight him by sea, we shall fight him in the air, until with God's help we have rid the earth of his shadow and liberated its peoples from his yoke. Any man or State who fights on against Nazidom will have our aid. Any man or State who marches with Hitler is our foe.

June 22 WINSTON CHURCHILL
(On the invasion of Russia)

Vitebsk in flames. A hundred Russian cities shared its fate

Lord Beaverbrook arrives back in London from Moscow where he laid the foundations of all-out aid to the U.S.S.R.

Russia needed help badly. By July 1, the Germans had captured Riga and reached the Berezina; four days later they were at the Dnieper. China broke off relations with the Axis Powers; in London, Russian and Polish representatives met to discuss collaboration against Germany. In the midst of all these world-shattering events Peru and Ecuador had a little three weeks' war of their own. The Russian counter-attacks started in White Russia and on the Latavian frontier; in the middle of July the Battle of Smolensk began, raging for four weeks and Hitler spoke of the division of spoils in conquered territory, saying, 'we now have to face the task of cutting up a giant cake according to our needs'. Bessarabia was evacuated by the Russians and Rundstedt launched his drive towards the Black Sea. In mid-August Marshal Budenny began to withdraw across the Dniester and the German attacks on Leningrad were intensified with Voroshilov's forces within the first ring of the city's defences. The great Dnieper Dam had to be destroyed, Tallinn, the capital of Estonia, fell to Hitler's armies. But by September the Russian counter-attacks began to be effective; from Gomel to Smolensk, from Leningrad and the Valdai Hills to Kharkov they fought back fiercely. They could not stem the German advance; Kiev fell after a battle of forty-five days and German parachutists landed in the Crimea.

A Soviet Military Mission had arrived in London less than three weeks after the German invasion. An Anglo-Soviet agreement was signed in Moscow, stipulating no separate peace with the enemy. A Polish army under General Anders was formed in Russia and in mid-September Lord Beaverbrook, as Minister of Supply, headed a British mission to Moscow. He pledged a whole week's British tank production for Russian use. The British and American delegations completed their work within three days in Moscow and announced that the U.S.S.R. would be provided with almost everything she asked for.

The R.A.F. started a daylight offensive over Europe which went on, almost unbroken, for three weeks, directed mostly against harbours and shipyards in enemy territory; Moscow had its first air-raid. Britain was almost free of bombs—except for Newcastle which had a bad raid in September.

By mid-July Syria and Lebanon were under Allied control. In August British and Russian troops entered Iran with the British in Abadan and the Russians in Tabriz. Iranian resistance only lasted four days; the Shah abdicated and was succeeded by his son. The Allies occupied Teheran and established zones of influence. The Mufti of Jerusalem fled to the Japanese Legation.

'Colonel Britton' of the B.B.C. announced the mobilization of the 'V Army' in occupied Europe; Goebbels made a somewhat clumsy effort to steal the 'V for Victory' sign. Nazi plots were discovered in Argentine, Chile and Cuba. Churchill and Roosevelt met in the North Atlantic and issued a statement of common war aims which became known as the Atlantic Charter. It established the famous Four Freedoms.

Laval and Deat, the French quislings, were wounded at a Versailles military ceremony and a wave of arrests and executions started in France. Canadian, British and Norwegian commandos raided the Spitzbergen, wrecked the coal-mines and brought back the whole Norwegian population.

America occupied bases in Iceland. The Japanese invaded Indo-China; the U.S. denounced them as aggressors, froze their assets, cut off oil-supplies and banned Japanese silk from America. The period of military service was extended—by a single vote—to eighteen months. American merchant ships were to be armed.

'Colonel Britton'—Freedom's spokesman

The birth of the Atlantic Charter—on a battleship in mid-Atlantic

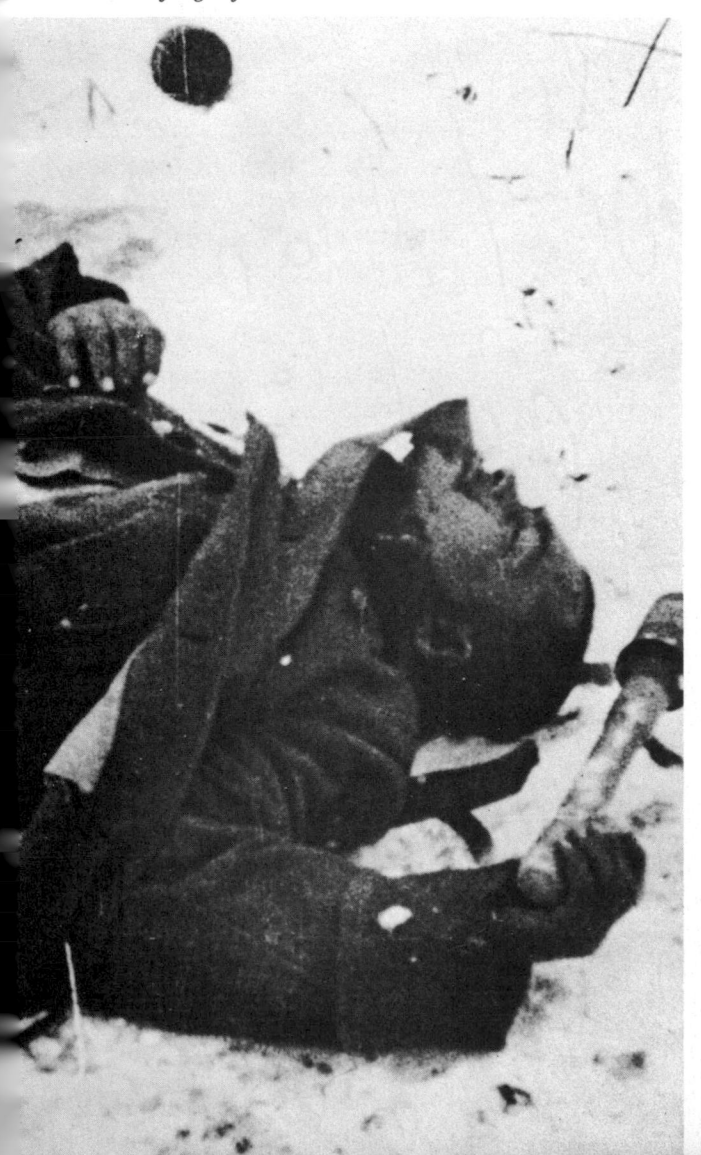

Russian cavalry attack German positions in the snow

General Winter fought for Russia

Early in October Hitler issued an Order of Day: 'Today is the beginning of the last great decisive battle of this year.' The Germans launched a two-pronged attack on Moscow and made substantial gains. Two weeks later the government and the diplomatic corps left Moscow for Kuibyshev. After three weeks' fighting the Germans were within sixty-five miles of Moscow. Kharkov fell to them and they renewed their offensive in the Crimea; by early November they had captured Simferopol, its capital. But by late November the Red Army threw the invaders back at Moscow, retook Rostov and was equally successful at Tula and Mariupol. In December they took the offensive along the whole of the Eastern Front. Five days after the start of their offensive Hitler's forces were in retreat along the entire front, the Russians had landed in the Crimea and proved that General Winter was on their side. Lord Beaverbrook declared in a Manchester speech: 'I put my faith in Stalin's leadership and I believe in Russian resistance.'

In December, the Imperial Forces started their offensive in the Eastern Desert. There had been a daring commando raid, led by young Colonel Keyes, on Rommel's headquarters—the future Field-Marshal escaped by the sheer accident of attending a birthday party. Next day General Cunningham's forces made a fifty miles' gain, driving close to Tobruk. After another five days General Ritchie succeeded in relieving Tobruk. When the tank battle resumed early in December, Rommel drew off; ten days later his front broke and he retreated into Tripolitania.

Rommel, the 'Desert Fox', speaks to his men

Ritchie and Cunningham

Occupied Europe began to fight back against the quislings and the Germans alike. Pétain had ordered the arrest of General Gamelin and of the political leaders, Daladier, Blum, Reynaud and Mandel. When a German major was shot at Bordeaux, the Germans executed fifty hostages; three weeks later the Paris Press announced that two Spaniards had been arrested as the real killers. The commander of the Nantes region was also assassinated and fifty more patriots paid for the death of one Nazi. Rosenberg was appointed Reich Minister for Occupied Eastern Territories and began his terror régime of slave labour and extermination. On the fifth anniversary of the Anti-Comintern pact seven new countries joined it—only one of them (the pro-Japanese puppet government of Nanking) not under German occupation.

Anti-Allies propaganda took many forms in Vichy France

The war in the air was a race of endurance. There were twenty light raids on Britain during November, widespread but not serious, with Merseyside suffering most; the R.A.F. bombed Berlin, Cologne and Mannheim. One of these raids, with 300 planes, was the heaviest attack in the first two years of the war.

The sea-war highlights were the destruction of two large enemy convoys south of Taranto and the sinking of the *Ark Royal*—with a single casualty—in the Straits of Gibraltar.

THEIR OWN DEATH WARRANTS

The day of infamy—Japanese assault on Pearl Harbour

The second great climax of the year was December 7—'a date which will live in infamy', as President Roosevelt put it—when Japanese bombers swooped down on Pearl Harbour, sinking or damaging nineteen ships of the U.S. Pacific Fleet. At the same time they attacked Manila, the International Settlement at Shanghai and targets in Malaya, Thailand and Hong Kong. For a week there had been a state of emergency in Singapore and Hong Kong as reports of Japanese troop concentrations and other warlike moves came in; but Japanese envoys had been negotiating up to the last moment in Washington and the attack followed the Hitler pattern of unprovoked and sudden aggression. The same day all Allied governments declared war on Japan. The Axis front was now complete; the whole world was at war.

The last three weeks of 1941 brought a series of spectacular successes for the Japanese. They landed in Thailand, North-East Malaya and the Philippines. In a single day Thailand ceased resistance. One of Britain's worst blows was the sinking of the *Prince of Wales* and *Repulse* off the Malayan coast. By December 10 Guam had surrendered; after a siege of seventeen days, Hong Kong fell. Within ten days of their attack the Japanese had landed in North Borneo, were within ten miles of Penang and had launched their major attack on the Philippines. Manila was declared an open city which did not save it from heavy air attacks and by the last day of December the Japanese were closing in on the Filipino capital.

A day before Pearl Harbour Britain had declared war on the three German satellites, Hungary, Finland and Rumania. Italy and Germany had declared war on the United States. Two days before Christmas, Churchill, Lord Beaverbrook and British Service chiefs were in Washington to discuss full Allied co-ordination of the war effort. These were dark hours; but at last the two great Anglo-Saxon democracies were full partners in the fight. Admiral Nimitz had replaced Husband E. Kimmel as Commander of the U.S. Pacific Fleet; MacArthur was made a full general and the Americans were jolted into the grim realities of war in the twentieth century. The isolationist illusion was dead.

The end of the 'Prince of Wales' off the coast of Malaya

The death of the 'Repulse', a proud battleship goes down to her doom

The fall of Hong Kong—the first Japanese troops enter the Crown Colony and the 'New Order' comes to Asia

The surrender of Rangoon—Japanese infantrymen march into the Burmese capital

The day before Pearl Harbour Fermi and his fellow-physicists (above) *reached the point in their work on the atomic pile where they realized that an all-out effort was needed and this effort was soon authorized by President Roosevelt*

But while every day brought new shocks it also brought books and films and plays. Disney's *Fantasia* broke new ground; *How Green Was My Valley* won an Oscar for its director John Ford, while Joan Fontaine and Gary Cooper shared the acting awards. The free world was reading Lin Yutang's *With Love and Irony*, Hemingway's *For Whom The Bell Tolls*, James Hilton's *Random Harvest* and Alice Duer Miller's *White Cliffs*

Joan Fontaine won an Oscar

Roddy McDowell in 'How Green Was My Valley'

London 1941: In business—but not quite as usual

1942 to 1945 The World at War

Battle

They said . . .

We came here with hope and determination. We leave here friends in fact, in spirit, and in purpose.

> December. The final sentence of the Teheran declaration, signed by Roosevelt, Stalin, and Churchill

In ten years Hitler has led us from poverty and impotence to victory. He is now leading us to the greatest of victories.

> January 30, 1943 GOERING

Some time next year . . . but it may well be the year after . . . we might beat Hitler, by which I mean beat him and his powers of evil into death, dust and ashes.

> March 21, 1943 WINSTON CHURCHILL

Our first duty is to win the war. But to win the war we must keep the vision of a better future. We must never cease to strive for its fulfilment. No lesser vision will suffice to gain the victory over those who seek world domination and human enslavement.

> May 12, 1944 MACKENZIE KING, P.M. of Canada

The tide has turned. The free men of the world are marching together to victory. I have full confidence in our courage, devotion to duty and skill in battle. We will accept nothing less than full victory.

> June 6, 1944 EISENHOWER'S ORDER OF THE DAY

Only the British and American troops succeeded in carrying out with credit the vast plan of forcing the Channel and effecting the mass landing of troops. History will record this deed as an achievement of the highest order.

> July 14, 1944 STALIN

We shall have failed, and the blood of our dearest will have flowed in vain, if the victory which they died to win does not lead to a lasting peace, founded on justice and good-will. To that, then, let us turn our thoughts, on this day of just triumph and proud sorrow; and then take up our work again, resolved as a people to do nothing unworthy of those who died for us, and to make the world such a world as they would have desired for their children and for ours.

> May 8, 1945 H.M. KING GEORGE VI

I told you hard things at the beginning of these last five years; you did not shrink and I should be unworthy of your confidence and generosity if I did not still cry: Forward, unflinching, unswerving, indomitable, till the whole task is done and the whole world is safe and clean.

> May 13, 1945 WINSTON CHURCHILL

Sir Stafford Cripps went to India

THERE HAS BEEN no other war during which the belligerents thought so much about the peace at its end. Perhaps the Allies had learned from the muddle that followed 1918 and were determined to avoid it. The Atlantic Charter was followed by the United Nations Declaration; on New Year's Day 1942, twenty-six nations signed it in Washington, with Churchill and Roosevelt present. Two weeks later there was a conference of the Allied Governments at St. James's Palace, London, where they pledged themselves to punish the Axis war criminals. A Pan-American Conference in Rio decided to break with Hitler and his allies—with Argentine the sole objector. At the end of January the Chief of Staffs Committee established the Pacific Council in Washington and set up an Anglo-U.S. Combined Raw Materials Board. In February a Master Mutual Aid Agreement was signed between America, Britain, Australia and New Zealand which served as pattern for many others. Sir Stafford Cripps went to India in March to discuss the future of the sub-continent with Indian leaders. In May the twenty-year Anglo-Soviet Treaty was signed in London, providing full co-operation during and after the war. The first Moscow Conference followed in August with Churchill, Harriman and Stalin as chief participants. In November the Allied Ministers of Education held their first meeting in London. In December the Beveridge Report forecast the establishment of the Welfare State, even though no one could foresee the exact date by which anybody could benefit from it. But this time, Britain's leaders wanted to do all they could to bring social justice to their people.

The Anglo-Soviet Alliance: Churchill and Eden meet Molotov and Maisky in London

The surrender of Singapore is signed—another bastion has fallen

It needed faith and courage to start planning a world that presupposed an Allied victory. There was little cheer on the battle fronts. On January 2 the Japanese entered Manila and Cavite Naval Base; there were further landings on the west coast of Malaya. On the night of January 10–11 the Emperor's forces invaded the Netherlands East Indies. Kuala Lumpur fell; New Britain and Borneo were also attacked. Within a few weeks all the Far Eastern bastions had fallen: the naval base of Amboina in the Dutch East Indies, the oil-refineries of Sumatra —and the hardest blow of all—Singapore which surrendered on February 15 with 60,000 British and Imperial prisoners. It seemed that nothing could stop the Rising Sun: Bali, Portuguese Timor, Java, Rangoon, the Andaman Islands, all were occupied by the end of March. Japan threatened to dominate all Asia.

To destroy the white man's prestige the Japanese force Australian soldiers to sweep the streets

In North Africa the see-saw in the Western Desert continued. Bardia was retaken by the Imperial Forces who took 8000 prisoners and liberated 1000 British captives. Rommel's brief counter-attack ended in his withdrawal under cover of a sandstorm. But he started a second counter-offensive and won a tank battle near Agedabia. He took Benghazi: fighting on a larger scale started again in the middle of February.

The Russians did better; they recaptured almost the whole of the Kerch peninsula, returned to the province of Smolensk. Timoshenko's new offensive gained sixty-five miles in ten days and cut German lines, breaking through on a broad front. In the last days of January the attack had carried the Russians into the Ukraine; German resistance stiffened when the Red Army reached White Russia. March saw the launching of a new offensive in the Crimea. The war in the air became greatly intensified. Throughout January the R.A.F. was bombing Germany and the ports of occupied Europe; there were no serious air-raids in the United Kingdom but Malta was still being battered continuously and still holding out.

A gunner's grave in the West African desert

H.M.S. 'Campbeltown' at St. Nazaire—two minutes before being blown up

In February half a dozen German cities were attacked and the continental harbours were also bombed. In the Mediterranean Malta had no respite and the main Allied targets were Sicily and the enemy-held North African strongholds. March brought many daylight sweeps while a few German raiders were over Dover and the South Coast. Malta's ordeal continued; the Allies attacked the Greek islands and Sicily. In the Far East air attacks were used to strategic purposes, mainly against Japanese shipping.

In the vast prison of Europe a Norwegian puppet government was set up under Quisling and commandos raided Helle Fjord in Norway. At Riom the trials of former French ministers opened and were abruptly broken off when the accused turned into accusers. At the end of March came the brave and brilliant Combined Operations raid on St. Nazaire, a miniature D-Day, which succeeded in jamming the main dock gate.

The 'Scharnhorst' and her companions escape through the Channel

In the Pacific a series of naval battles began with a five-day engagement in the Macassar Straits in which many Japanese transports were sunk or damaged. There was an American raid on Wake and Marcus Islands in February, a few days before the Battle of the Java Sea against the Japanese fleet protecting a huge invasion convoy. In this, Allied losses were considerable. Seven Japanese ships were knocked out when another invasion fleet headed for Port Moresby; but this did not prevent their landing in the Solomons. Late in March there was a three days' naval action in the Mediterranean which brought a British victory over the Italian forces. It was a galling setback for the Royal Navy when the *Scharnhorst*, *Gneisenau* and *Prinz Eugen* escaped from Brest; the three German warships could not be intercepted by air attacks.

American troops arrived in Ulster and Mr. de Valera duly protested against their presence so close to neutral Eire. Lord Beaverbrook became Minister for Production but a fortnight later left the government and went to America to handle production and supply problems. Mr. Attlee did two jobs, Deputy Prime Minister and Secretary for Dominions; Sir Stafford Cripps became Lord Privy Seal. In Egypt Nahas Pasha formed a new government after British tanks had surrounded King Farouk's palace. S.S. *Lafayette* (ex-*Normandie*) was seriously damaged by fire in New York harbour. General MacArthur was appointed C.-in-C. Allied Forces,

The Baedeker raids: Exeter

Norwich

Australia; General Gordon Bennett, having escaped from Singapore, joined him. The Duke of Aosta died in Nairobi. In the States Donald Nelson was appointed War Production Chief. Carole Lombard, the film star, was killed in a plane crash while on a cross-country tour for a Victory Loan drive.

April brought Allied raids on Cologne, Hamburg, the Ruhr and Rhineland, the Skoda works at Pilsen and factories in France. In retaliation Hitler started his Baedeker raids, announcing attacks on British towns starred in the famous guide-books. Exeter, Bath, Norwich, York, suffered badly and almost a thousand people were killed. In the Mediterranean Malta had its two thousandth alert and the Germans also bombed Alexandria. In the Far East the Japanese attacked Darwin in Australia, Port Moresby in New Guinea and the first raids were made on India. In May the R.A.F. continued its daylight sweeps and night attacks on German cities; the Baedeker raids were concentrated on Exeter, Hull and Canterbury. Malta was bombed daily up to May 9 when in three days 112 enemy planes were lost and the attacks slackened. In June the R.A.F. targets were Danzig, Bremen, the Ruhr, U-boat yards, while the Germans kept mostly to coastal regions, switching later to the Midlands. Malta was again under continuous attack.

Bath

Japanese heavy cruiser under American air attack (Midway)

The U.S.S. 'Lexington' dies gallantly

The Japanese carrier 'Ryukaku' is hit by a torpedo

In the Far East things were still going badly for the Allies. On April 9 General Wainwright's forces surrendered on Bataan though the General and the remnant of his depleted army escaped to Corregidor. Lashio, in Burma, fell to the Japanese by assault; they also landed at Bougainville in the Solomons. The first American raid on Tokyo, Kobe, Yokohama was only a gesture to bolster up the home front. On May 1 the British had to evacuate Mandalay and though the naval battle of the Coral Sea ended with an Allied victory, three days later Corregidor, the last epic stand of the Americans in the Philippines, fell to the enemy. Japanese forces swarmed up the Burma Road and crossed the Chinese frontier; they captured the last British-held port in Burma. General Stilwell reached Delhi after twenty days' fantastic trek through the Burmese jungle. Early in June came the Battle of Midway Island which went in favour of the Allies. In the middle of the month the Japanese landed in the Aleutian Islands, taking Attu and Kiska. India was threatened by invasion: negotiations between Britain and Gandhi's representatives had failed. Considerable British forces arrived in the endangered dominion.

The Norwegian bishops resigned in protest against Quisling; Bardossy, the pro-Nazi Hungarian Premier quit and was succeeded by Miklos Kallay.

An explosion in Tangier killed 24 people; the Spanish police blamed the British and there were some anti-British riots.

In the United States nation-wide gas (petrol) rationing started in mid-May creating car-pools, innumerable jokes and the strange sight of uncongested highways.

The Free French flag flies at Bir Hakeim

There were new jobs for politicians and military leaders. Lord Mountbatten was appointed Chief of Combined Operations; in France Laval returned to power. General Giraud escaped from his prison fortress and reached Switzerland. Hitler appointed himself 'Supreme Law Lord' with absolute powers. Lord Gort became C.-in-C., Malta.

In May the Germans launched a new offensive on the Kerch peninsula while the Russians attacked in the Kharkov sector where the battle continued until the end of June. Sevastopol was hard pressed but the garrison held out. Hitler's armies were more successful in Africa where the third German counter-offensive threw the Imperial and British forces back. The Free French's gallantry made their stand at Bir Hakeim one of the finest chapters in the African war. Tobruk fell on June 21, a dark day for Britain with the Germans claiming 25,000 prisoners; by June 24 they were fifty miles across the Egyptian frontier, took Mersa Matruh and continued their advance towards Alexandria. On the first day of July the Battle of El Alamein began on a forty-mile front.

Lord Louis Mountbatten

The fall of Tobruk after many months of stubborn resistance

British soldiers in Madagascar

'A German taken prisoner is a free German'

British forces landed on Madagascar; the Vichy French resisted but gave in after two days' token fighting. On May 26 a twenty-year Anglo-Soviet Treaty was signed by Molotov in London, providing for full collaboration during and after the war. Two weeks later came the razing of Lidice, adding another name to the growing and terrible roster of German terror, with every male inhabitant shot and women and children deported.

July brought increased R.A.F. attacks on Germany, including Danzig, Bremen, the Ruhr and many other targets. The first thousand-bomber raid on the last day of May had proved the growing air strength of Britain. The attacks continued throughout August, striking at Gdynia, Nuremburg, Frankfurt and a dozen other targets while the Germans mostly kept to hit-and-run coastal raids. The Russians bombed Königsberg, Warsaw, Berlin. The attacks on Malta were still continuous but on a reduced scale. September brought little variation in the targets within Germany though a good many were now in occupied territory and the R.A.F. made a brilliant low-level attack on the Oslo headquarters of the Gestapo. Russian bombs fell on Budapest, Vienna, Bucharest, Königsberg and Ploesti for the first time. Sicily and North Africa were under attack by the Allies; the Malta raids were much reduced in scale. In the Far East the Japanese-held islands and Burmese cities were the main targets. After a day's hard fighting, the Germans withdrew from El Alamein. The end of August brought the battle of Alam Halfa in which they suffered heavy losses. Early in September British troops withdrew from liberated Ethiopia. Mobile columns raided Benghazi, Barce and Tobruk, now in German hands; but otherwise the North African fighting seemed to die down.

The Germans again took the offensive in Russia. They captured Sevastopol and reached the Don on a broad front. Rostov and Voronezh, fell to them, their advance in the Caucasus continued and they crossed the Kuban river. The Russians counter-attacked on the Moscow and Leningrad fronts and reached Stalingrad—their Waterloo-to-be, where the Russian counter-offensive began in the last week of September.

The Battle of Stalingrad begins

Americans landing in New Guinea

'light for a dark 'un'

The Allies began to rally in the Pacific. On August 7 American forces landed in the Guadalcanal-Tulagi area (Solomons). A Chinese offensive was successful in Kwangsi and other provinces. When the Japanese landed in South-East Papua, they met with strong resistance. They crossed the Owen Stanley Range and were checked only forty miles from Port Moresby. Late in September the Australians resumed their offensive in New Guinea. The Ministry of Greater East Asia, set up in Tokyo, marked the beginning of a systematic exploitation of the vast territories the Japanese had temporarily conquered.

But the initial victories of the 'New Order' in Asia were deceptive. The slumbering Democracies had awakened and then struck back. American forces held most of Guadalcanal, the Japanese fleet retired from the Solomons. By early November British forces had occupied almost the whole of Central and North Papua and at the end of the month the Americans beat off another Japanese attempt to land reinforcements in the Solomons. Allied successes continued in New Guinea to the end of the year.

An Aussie at Attape

At Dieppe the Canadians crashed into occupied Europe

There was grave trouble in India where Gandhi and members of the Congress Working Committee were arrested, also riots in Bombay and Delhi where troops had to be called out.

Britain and Russia declared the Munich Agreement null and void. The First Moscow Conference brought together Churchill, Harriman and Stalin in Moscow. The first British newspaper in the U.S.S.R.—*British Ally* —was published in Russian; the ban on the *Daily Worker* was removed in Britain.

The Dieppe Raid brought a little comfort to enslaved Europe; for nine hours Canadian troops held the town and harbour and did considerable demolition; but the losses were heavy.

In France conscription of workers for Germany began, setting the pattern for slave-labour on a vast scale. Quisling reintroduced the death penalty in Norway; the Rumanian dictator, Antonescu, followed the Führer's example in declaring himself supreme legal authority. Late in September the first British liaison mission arrived in Greece to join the guerrilla forces.

The last quarter of the year brought many many night raids on Germany and sustained daylight attacks; the only heavy raid in Britain was on Canterbury. In the Mediterranean area Genoa, Turin, Crete and North African targets were attacked; after sixteen days of concentrated raids, Malta got a respite, due to heavy enemy losses. The bombing of Germany and occupied Europe continued in November while over Britain there were only single German planes. Turin, Sicilian, Sardinian and Cretan airfields were battered by the Allied planes; in the Far East many island targets with Burma and Thailand also received attention. The Japanese sent only a few bombers against Darwin and Port Moresby. The final month of 1942 brought Allied raids on Frankfurt, Munich, Karlesruhe and many other German cities. There were only a few attacks on Britain. Naples, Palermo, Taranto, Sicily and Crete were primary targets in the Mediterranean area. Malta had 'received' 14,000 tons of bombs during the year with 1468 civilians killed. The Japanese bombed Calcutta and Chittagong. In America Admiral Leahy was named Roosevelt's Chief of Staff; Mr. Cordell Hull forecast the establishment of an 'international agency for peace'. The President ordered the stabilization of prices and rents, appointing James Byrnes to control living costs. In November Thomas Dewey was elected Governor of New York with a comfortable majority. John Barrymore, the 'Profile', died, so did Brigadier Cornelius Vanderbilt. And the first anniversary of Pearl Harbour was observed throughout the U.S. with solemn pledges for victory.

The Place

Triumph came at long last in Africa. General Montgomery's 8th Army opened the attack on the night of October 23–24 at El Alamein. It was 'a famous victory'. General Thoma, Commander of the Afrika Corps and a great many prisoners were captured as the Axis forces started to retreat westwards. By November 4 the retreat was almost a rout Rommel and his Afrika Corps were on the run.

The Tools and the man

Monty—the Victor

'After the war when a man is asked what he did, it will be sufficient for him to say, "I marched and fought with the Desert Army." '
WINSTON CHURCHILL

'*Don't give me that stuff about a black-out accident—here's a picture of Montgomery with his knuckles bandaged.*'—by Neb

55

The welcome in North Africa

'Marshal forwards and backwards'

During the night of November 7–8 came the Allied landing in North Africa. Under General Eisenhower's command American and British forces went ashore at many points on the French North African shore. Roosevelt, De Gaulle and General Giraud broadcast to the French people. Pétain gave orders to resist but Algiers had surrendered by the end of the first day and rapid advances were made at Oran. Off Casablanca French warships were destroyed and damaged. German troops promptly arrived in Tunisia; so did General Giraud who was smuggled from France in a British submarine. Casablanca capitulated on November 11 and Admiral Darlan ordered all French commanders to cease hostilities. Hitler sent his troops into unoccupied France, occupying Corsica and Nice, reaching the Spanish frontier the same day. By November 12 French resistance in North Africa had ceased everywhere.

Montgomery's forces swept forward; by the time they captured Tobruk they had taken 30,000 prisoners and cleared Cyrenaica of Axis troops. The advance continued; the German counter-attack did not begin until December 1. Rommel was outflanked at El Agheila; French forces thrust forward from the Chad under General Leclerc and the year ended with victory within sight in Africa. It seemed that the Japanese had also been brought to a halt. In New Guinea the Australian advance continued; in October there was a landing on an island off the Papuan coast.

The Allied advance in North Africa

Darlan and Eisenhower—uneasy and temporary associates

In Russia the great Battle of Stalingrad (*above*) raged uninterrupted. The counter-offensive of the Red Army started on November 22 and gained in a single day 24,000 prisoners. In December the Russians advanced on the Middle Don and bagged another 13,000 Germans, getting half-way between the Don and Donetz. The year ended with the Nazi troops in retreat and many towns recaptured.

Rooftop in Stalingrad

H.R.H. The Duke of Kent

On Christmas Eve Admiral Darlan who was acceptable to the Americans (but to nobody else) was assassinated in Algiers. General Giraud was promptly elected as High Commissioner in French Africa. The Duke of Kent's tragic death came in an air crash.

57

The two Hermiones (Baddeley and Gingold) brightened the London blackout in 'Sky High', one of a brilliant series of wartime revues

De Gaulle and Giraud shake hands

THE CASABLANCA CONFERENCE, in mid-January 1943, was the first of a series of historical meetings between the Allied war leaders. In North Africa Roosevelt and Churchill hammered out the 'unconditional surrender' policy, made plans for the invasion of Sicily and set the date of the cross-Channel invasion for 1944. De Gaulle and Giraud were coaxed into shaking hands to assure a united war effort of the French Empire and the Free French Forces. After Casablanca Churchill and Sir Alan Brooke met President Inonu at Adana and reached agreement with Turkey to support the Allies in exchange for war materials and territorial guarantees. The Second Washington Conference took place in May with Roosevelt, Churchill and their staffs discussing current war problems; in August they met at Quebec where plans for the invasion of France were finally approved, including the pre-fabricated Mulberry harbours which played such an important part in the success of D-Day.

Mackenzie King, F.D.R., and Churchill in Quebec

'Begging your pardon sir—Sergeant Krautz and the 472nd Panzer Grenadier Division withdrawing to pre-arranged line as ordered sir'

The Second Moscow Conference, in October, with Cordell Hull and Harriman representing the U.S.A., Anthony Eden and General Ismay Britain, discussed post-war security and co-operation; it set up the European Advisory Council; dealt with the future of Italy and Austria and the punishment of war criminals. A month later, at the First Cairo Conference, Roosevelt, Churchill and Chiang Kai-shek worked out details for further military operations against Japan and decided that the Japanese must restore all their conquest after the Allied victory. Six days later the Teheran Conference opened —perhaps the most important one of the whole war. At least one historian picked November 30, 1943, as 'one of the decisive days in world history'. Today we know that in the Persian capital President Roosevelt took Stalin's side, rejecting Churchill's plan for an Anglo-American invasion of the Balkans which would have struck at the 'soft underbelly' of Nazi Germany. Stalin demanded an Anglo-American landing in France and got it. He got a good deal more— the Kuriles, half of Sakhalin, wide privileges in China against his promise to enter the war against Japan two months after the end of the European war.

Stalin toasts Churchill (on his 69th birthday) after Russia made the best bargain in Soviet history—'one of the decisive days in world history'

The great turning-point of the war began with the spectacular Russian victories. By January 18 they had raised the siege of Leningrad and their advance in the Caucasus continued. The next day their offensive began at Voronezh which ended in a shattering defeat for the German satellites—of the 52,000 prisoners the majority were Hungarians and Italians. By January 31 General Paulus and sixteen other generals had been captured at Stalingrad and two days later the remaining German forces capitulated. Over 150,000 of them had fallen and in two days 45,000 prisoners were counted. Hitler's lunatic policy of no withdrawal had failed at a tremendous cost. On February 16 the Russians took Kharkov.

The loser at Stalingrad: General Paulus

The Germans had some successes in the Donetz Basin where their strong counter-attacks drove the Russians back; in July they made some slight gains in the Orel, Kursk and Byelgorod sectors at heavy cost. The Russians launched their offensive north and east of Orel; by early August they had captured the important junction. Kharkov which had changed hands three times was retaken by storm and late in the month the Russians had other successes near Smolensk and in the Crimea. Their advances continued with the recapture of the entire Donetz Basin and by the middle of September they had cut the Poltava-Kiev railway; the two cities fell to them in the last week of the month. In October a new Russian offensive started on the front from Vitebsk to the Taman penin-sula and they crossed the Dnieper; the

DNIEPER BEND

great dam at Dnepropetrovsk was recaptured after three weeks of heavy fighting. By November 1 they had cut German land communications with the Crimea and with the fall of Kiev on November 6, much of the Ukraine had been liberated. Gomel fell to them three weeks later and their successes continued to the end of the year. The work of planning for the post-war world continued in 1943. On January 17 Allied governments issued a declaration against the acts of dispossession in Axis-occupied territories. In April planning for the relief of civil population in the Balkans began in the Middle East and a conference on refugees was held in Bermuda. The United Nations Food Conference was held at Hot Springs, Virginia. In August the Allied governments warned neutrals not to give asylum to war criminals. In October a final agreement was signed (with the exception of Russia) to establish a U.N. Commission for the investigation of war crimes. UNRRA (United Nations Relief and Re-habilitation Administration) came into being in November with forty-four Allied and Associated nations signing an agreement. In North Africa there was some hard fighting before final victory. The 8th Army opened its new attack in mid-January; the Germans counter-attacked in Tunisia, using Tiger tanks for the first time and destroyed much Allied equipment but British industry was working all out and the equipment was replaced.

Massed pipers led the victory parade in North Africa

Sic transit gloria. . . . A Desert Rat turns his back on the Führer and lights up

In February the Germans still had some initial successes against the American forces, breaking through the Kasserine Pass; they were thrown back after five days of bitter fighting. In North Tunisia General von Arnim slowly drove back the British in a series of battles lasting until the last week of March. The 8th Army attacked the Mareth Line and drove a wedge in it but had to withdraw under counter-attacks. The offensive was renewed five days later and for the first time low-flying planes supported the ground forces. The British 1st Army also went over to the offensive and took 8000 prisoners in a single day. In the three days April 6–8 the 8th Army broke through Rommel's defence and joined up with the Americans. The final assault on Tunis started on May 6, by next day both Tunis and Bizerta were captured and in North-East Tunisia the Germans surrendered unconditionally. On May 12 all organized resistance in Tunisia ended and General von Arnim was taken prisoner; the final bag was 219,000 and the Axis had been driven from Africa. Italy was the next objective.

The 8th Army breaks through at Gabes

General Patton—the two-gun General

In January President Roosevelt had sent his $100 billion war budget to Congress. In February, Dwight D. Eisenhower, a full general, was appointed to command the Allied armies in Europe. On the home front the President curbed prices and wages and regulated the changing of jobs; in June the House of Representatives voted a drastic anti-strike bill.

Limited successes were also achieved against the Japanese; they were ejected from Papua and began to withdraw their forces from Guadalcanal. Allied forces from India raided Burma without casualties; in March the Battle of Bismarck Sea ended with the wiping out of an entire Japanese convoy bound for New Guinea. Also in February the Chinese gained an important victory, throwing the Japanese back over the Yangtze. Washington disclosed that American airmen, brought down during a raid on Tokyo in 1942, had been executed by the Japanese warlords.

In May American troops landed in the Aleutians; in ten days all organized Japanese resistance had ended on Attu. Wingate's commandos spent three months on an epic raiding expedition in Central Burma, far behind the enemy lines. Late in May the Chinese launched a new counter-offensive on the Hupeh-Hunan border and routed the Japanese. In June came landings in New Georgia where three islands were occupied by the Americans; a naval battle in July ended with several Japanese warships being sunk. In August, U.S. and Canadian forces landed on Kiska, another Aleutian island. Lord Mountbatten was appointed Supreme Allied Commander in South-East Asia. A large-scale Allied invasion of New Guinea began in September where American paratroops surrounded 20,000 Japanese and Australians captured Lae and Finschafen. A Japanese counter-offensive in China gained some ground in October; by the middle of the month the entire New Georgia group in the Solomons was in Allied hands. November brought a landing on Bougainville and the Gilbert Islands. The outer defences of Japan were gradually being reduced though at great cost and at a painfully slow pace.

Japan also found quislings: she recognized Burma as an independent State and Ba Maw, the puppet Premier, declared war on Britain and America, Subhas Chandra Bose formed a provisional 'Free India' government in Singapore.

The future well-being of the world depends upon the extent to which Marxism, as it is progressively modified in Russia, and Democracy as we are adapting it to twentieth-century conditions, can live together in peace.

HENRY WALLACE

The bleak Aleutians: a wounded man carried to safety on Attu

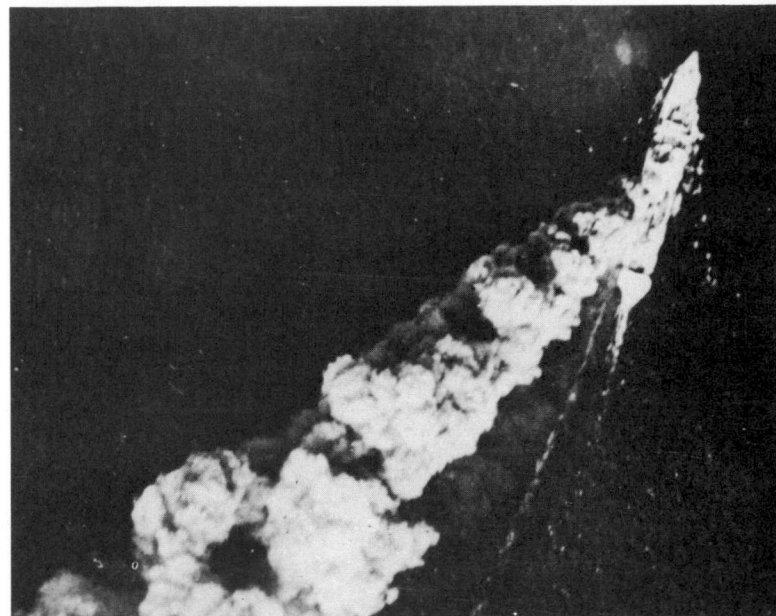
Battle of the Bismarck Sea. A Japanese ship burns

Wingate—their battle was behind Japanese lines

The invasion of Sicily

Mobile first aid post

The main event of 1943 was doubtless the collapse of the Axis, the rapid and inglorious end of Mussolini's Fascist dictatorship.

In April Hitler and the Duce met at the Führer's headquarters. A month later the fighting in Africa ended. Within four weeks the Allies were on their way to the Italian mainland. Pantellaria surrendered to a squadron of bombers; Lampedusa to a handful of commandos. On July 9 U.S. and British paratroops landed in Sicily. Churchill and Roosevelt called on the Italian people to surrender; the Italian forces on the big island obeyed this call with alacrity. Palermo and Enna fell rapidly; Rome's marshalling yards were bombed. After a stormy meeting of the Fascist Grand Council, Mussolini was arrested on July 25 and Badoglio became Premier. There were peace demonstrations in Milan and Turin. The Fascist Party was dissolved. By mid-August all resistance had ended in Sicily and the Lipari Islands (Mussolini's concentration camp) had surrendered. On September 3, troops of the 8th Army landed between Reggio and Catona and made swift advances. The same day the Italian armistice agreement was signed secretly. On September 8 Italy surrendered unconditionally; the 8th Army advance continued. Mussolini was rescued from imprisonment by German commandos on September 12. The German H.Q. near Rome was heavily bombed. Next day came the Salerno landing by the U.S. 5th Army. The Italian battle fleet left Spezia and arrived almost intact in Malta. In the Aegean Italian garrisons joined the Allies but the Germans soon reoccupied the islands. The Germans occupied Northern Italy.

They 'rescued' the Duce

RECONDITIONED CAESAR—

—ALMOST AS GOOD AS NEW

by ILLINGWORTH

As the tide of German victories receded, resistance grew in the occupied territories and Nazi reprisals became more savage. Laval set up the Vichy Militia, introduced compulsory labour service. Norwegian commandos destroyed the German heavy water installations at Norsk Hydro, near Ryukan, thereby practically knocking Germany out of the atomic race. King Boris of Bulgaria died (some spoke of his being murdered) and was succeeded by his infant son. French commandos landed at Ajaccio in Corsica in the middle of September; after three weeks the island was completely liberated. In Yugoslavia partisans captured and held Split on the Adriatic for twelve days; in Greece there was disunity among the two main resistance groups. General Mihailovitch captured Kotor in Dalmatia.

There was some painful disputes among the Allies. The Americans complained through their Moscow Ambassador that the Russian people weren't told of American aid. Next day Moscow broadcast a full statement and Litvinov made a speech of thanks in Washington. Far more serious was the Katyn affair. Eight thousand Polish officers were found massacred in a deep pit and the exiled government demanded an International Red Cross investigation. Moscow replied that this was a Gestapo frame-up and broke off relations with the Poles who thereupon dropped the appeal to the Red Cross. But the dispute sharpened. In July General Sikorski, the Polish Premier, his daughter and several Polish leaders—together with Colonel Victor Cazalet—were killed in a plane crash near Gibraltar. The tension persisted to the end of the year. Today it is generally accepted that the Russians were responsible for the mass-executions of Katyn.

In the United States violent race riots broke out in Detroit and claimed twenty-three dead before the army quelled them. There was a rail disaster in Philadelphia costing seventy-five lives. Sumner Welles retired and Edward Stettinius was appointed as Under-Secretary of State. The U.S. Senate voted, by a huge majority, for the United Nations plan. Widespread strikes led to the Federal authorities' seizure of the railroads.

A provisional government was established in Yugoslavia and Tito was raised to the status of full Allied Commander

R.A.F. 'Dam-Busters' flooded a large area and affected two-thirds of the Ruhr's water-supply

Sir Harold Alexander and Sir Claude Auchinleck, liberation commanders

On Christmas Eve the names of the commanders of the European liberation armies were announced —Eisenhower, Sir Maitland Wilson, Sir Harold Alexander, Sir Bernard Montgomery and General Spaatz headed the list.

In Britain the problem of India was causing considerable headaches. In February Gandhi started a three weeks' fast in protest against his detention. He ended his fast on March 3 but the agitation for independence did not lessen. In April the Moslem League Conference at Delhi passed a resolution demanding the establishment of 'Pakistan'. In June, Field-Marshal Wavell was appointed Viceroy of India. The autumn brought a disastrous famine in Bengal. An All-India Food Conference opened and set up relief camps for famine victims but hundreds of thousands died before relief became effective.

General Mark Clark and Sir Maitland Wilson

Monty and Bradley

General Carl Spaatz

Field-Marshal Wavell in Burma

Sir John Anderson, Chancellor of the Exchequer

In the air and on the oceans the global war brought Allied successes while enemy attacks on Britain were on a much smaller scale. The Battle of the Ruhr opened in May with almost continuous R.A.F. bombing of the great industrial centres while German attacks on Britain increased in strength. Mosquito night raids became the rule; in July the R.A.F. dropped 2300 tons on Hamburg which killed 20,000 and injured 60,000; 'window' strips of metal foil were used against enemy radar for the first time. The Reich was being battered into rubble and the scale and range of the Allied attacks were constantly expanded.

Moscow dissolved the Comintern 'to show her good intentions'; Stalin agreed to the election of a Patriarch and the establishment of a Holy Synod under the Metropolitan Sergius. The Archbishop of York visited Moscow at the invitation of the Orthodox Church.

In Britain Bevin announced registration of women up to the age of fifty; Sir Kingsley Wood, the Chancellor of the Exchequer died. He was succeeded by Sir John Anderson. Lord Beaverbrook became Lord Privy Seal. Sir Dudley Pound was followed by Sir Andrew Cunningham as First Sea Lord. Britain and Portugal signed the Azores Agreement which gave the U.K. a naval base—under the terms of an Anglo-Portuguese Agreement of 1373. Lord Woolton became Minister of Reconstruction. Sir Oswald Mosley was released on health grounds.

Lord Woolton boosts potatoes

Lord Beaverbrook, Lord Privy Seal

Sir William Beveridge, architect of Welfare

Leslie Howard—most beloved of British film actors

There were running battles with German E-boats in the Channel; late in December the *Scharnhorst* was at long last sunk off the North Cape by the Home Fleet.

De Valera was elected Prime Minister of Eire. Labour won the elections in New Zealand and Australia. A military coup in the Argentine ousted Castillo. General Chang Ching-ui, puppet Premier of Manchukuo, ran amok, killing a number of quislings and Japanese officials, poisoned his family and committed suicide. Leslie Howard, one of the most beloved film stars, died when his plane was shot down between Lisbon and London in the belief that it carried Mr. Churchill. This was the year—1944—in which Henry Wallace coined the phrase about 'the Century of Common Man', Otto Stern won the Nobel Prize in Physics, George Hevesy de Heves in Chemistry, Henrik Dam and Edward A. Doisy shared it in Medicine. The Beveridge Report was published; Bolivia, Brazil, Columbia, Iran and Iraq joined the United Nations.

Sir Oswald Mosley—his health brought release

From 'Desert Victory', film of the year, made by the Army. An El Alamein piper leads the charge on German positions

A wounded German prisoner gets a helping hand, and shoulder, from his captors. ('Desert Victory')

Churchill visits bomb-scarred Liverpool

The Allied armies returned to Europe. Trucks go ashore—transportation for the greatest sea invasion of history

1944 WAS THE 'year of miracles', the beginning of the end.

Early in January General Montgomery arrived in Britain, to take over command of the British group of invasion forces. The pre-invasion bombing of France began in March with almost round-the-clock attacks on rail centres and industrial targets. In April the transmission or receipt of code telegrams by diplomatic missions in London was banned, diplomatic bags were to be censored and no diplomat or his family, with the exception of American, Russian and Dominion citizens, was allowed to leave the country. In May the Low Countries, Norway and the Big Three signed an agreement on the administration of the countries to be liberated.

The night of June 5–6 brought D-Day, the landings between Cherbourg and Le Havre, supported by tremendous air and naval forces. Churchill made a statement in the House. H.M. the King broadcast to his people and De Gaulle spoke to the French.

In a single day Bayeux was liberated. The Bayeux–Caën road was cut, all beach-heads were cleared of the enemy and almost all German coastal batteries were silenced by naval guns. Next day Allied air forces began to

Safely ashore—tanks line up for the drive towards Hitler's Reich

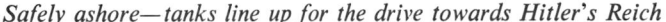

The liberators march in. Old friends bring freedom back to France

operate from airstrips in France, established mostly by the air-borne troops which had landed on the night before D-Day from a thousand troop carriers and gliders behind the German defences. Within a week the beach-heads were merged on a front of fifty miles. Churchill, Field-Marshal Smuts, Eisenhower and Montgomery visited Normandy. On June 26 Cherbourg was liberated, with the Admiral commanding the Normandy sea defences among the prisoners. Caën fell on July 9, St. Lô on the 16th when British and Canadian troops broke through in Normandy. Two weeks later the Americans had also broken through on their sector: Granville and Avranches fell. Early in August the Germans used 'human torpedoes' and explosive motor-boats against the Normandy anchorage, causing some damage but themselves suffering great losses. The pace quickened now: Rennes was liberated and the German counter-attack against Avranches collapsed after six days when a general retreat began. Nantes and Angers fell; the Americans crossed the Loire. The first *Pluto* pipeline from the Isle of Wight to Cherbourg was now in operation. St. Malo and Alençon were freed.

At the alert looking toward Caen   *'Pluto' carried supplies across-Channel*

Free French and British soldiers bring liberation to Paris

On August 15 the Allies landed on the south coast of France, at many points between Toulon and Nice. Progress was rapid both in the north and the south. The Free French forces liberated all Haute Savoie; the Falaise gap was closed and General Patton's forces crossed the Seine. By August 20 eight departments in Brittany, the Pyrenees, the Alps and the Massif Central were clear of the 'potato bugs' as the French had nicknamed the oppressor. Three days later came the glorious, confused and unexpected liberation of Paris from within. For two days there was desperate fighting in the city; on August 25 General Leclerc's armoured division reached it in a headlong dash and organized resistance was crushed. American and Free French forces met on the outskirts of Bordeaux; Marseilles, Grenoble were freed and the French Resistance took over the frontier station of Hendaye. De Gaulle entered Paris and broadcast to the nation, narrowly escaping being shot during next day's ceremonial parade.

Leclerc—the tank commander

The Vichy Militia, making a last hopeless stand, sniped from the rooftops and Parisians ducked

Leaders of Free Europe, Churchill and De Gaulle, with the Arc de Triomphe in the background, receive the plaudits of Paris

Brussels jubilantly greets its liberators

Flooded Walcheren

The Arnhem fighting

The advance continued almost without a pause; the Marne was crossed three days after the liberation of Paris, Toulon was cleared of the enemy and General Eberbach, the Commander of Amiens, was captured at his break-fast table. On September 1 the Canadians reached the Channel at Le Tréport, taking Dieppe and Rouen and next day the Allied forces crossed the Belgian frontier. Brussels was liberated by the British; next day Antwerp, Lille, Louvain and a score of other cities were freed.

The Americans, having taken Namur and Charleroi, linked up with their allies. By September 10 when Luxembourg City was liberated, the Allies were only fourteen miles from the German frontier. Far to the west there was still a lot of mopping up to be done; Le Havre surrendered on September 12, the same day as the American 1st Army crossed the German frontier, capturing Eupen and Malmedy. British patrols probed into Holland. The Maginot Line was captured intact. On September 15 the Siegfried Line was broken east of Aachen. Two days later the first Allied airborne army landed in Holland where it took Nijmegen and Eindhoven; but at Arnhem there was a tragic setback which cost 7000 in killed, wounded and missing. On the last day of the month Calais fell.

Walcheren Island, where the R.A.F. had breached the dikes, causing extensive flooding, wasn't occupied until early in November by which time the first German cities, Aachen and Gelsenkirchen had fallen.

The last, desperate throw of the Germans came in mid-December when Rundstedt launched a strong offensive in the Ardennes with considerable initial success. But American resistance stiffened and by Christmas Day the surrounded garrison of Bastogne was relieved; on the last day of the year the American counter-offensive started and the Allies were poised for the final assault on the Reich.

Progress in the East had been even more spectacular. By January 6, 1944, the Russians had crossed the 1939 Polish frontier. By the end of the month they were in the Carpathian foothills, crossed the Pruth and were within sixteen miles of the Ruthenian frontier. They entered Rumania on April 2, recaptured Odessa and cleared the Crimea. On the last day of July they were within twelve miles of Warsaw where they, inexplicably, stopped. The tragic rising of the Polish Underground Army lasted for almost two months, with the Allies dropping arms and food to the resistance; but the Poles were defeated by the Germans while the Russians watched the struggle from Praga, the Warsaw suburb across the Vistula.

Long before that Rumania had accepted the Russian armistice terms and declared war on Germany; the Finns asked for armistice negotiations and signed one in September; in a single day Russia declared war on Bulgaria, Bulgaria declared war on Germany and asked for an armistice with Russia. On September 23 Russian and Rumanian troops crossed the Hungarian frontier. On October 1 the Red Army entered Yugoslavia by agreement with Marshal Tito. A three-pronged attack on Hungary began from east, north and south. Riga, the Latvian capital, fell on October 13; five days later the Red Army was in Czechoslovakia and next day the first important

General Bor-Komorowski—Commander of the Polish Underground Army

After the Warsaw rising

Stulpnagel—forced to kill himself

'THESE AMATEURS—I DIDN'T MISS!'

city in East Prussia fell to them. By the end of the year they were fighting in the streets of Budapest and Hitler had lost practically all his *Lebensraum* in Eastern and Central Europe.

As the 'Twilight of the Gods' cast its long shadows over Germany, Hitler mobilized schoolchildren for war purposes. Berlin was being battered into ruins; in February 1944, 2500 tons rained down on the German capital in a single night. Goebbels was appointed the sole administrator of the city in April. On July 20 the ill-fated attempt to kill Hitler by a bomb which Colonel von Stauffenberg carried into the Führer's East Prussian Headquarters misfired. General Beck, the head of the plotters at the War Ministry announced Hitler's death in Berlin—prematurely, as it turned out. The Nazis exacted terrible vengeance. Beck and Stauffenberg were shot the same night, General Stulpnagel and Rommel were forced to commit suicide. Himmler was appointed C.O. of the 'Home Army'. The purge continued for weeks; eight high-ranking officers were hanged for complicity in the bomb-plot, seven civilians, headed by Karl Goerdeler, were also executed. In October all able-bodied Germans between sixteen and sixty were conscripted.

The liberation of Europe and the planning of the post-war world proceeded side by side; but at the same time trouble started in several of the liberated countries almost as soon as the Germans departed. In January Ciano, Marshal de Bono and others were tried in Verona for overthrowing Mussolini; five of them were executed—including Ciano. Edda, Mussolini's daughter fled to Switzerland.

After the explosion at Hitler's H.Q. Circle marks where the Fuhrer stood

Ciano's execution. He is extreme right—and inset

The battered Abbey of Cassino

Progress in Italy was disappointingly slow at first. In January 22, 1944, came the Anzio landing with little initial opposition; but later the Germans counter-attacked with great force and stubborn persistence, renewing their offensive three times. The 5th Army broke into the Gustav Line. The ancient Abbey of Cassino was bombed and shelled after previous warning and reduced to rubble; it was the middle of March before most of the town was occupied. Rome was liberated on June 4 and King Victor Emmanuel fulfilled his promise by transferring his powers to Crown Prince Umberto. Badoglio resigned and Bonomi formed a cabinet in which Count Sforza, Benedetto Croce and the Communist Togliatti were members. Progress was more rapid now; Florence was liberated on August 11; at the end of the month the 8th Army attacked the Gothic Line in the Adriatic sector and broke through after two days. In September the Republic of San Marino declared war on Germany—a little belatedly but with enthusiasm.

New Zealand troops at Cassino

The Roosevelts and Churchills meet at Quebec (with Field-Marshal Smuts and Mackenzie King)

Elsewhere the Resistance movements came into their own. Marshal Tito, with some help from the Red Army and the Allied forces, captured Jajce and the island of Korcula. He and Major Randolph Churchill narrowly escaped capture by German paratroops in May. In August Tito and Winston Churchill met in Italy and by mid-September all Dalmatian islands were liberated. Belgrade and Dubrovnik were freed jointly by Russian and Yugoslav forces in October; three weeks later Tito's troops entered Monastir, controlling the Serbo-Greek frontier. In November British troops went into action in Herzegovina and Montenegro; Tirana and Durazzo were liberated by Albanian patriots.

The post-war world began to take shape and forecast troubles in many parts of the globe. Talks on Arab unity began between Egypt, the Lebanon, Syria and Iraq in January. The Soviet Government proposed that the Polish-Russian frontier should be established on the 'Curzon Line' of 1919; the Polish Government protested vigorously and the Russians refused American mediation in the matter. The Americans backed free Jewish immigration into Palestine in spite of Arab protests. UNRRA's European Committee had its first meeting in London. Lord Beaverbrook and Adolf Berle started discussions on the problems of post-war aviation. In May the Conference of Commonwealth Prime Ministers surveyed foreign policy, agreed on strategy and declared the need of a post-war world organization for peace and security. An official committee was set up to advise the British Government on works of art stolen by the enemy. Iceland broke away from Denmark and declared herself a republic. A report by the Inter-Allied Committee of Experts was published on the future of the Court of International Justice. Tito reached a compromise agreement with Subasitch, Premier of the exiled Yugoslav Government. On July 1 the International Monetary Conference opened at Bretton Woods; a monetary fund and an international bank for reconstruction and development were established. Moscow formed a Polish National Committee for Liberation in Lublin over the protests of the Polish Government in London. Anglo-American oil-talks began in Washington with Lord Beaverbrook and Cordell Hull heading the delegations. Mikolajczyk, the Polish Premier arrived in Moscow on August 1 for conferences with the Communist Committee of Polish National Liberation. The Inter-Governmental Committee on Refugees met in London; six days later British, American and Russian delegates started their discussions at Dumbarton Oaks on post-war security and agreed on the foundations of the United Nations Organization. In September, Benelux began by the customs union between Belgium, Luxembourg and Holland. At the Second Quebec Conference Churchill, Roosevelt and Eden made plans for the Pacific War and ending the fighting in Europe, declared their readiness to help Italy and agreed on the handling of the post-war European problems. The Third Moscow Conference was attended by Churchill, Eden, Stalin and the Polish Premier and achieved a somewhat uneasy compromise over the Polish-Russian dispute. In December France and the U.S.S.R. signed a treaty of alliance.

Molotov, Harriman, Churchill, Stalin and Eden in Moscow

The raid on the Gestapo headquarters at the Hague

Throughout Europe the ferment of resistance and liberation was reaching explosive stages. The R.A.F.'s pin-point bombing had freed a hundred prisoners of the Gestapo in Amiens. In April British commandos captured General Kreipe, the German C.-in-C. on Crete—and hauled him across the island to captivity in Cairo. In May a squadron of Mosquitoes destroyed a single house in The Hague containing Gestapo and forced labour files. King Leopold of Belgium and the Crown Prince were taken to Germany by the Nazis. Late in June Philippe Henriot, the Vichy Minister of Propaganda, was assassinated in Paris. The Danes began a general strike in Copenhagen where a state of siege was declared; five days later the strike ended—with the Germans giving in to the Danes' demands. The S.S. destroyed the village of St. Gingolph in France, killing and deporting all inhabitants.

In September the Greek Government moved from Cairo to Caserta, in Italy. The Germans began to withdraw from the Aegean Islands, starting with Mytilene and Samos. September brought another general strike in Denmark and retribution for Antonescu and other Rumanian quislings who were arrested. Britain formed a Jewish Brigade Group. Prince Charles was elected Regent of Belgium. At Caserta the Greek Prime Minister, two guerrilla leaders of General Scobie signed an agreement on the liberation of Greece.

Athens liberated

EDES and EAM clash in Athens

On December 1 most of Crete was free; Athens, however, was under martial law with British tanks patrolling the streets, and fighting between the Right and Left-wing resistance forces continued. Churchill and Eden hurried to Athens where Archbishop Damaskinos took the oath as Regent. Trouble was still to come.

In Hungary October saw the tragic retribution overtaking Admiral Horthy. He was arrested by the Germans and Szalasi, a half-illiterate quisling of Armenian origin, instituted a reign of terror.

British forces landed on October 5 on Greek mainland, in Albania and on several islands; five days later serious clashes began between EDES and EAM, the main Greek resistance groups. Athens was liberated on October 14 and a landing made on Corfu; Lemnos, Thebes, Lamia fell and by November 4 Greece was clear of Germans except for small groups.

Britain was still enduring a heart-breaking ordeal in this year of decision. On the night of June 13–14 the first pilotless aircraft—also known as 'doodle-bug', 'buzz-bomb' or 'V-1'—landed in South England. The attacks continued day and night for the rest of the month, causing great damage and many casualties; in August over 1100 people were killed and the strain on wardens, rescue workers, hospitals was considerable. By September there were far fewer flying-bombs, and they were now mainly launched from aircraft as the R.A.F. had battered some launching sites and others had been captured. But on September 8 the first V-2 landed at Chiswick, London; later when the port of Antwerp was opened, Belgium shared England's peril and discomfort. The flying-bomb and the rocket continued to kill and maim people through the rest of the year.

Cause . . .

. . . and effect (V-1)

Cause . . .

. . . and effects (V-2)

'*And gentlemen of England now a-bed*
Shall think themselves accurs'd they were not here
And hold their manhoods cheap while any speaks
That fought with us upon St. Crispin's day. . . .'

The film of the year was Shakespeare's *Henry V* in which Laurence Olivier's 'Harry the King' summed-up the spirit of embattled England.

On 'Crispin's Day' 1944, the people of England were not a-bed. By night the Prime Minister, Winston Churchill, went out and watched rockets cascade on the capital—in the last desperate Nazi onslaught. The free world was striking with deadly effect towards the heart of the Reich and the days of Hitler's tyranny were numbered.

G.I.s and Red Army soldiers clasp hands on the Elbe

On April 21, 1945 Russian troops reached the suburbs of Berlin; the Americans cleared the Harz and started down the Danube valley while the British were on the outskirts of Bremen. After only two days the Russians broke through the north and east defences of the German capital. Göring sent a telegram to his besieged Führer, proposing to take over as his deputy; Hitler replied by ordering his arrest which took place next day. On April 24 Count Bernadotte transmitted a verbal message from Himmler (whom he met at Lübeck) to the British Legation in Stockholm, offering surrender to Britain and the U.S.A. only; this was refused. The Americans liberated Dachau. Next day Bremen and Stettin surrendered and the Allies stood along the Swiss frontier from Basle to Lake Constance. De Gaulle, showing his mettle again, refused to evacuate Stuttgart to make place for the Americans. The 7th American Army reached the Austrian border. On the same day in the *Führerbunker* Adolf Hitler married Eva Braun, made his will and appointed Admiral Dönitz his successor. On April 30 he and his two-day bride committed suicide; the bodies were burned in the courtyard. Goebbels poisoned his wife and children and then killed himself. Disintegration of Germany was only a question of days.

Admiral Dönitz—Hitler's successor

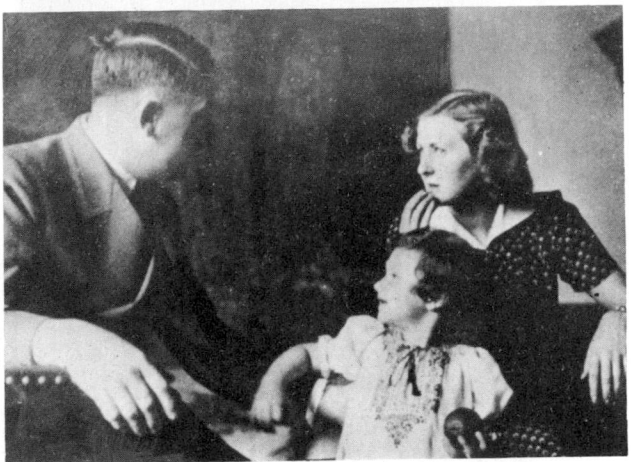

Hitler and his wife Eva Braun

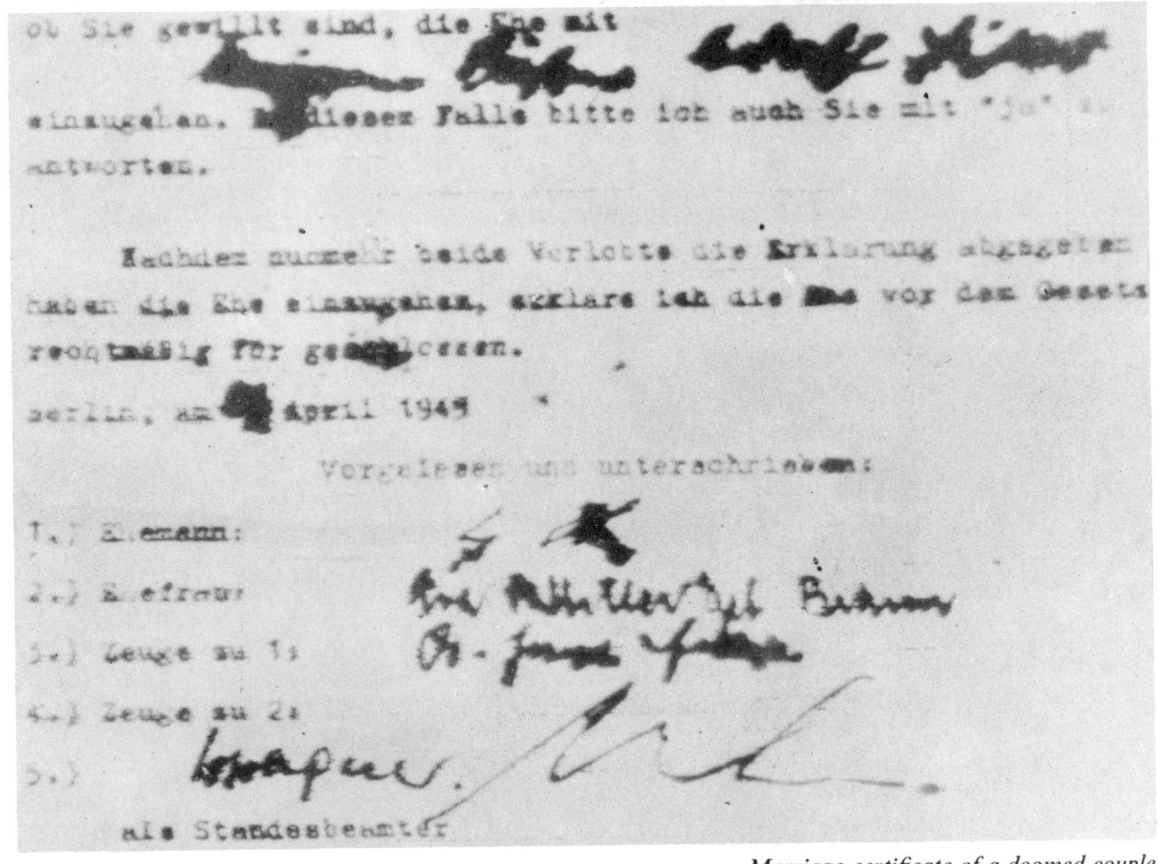

Marriage certificate of a doomed couple

On May 4 all enemy forces in Holland, North-West Germany and Denmark surrendered unconditionally. The unconditional surrender of the whole Reich was signed on May 7 by General Jodl at Rheims, General Eisenhower's headquarters and on May 8 the free world went wild celebrating VE Day.

General Krenzl signs the surrender

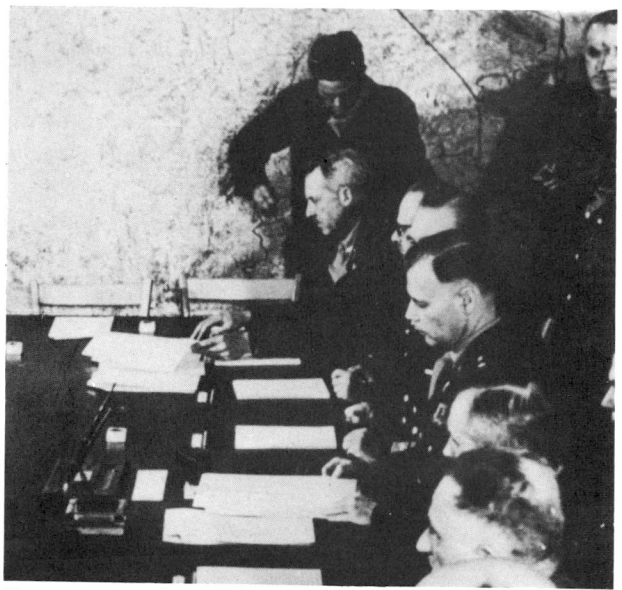

German surrender at Rheims

Churchill on VE Day

VE Day in Whitehall

'*Lest we forget*'—*prayer in Westminster Cathedral*

89

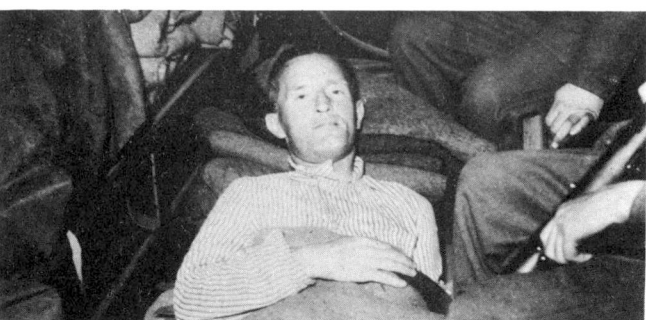

Lord Haw-Haw—the radio traitor

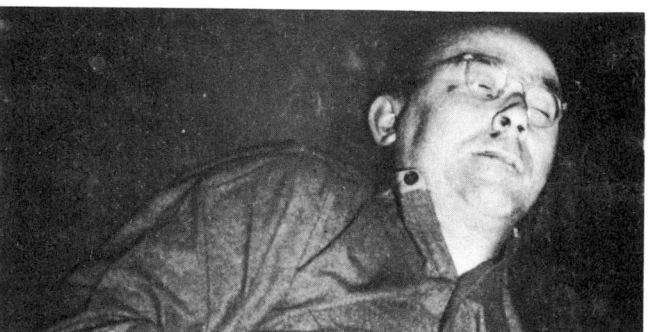

F.D.R.'s last picture—with Falla

Himmler—death of an evil man

David Lloyd George died on March 25 and eighteen days later the world was shocked into stunned grief by the death of Franklin Delano Roosevelt who had overcome such grievous physical handicaps to lead his country through economic disaster and the greatest war in American history. He was succeeded by Henry Truman, the Vice-President, perhaps the personification of Henry Wallace's 'Common Man', the ex-haberdasher, ex-artillery officer from Missouri, who took on one of the toughest jobs in history.

It was Truman who had to launch the San Francisco Conference which was to realize Roosevelt's dream of the United Nations. By June 23 the text of the Charter was completed and two days later it was approved at a plenary session.

The first half of the year also brought notable advances in the war against Japan. On January 9 MacArthur fulfilled his promise and returned to the Philippines; 100,000 Americans landed safely on Luzon. Akyab in Burma fell to the Allies. The land route to China was reopened in the last week of the month. The main air base on Luzon fell on January 25. On February 4 American troops entered Manila but it took them twenty days to clear out the Japanese. The Australians landed in New Britain.

After two months of continuous bombing and shelling troops invaded Iwojima; naval forces attacked air bases in and near Tokyo. Corregidor was liberated, the Chinese captured Lashio. No wonder that in Japan all men from 12 to 60 and all women from 12 to 40 were conscripted for essential war work. Fighting started in Hanoi between the Vichy-French and the Japanese when the latter took over the administration of Indo-China. On March 15 the American flag was hoisted over Iwojima; the French surrounded Japanese forces in Tonkin and Laos. Cebu, the second largest Filipino city was captured on March 27; on April 1 came the invasion of Okinawa in the Ryukyu Islands where five days later American military government was established and the Katchin peninsula was isolated. MacArthur was appointed to command all Pacific Army forces and Admiral Nimitz the Allied Navy. The Japanese Cabinet resigned and Baron Suzuku formed a new one. April also saw a decisive Allied victory in Central Burma. The campaign in the Central Philippines ended on April 22 with the capture of Cebu Island; the Australians landed on Tarakan off Borneo. By VE Day the Japanese were trapped in the Arakan-Irawaddy area and Okinawa was almost conquered.

The immense bill for the gory years was being presented all over the world and in many different ways. In Britain a Colonial Development and Welfare Bill envisaged the spending of £120 million in the next ten years. The toll of lives in the British Isles from September 1939 to September 1944 added up to almost 58,000 dead and over 70,000 injured. The total Commonwealth and Empire casualties up to the end of February 1945 were 1,126,802 in the armed forces, 34,161 in the Merchant Navy.

The round-up of quislings began. Laval was arrested in Barcelona; Pétain in France. Quisling and four of his ministers surrendered in Norway; Terboven, the Gauleiter and General Rediess, the chief of the German police,

Hoisting the flag on Iwojima

committed suicide. King Leopold of Belgium and General Bor-Komorowski, the heroic leader of the Warsaw rising were liberated. A British relief expedition reached the Channel Islands; the long and thorny dispute over Trieste began with Britain and America opposing Tito's Yugoslav administration. The Austrian Republic was re-established and the *Anschluss* declared null and void. There were strikes and riots in Syria and the Lebanon because French troops had landed. Tito withdrew his troops from Carinthia. Field-Marshal Montgomery was appointed C.-in-C. of the British Occupation Forces in Germany. In Britain the Labour Party rejected Churchill's proposal for the continuation of the Coalition Government. The Lend-Lease balance sheet showed that America had given Britain $12,775 millions' worth of aid, Russia received $8,409 million while the United States had collected $5,000 millions' worth from the Allies.

Himmler was found wandering in a sergeant's uniform, recognized, arrested and committed suicide at Lüneburg. Lord Haw-Haw, William Joyce, whose nasal voice had prophesied disaster for Britain over the German radio was also captured, and brought to Britain to stand trial for treason.

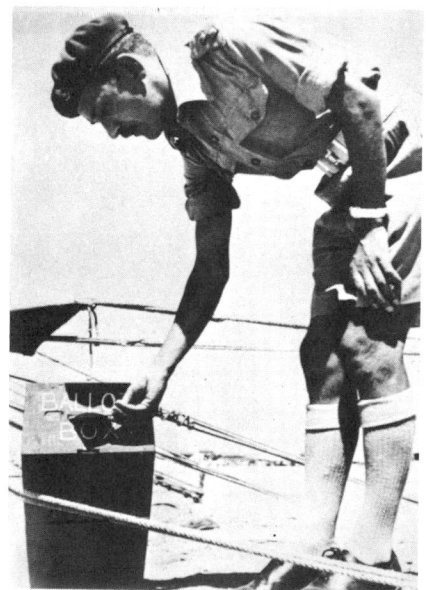

The American delegation to UNO

The exchange of Russian citizens, of British and Allied prisoners began. The Belgian Socialists demanded the abdication of King Leopold. There was a war crimes conference in London with sixteen nations participating. America and nine European countries set up the European Coal Organization. Ribbentrop was captured in Hamburg. The Allied Reparations Committee met for the first time in Moscow. The World Security Charter was signed by fifty nations in San Francisco, the statute of the Court of International Justice was approved and a preparatory commission for UNO established. Stettinius, Byrnes, Connally and Mrs. Roosevelt were appointed permanent UNO delegates; in July Byrnes was appointed Secretary of State.

Election 1945—the soldier's vote—

and the civilian's voice

As soon as the European war ended, the pressure on Japan increased rapidly. By May 18 all Japanese on Luzon were trapped in three pockets. Chinese troops advanced north from Foochow. Chiang Kai-Shek was succeeded by Dr. T. V. Soong as Premier of China; Chiang remained President and Generalissimo. In June, Osaka, Kobe, Tokyo were battered—by the end of the month all synthetic fuel plants and 80 per cent of Japan's war arsenals were destroyed. There were landings on Labuan and Sarawak, with fast progress; Okinawa was cleared after eighty-two days' hard fighting.

Mr. Churchill resigned on May 23 and formed a caretaker administration three days later. In Canada Mackenzie King returned to office though with a reduced majority. The General Election took place on July 5 in Britain; the result was something of a shock. The great wartime leader was 'dismissed' by the electorate; Labour won a landslide victory and Clement Attlee became Prime Minister on July 25 with Ernest Bevin Foreign Secretary, Sir Stafford Cripps

The scar of the Atom Bomb—in New Mexico

President of the Board of Trade and Hugh Dalton Chancellor of the Exchequer.

In June 1945, after the breakdown of negotiations, there was bitter fighting in the Levant with much damage to Damascus and Homs. Churchill ordered British forces to intervene, enraging the French; but by June 3 French troops were evacuated from Beirut and Damascus, and the long negotiations for the independence of Syria and the Lebanon started afresh. There wasn't much progress in the Indian problem where the Congress leaders were released but the Viceroy's Conference with Gandhi and Jinnah ended without an agreement at Simla. An Allied Food Conference was held in London; UNRRA reached Czechoslovakia and the Austrian Zones of Occupation were fixed. Moscow sentenced twelve of the sixteen kidnapped Polish leaders for 'criminal conspiracy'. A Polish Government of 'National Unity' was formed.

Potsdam I—Churchill—Truman—Stalin

The last six weeks of the Far Eastern war began with the round-the-clock bombing of Japan. Australians landed at Balikpapan and on July 5 MacArthur announced the liberation of the whole of Philippines. There were new landings in Borneo and, after eight weeks' hard fighting, the battle in New Guinea ended in an Allied victory. Next day, July 16, was the grim, decisive date upon which a new era, the Atomic Age opened—the first atom bomb was exploded in New Mexico. When the Potsdam Conference opened the next day, with Truman, Stalin, Churchill and Eden (the two British leaders were a week later replaced by Attlee and Bevin) the President of the United States was about to make one of the most momentous decisions in history—order the dropping of the atom bomb on Japan. The Conference agreed on the principles to govern Germany, the peace treaties with the satellites and the future of Poland; in most questions the Russian point of view prevailed.

Potsdam II—Attlee—Truman—Stalin

Then, on August 6, 1945, the Bomb fell on Hiroshima. Four square miles were completely devastated, about 160,000 people were killed or injured. Two days later Russia declared war on Japan. On August 9 the second atom bomb was dropped on Nagasaki. For five days the Japanese temporized, trying to bargain about the status of the Emperor. Then, at midnight on August 14, Attlee and Truman announced that Japan had accepted the Allied demand for unconditional surrender. August 15 was VJ day and the end of the most deadly and ruinous war in history.

Brighter than the sun

The Atom Bomb's aftermath in Hiroshima

Before that momentous landmark, the Liberals won the Canadian election, Mr. Chiffley was elected Australian Premier and De Valera declared Eire an independent republic. The Allied *Kommandatura* was established for Greater Berlin and the property of all members of the Nazi Party was confiscated. The German casualties, as captured secret documents revealed, were over four million from 1939 to November 1944—with almost 1,120,000 killed. British, American and French troops entered Vienna. Jan Masaryk returned to Prague after six years in exile. Laval was arrested by the U.S. Army Air Force and handed over to the French. The Director-General of UNRRA forecast that at least £375 million extra money will be needed to keep Europe from starvation during the coming winter. Pétain was sentenced to death but this was commuted to life imprisonment. Britain and U.S.A. offered to share their radar secrets with the rest of the world.

The aftermath of the Far East war led to fast developments. The Japanese armies surrendered one by one. The Russians occupied Harbin and Mukden and the long, tragic clash between Chiang Kai-Shek and the Chinese Communists began. Quisling's trial ended with his execution. Stalin announced the occupation of all Manchuria, the Kurile Islands and South Sakhalin. Lend-Lease ended; so did many wartime controls in America where unemployment began to rise. There were mass suicides in Tokyo as a series of surrender agreements were signed from Singapore to Bougainville, from the East Indies to the Ryukus. In China one million Japanese troops laid down their arms. Mao began discussions with Chiang Kai-Shek; on September 8 General MacArthur entered Tokyo. Tojo committed suicide, Japanese war criminals were arrested and the Black Dragon Society was outlawed. New York acclaimed General Wainwright and a clash between MacArthur and Dean Acheson, the new American Secretary of State began over U.S. policy in Japan.

In Britain Sir Stafford Cripps was the first to utter the nasty word 'austerity'. Lord Haw-Haw was sentenced to death; the Foreign Ministers' London Conference ended in dead-lock. The demands for opening Palestine to Jewish immigration began to be voiced. The Bank of England was nationalized. British troops were in action against Indonesians for whom the end of the war brought a resurgent nationalism and a desire to end Dutch rule.

The Nuremberg War Crime Trials opened on November 22.

British troops fight in Java

The call to Indonesian independence

Ready to give up–

–The Japanese surrender

Crime . . .

Revenge—a murdered guard (Dachau)

The living (Buchenwald)–

He survived (Belsen)–

–They didn't (Gardeleben)

–And the dead (Nordhausen)

and punishment

Von Neurath, former Protector of Czechoslovakia, was arrested in September; Laval was sentenced to death and executed; Ley, the Nazi leader, committed suicide. Kramer, the Beast of Belsen, was sentenced to death but Krupp was not tried as a war criminal. Hess was found sane enough to be tried; Nazi commanders and guards of Dachau were sentenced to death. Retribution also came to the Japanese war criminals: Togo and Homma were arrested in September; Yamashita's trial began late in October. In December fifty-nine Japanese leaders were taken into custody and the trials continued well into 1946.

The Beast of Belsen and his Mate

Mussolini and his mistress—in the main square of Milan

Generalissimo Chiang Kai-Shek—leader of Free China

Sir Alexander Fleming, the man behind the discovery of Penicillin

The well-dressed lady of 1945

Padded and square shoulders were still the fashion for British women while in Paris women piled immensely high turbans upon their pretty heads—which were designed originally (a good excuse) to annoy the 'potato-bugs', the Germans, by using as much material as possible. Nylons were still something mythical, existing on the other side of the Atlantic but rarely glimpsed in London. Restaurants could still not charge over five shillings for a meal—though some charged four times as much by cleverly invented extras. Food was terribly important—the gastronomic nadir was reached by the introduction of whalemeat about which there were innumerable jokes but precious little relish.

The song-hits were 'Till the end of Time', 'Laura', 'Don't Fence Me In', 'There goes that Song again'. The best-sellers in the bookshops included *Left Hand, Right Hand* (Osbert Sitwell), *Brideshead Revisited* (Evelyn Waugh), *Cannery Row* (John Steinbeck), *Dragonwyck* (Anya Seton), *Odd Man Out* (F. L. Green), *The Lost Weekend* (Charles Jackson), *London Belongs To Me* (Norman Collins), *Mine Own Executioner* (Nigel Balchin), *Anna and the King of Siam* (Margaret Landon), *Animal Farm* (George Orwell)—most of which ended up as films.

Norman Collins

Sir Osbert Sitwell

Evelyn Waugh

I think I'll celebrate the anniversary of our entry into the victorious war against the aggressors by clearing out the air-raid shelter

1946

and after

The search

for Peace

They said . . .

Our motherland has been transformed from a backward country into a world power, from an agrarian into an industrial country, and all in thirteen years.

February 9, 1946 STALIN

With the successful accomplishment of Comrade Stalin's strategic plan in 1944 the Soviet Union was in a position with its own forces and without the aid of the allies, to occupy all Germany and accomplish the liberation of France. This circumstance forced Churchill, who up to this time opposed the opening of a second front in Europe to undertake the invasion of western Europe.

· February 8, 1947 STALIN'S REVISED
OFFICIAL BIOGRAPHY

Come what may, nothing will ever shake my belief that this old country—old in history, old in experience, old in achievement—is at heart as young and vigorous as she has ever been.

May 15, 1947 H.M. THE KING AT GUILDHALL

(Russia) is a sealed book . . . what person can say what is happening inside the U.S.S.R.? We are invited to put our security in the pool with a nation which is determined not to reveal to the world what it is doing.

September 27, 1948 BEVIN

The horrors of the recent war are too alive in the minds of the people and the public forces in favour of peace are too great for Churchill's pupils in aggression to be able to overcome them and to deflect them towards a new war.

October 28, 1948 STALIN

To have a strong democracy we must have political under-standing between free democratic nations. To have any political understanding we must have a sound strategy for the defence of democracy. To have a sound strategy for defence we must have a firm and stable economic basis in all the countries concerned.

September 9, 1949 SIR STAFFORD CRIPPS

The last war showed that the German and Soviet peoples made the greatest sacrifices and that they have the greatest potentialities in Europe for executing great enterprises.

October 14, 1949 STALIN'S MESSAGE TO
THE EAST GERMAN GOVERNMENT

I reject the legal and the collective guilt of the Germans but like many of my compatriots I am profoundly conscious of a sense of collective shame.

December 11, 1949 CHANCELLOR ADENAUER

Mayor O'Dwyer of New York

AS AN AMERICAN newspaper put it, New Year's Eve 1945–6 was the first for six years on which 'men were not shooting at each other formally'. There was still a great deal of 'informal' shooting and the first year of peace was the least peaceful within human memory.

In the United States William O'Dwyer succeeded La Guardia, the 'Little Flower', as Mayor of New York. President Truman was having trouble with Congress; there was also trouble with American troops in India, Korea, Japan, the Philippines and Europe. The boys wanted to go home. Radar hit the moon for the first time, bouncing back and recording its impulses.

In Japan the Emperor gave his worshipping subjects a shock by denying his divinity. Chiang Kai-Shek signed a truce with the Communists; General Marshall mediated. Iran asked the Security Council to get the Russian occupation troops out of the country.

The United Nations soon settled down to many years of bickering and often abstruse argument. There was much dispute about the size of its permanent headquarters with New York the ultimate choice. The Security Council rejected the Russian demand to investigate the presence of British troops in Greece. Promptly the Ukraine asked that a similar investigation should be undertaken about Commonwealth forces in Java which 'menaced peace'; this was also rejected. Stalin proclaimed his new five-year plan for Russia.

In Egypt anti-British demonstrators rioted through Cairo and Alexandria

E. Phillips Oppenheim

George Arliss

Peron was elected President of the Argentine. France closed her frontier with Spain, accusing Franco of harbouring Fascists, Nazis and plotting against democracy. Truman, as the Gallup Poll found, was the choice of 65 per cent of the population. In the middle of March Attlee offered India full independence either inside or outside the Empire. E. Phillips Oppenheim, the novelist and George Arliss, the actor died.

Andrei Gromyko, the 'walk-out' delegate, listens at UNO

In his great speech at Fulton, Missouri, Winston Churchill coined the phrase 'iron curtain'; Stalin promptly called him a 'firebrand of war'. England, France, and the U.S. published captured German documents to prove Franco's co-operation with the Axis and called on the Spanish people to overthrow him—a singularly unsuccessful appeal. Japan drafted a new constitution, abolishing the armed forces forever, making war 'unconstitutional'. Soviet troops left Mukden and most of Manchuria, carrying off quite substantial 'souvenirs'—practically stripping all factories of machinery. Italy and Greece held elections—in Italy this was the first free poll since 1922; in Greece the Right-wing won and the leftist parties immediately accused it of terrorism. Two strikes were settled in the U.S.—that of Western Electric and General Motors workers—and another began when John L. Lewis called out his 400,000 miners who demanded higher wages and a union welfare fund to which employers would contribute. Herbert H. Lehman resigned after holding for three years the post of UNRRA Director; President Truman, after trying in vain for seven weeks to persuade the Senate of Mr. Pauley's fitness for the post of Assistant Secretary for the Navy, withdrew the nomination. The Security Council began its second session in New York; Iran made a second plea for Russian evacuation. Gromyko, the U.S.S.R. delegate walked out for the first (but not the last) time; the Persian complaint stayed on the agenda. The U.S. Government banned business building in favour of houses for veterans.

In Geneva the League of Nations met for the last time and dissolved itself, turning over its assets to the United Nations.

Twenty-seven Japanese war leaders were put on trial in Tokyo. General Marshall, with exemplary patience, arranged another truce between Chiang Kai-Shek and the Communists.

The U.N. Atomic Energy Commission met for the first time; the American and Russian plans for atomic control were presented and naturally differed in all essentials.

The first post-war atom bomb test took place on August 1 at Bikini Atoll; eleven old warships were destroyed, twenty-five put out of action. Of the goats, sheep and other animals 15 per cent perished. The second, three weeks later, was exploded under water and sunk a battleship, an aircraft carrier and eight other ships. American atom control was placed under a civilian board of five.

Winston Churchill—historic speech, Fulton, Mo.

Shigeru Yoshida—the Japanese Premier was attacked as a representative of the 'old ruling clique'

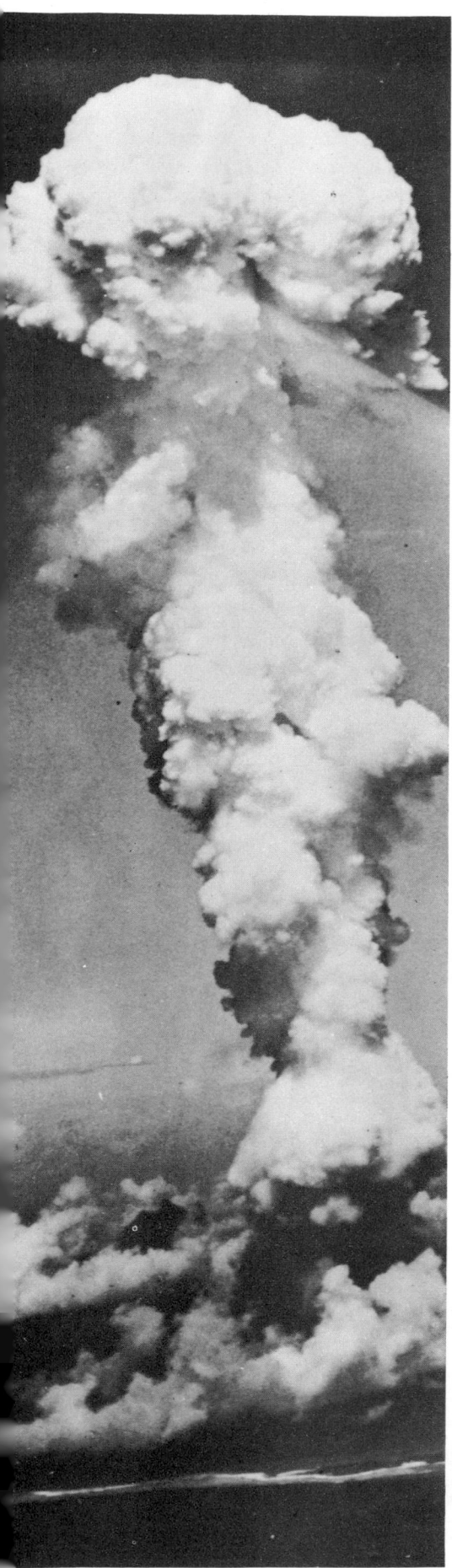

U.S.S. 'Nevada', target ship at Bikini

Violence exploded in the American South: Theodore G. Bilbo, the Mississippi Senator urged his constituents to do everything to prevent Negroes from voting. The £1000 million loan to Britain was finally approved; the British planned to buy machinery, food—and motion pictures—with it.

The Council of Foreign Ministers agreed to make Trieste a ward of U.N. and an international port. Molotov did not want a Federal Germany but a strong central government—and $10 billion in reparations. Once again the Ministers parted without agreement. On July 29 twenty-one nations met in Paris to discuss the peace treaties with Italy, Bulgaria, Rumania, Hungary and Finland—but many points were still in dispute. In the United Nations Russia vetoed the admission of Eire, Portugal and Transjordan (which had become an independent country with Emir Abdullah elevated to King); the Western Powers retorted by keeping out Albania and Outer Mongolia—but Sweden, Afghanistan and Iceland were admitted. Russia demanded an investigation of the number of troops Britain and the U.S. maintained in other than ex-enemy countries.

There was a slaughter of Jews at Kielce, Poland, the worst of the post-war pogroms. Thousands of Jews fled the country in terror.

Mushroom cloud over Bikini   *Theodore Bilbo—'stop negroes voting!'*

Seventy-one died. The King David Hotel outrage

Reacting to Bevin's previous statement that one million Jews could not be admitted to Palestine—as the Arabs would rise—Jewish illegal organizations threw a bomb into the King David Hotel at Jerusalem, killing seventy-one. Britain intercepted a number of ships bringing illegal European Jewish immigrants to Palestine and put them into detention camps on Cyprus. Tito's court condemned Mihailovitch to death and two days later he was executed. The Yugoslavs shot down an American Army transport plane that flew over their territory; all on board died. The U.S. sent a stiff protest. Russia asked Turkey for a share in the control of the Dardanelles. The British and American zones in Germany were merged economically; France and Russia refused a similar arrangement. Gertrude Stein, who wrote 'a rose is a rose is a rose' died at the age of seventy-two; the prophet of the shape of things to come, H. G. Wells, died in August, having become at the end of his life grimly pessimistic about mankind's future. Bread was again rationed in Britain; the suspicion began to grow in the minds of some people that winning a war *was* a costly business for which extreme austerity was the price.

H. G. Wells

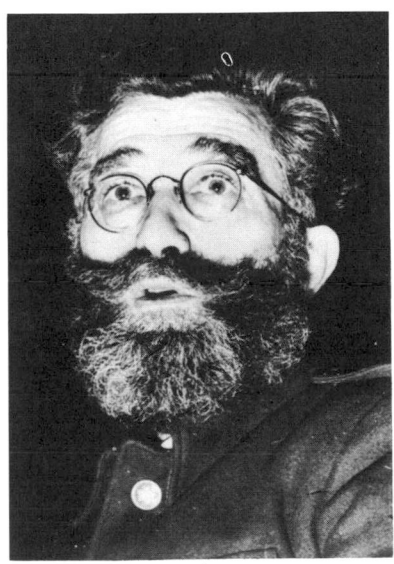

Gertrude Stein

Mihailovitch

The Nuremberg trial in October 1946, just retribution for the war criminals

Mao Tse-Tung—the new Red China was emerging under ruthless Communist leadership

David Lean brought Dickens to the screen in 'Great Expectations'. John Mills as Pip. Finlay Currie as Magwitch

Hermann Hesse won the Nobel Prize for Literature; those in Physics, Chemistry and Medicine were all scooped by Americans. We whistled or sang 'The Gipsy', 'Five Minutes More' and 'Surrender'. And peace, if not quite real, was wonderful. . . .

ON THE FIRST day of the second post-war year coal-mines were nationalized in Britain—so was the Cable & Wireless Ltd. Thirteen days later Sir Stafford Cripps had to announce emergency fuel plans for industry—the Big Freeze-Up began. By January 24 the whole of the British Isles (and most of their people) were shivering in the icy grip of the worst winter since 1940. In the first week of February the Government announced 'a most serious situation'. Electrical supply to many important industrial areas was cut off; its domestic use was reduced to a minimum. An emergency committee met under Mr. Attlee's chairmanship; its first decision meant further restrictions for housewives. It wasn't until February 24 that the factories could resume production, still with limited fuel.

Milk delivery by Pony Express sled

March brought great destruction by gales and floods; so much damage was done that the Lord Mayor opened a relief fund to which the Government contributed a million pounds.

Water, water, everywhere

Frontdoor fishermen

Nationalized—but the same old shifts—the same men

In Parliament Mr. Bevin attacked U.S. backing of Israeli insurgents and renewed refusal to implement the Anglo-American recommendation to admit 100,000 refugees and immigrants to Israel

King Paul and Queen Frederica of Greece

The gas and electricity cuts were to be continued throughout the summer and throughout the country. It was the wettest March on record in Great Britain. Snow and gales came back in April. Austerity was in full flower (or, to coin a phrase, in full wither). A serious transport strike in London lasted eleven days and the troops were called out. Australia and New Zealand came to the aid of the sorely-beset Mother Country with a joint gift of £35 million. There were two budgets instead of one—the first in April, the second in November. The second one led to the resignation of Mr. Hugh Dalton as Chancellor of the Exchequer as he had inadvertently disclosed some of his proposed tax provisions. The trade-gap was widening ominously. The meat ration was cut in July. Mr. Byrnes resigned as American Secretary of State and was succeeded by General Marshall. In June Marshall delivered his great speech at Harvard, formulating the momentous Marshall Plan for the reconstruction of Europe and for stopping the Communist floodtide. Of the twenty-two countries invited to a conference about Marshall Aid, sixteen accepted—the six Communist-dominated States stayed away.

In the Middle East the forecast was stormy. The Anglo-Egyptian talks broke down at the end of January and it was decided to submit the matter to the United Nations. The Palestine Conference met in London; after two weeks this problem, too, was dumped in UNO's lap. By the end of March British troops had been withdrawn from Cairo and Alexandria but they still stayed in the Canal Zone. The special session of the General Assembly of UNO opened at the end of April—the main subject being the Palestine question. This didn't help much; in the meantime thousands of Jews were put behind barbed wire on Cyprus and in Palestine itself; Jews and Arabs were killing each other and both sides were also busy killing the British.

On February 10 the Peace Treaties with Italy, Rumania, Hungary, Bulgaria and Finland were signed in Paris. France chose a new President—M. Vincent Auriol, probably the first French Head of State who had a famous aviatrix for a daughter. De Gaulle, in voluntary retirement, announced the formation of the 'Rally of the French People' (R.P.F.) which aimed at organizing 'a more real and efficient democracy'.

In the satellite country the 'salami-policy' started (this was the name Rakosi, the Hungarian Communist dictator gave to the gradual destruction of all opposition to Moscow). In January the Hungarian Government published reports of plots against the Government; there were many arrests and flights. The Polish General Election brought an overwhelming victory for the so-called Democratic bloc; Bierut, a Communist, was elected President and Cyrankiewicz, a left-wing Socialist, Premier. In April the Coalition Government in Finland resigned; in May, Ferenc Nagy, the Hungarian non-Communist Premier was blackmailed into resignation—by telephone, from Switzerland—by holding his small son as hostage in Budapest. King George II of the Hellenes died on April 1 and was succeeded by his brother, King Paul.

Rioting in Bombay

The winding-up of the British Empire was proceeding briskly if not without storms and snags. Responsible government was restored to Malta in September. On January 22 the Indian Constituent Assembly resolved on a sovereign independent republic. The future constitution of Burma was agreed in London by the end of the month. Mr. Attlee promised the transfer of power into Indian hands not later than June 1948; Lord Mountbatten was appointed as the last Viceroy. British policy on East Africa also held out promises of greater autonomy. A conference of Asian Relations opened in Delhi. The Constituent Assembly of Burma was elected; practically all seats were won by the Anti-Fascist People's Freedom League. Lord Pethick-Lawrence resigned as Secretary for India and was succeeded by Lord Listowel. In June Mr. Attlee made the momentous announcement that India was to be divided into two Dominions and that power would be transferred within ten weeks. Within a few days the terrible mass slaughter began and by September more than two million refugees were on the way—Hindus from the future Pakistan, Muslims from the future Dominion of India. Cholera and famine tripled and quadrupled the number of the dead.

The Baramula Convent, Kashmir, in which four nuns, a British Colonel and his wife were killed by tribesmen

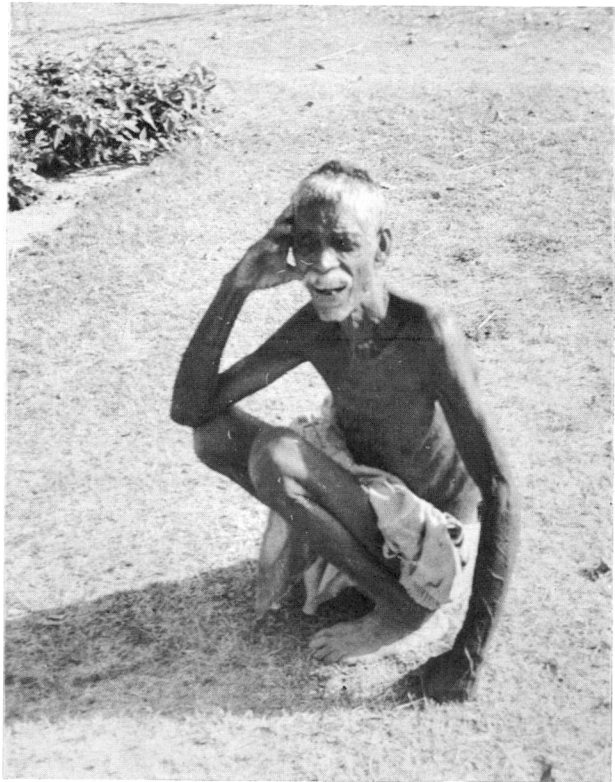

One of the two million famine-stricken refugees—for them freedom to die of starvation

Clement Attlee—India was to be divided and power transferred, within ten weeks

Ellen Wilkinson, Minister of Education

Lewis Douglas, U.S. ambassador

On January 26 a Danish airliner crashed near Copenhagen; among the twenty-two victims was Prince Gustav, the eldest son of the Crown Prince of Sweden. King Christian X of Denmark who had stayed with his people during the dark years of Nazi occupation died in April and was succeeded by his son, King Frederik IX.

A South Pacific Conference met in Canberra. The Dutch signed in March the agreement to establish the United Nations of Indonesia and the Netherlands-Indonesian Union. The U.N. Security Council approved American trusteeship over the former Japanese mandated islands. Chang Chun, Governor of Szechwan, became Prime Minister of the National Government of China. The new Japanese constitution came into force in May; Mr. Katayama, a Social Democrat, formed a new government three weeks later, on a coalition basis. Private trade with Japan was restored in June.

Ellen Wilkinson, the Labour Minister of Education, died in February and was succeeded by George Tomlinson. The White Paper on the Economic State of the Nation was published, debated for three days with a motion of censure which was defeated. The National Service Bill was published in March; but under pressure, the period of conscription was reduced by the Government to one year.

Mr. Lewis Douglas became American Ambassador to Britain; Mr. Attlee delivered what became the first 'Party Political Broadcast', the forerunner of politics on television. The Royal Commission on the Press was appointed; Sir Edwin Plowden became Chief Planning Officer of the Government—and there was a lot of planning to do. The Butler Act, raising the school-leaving age to fifteen, came into force on April 1. Lord Pakenham took over responsibility of the administration of the British Zones in Austria and Germany. The Allied approach to the ex-enemy continued to be humane and confused. German industry quietly planned a resurgence.

'Just like the pictures, ain't it ducks? Pity they're scrapping for our one and ninepences instead of for our charms alone.'

The first British Industries Fair since 1939 opened in May

King George VI and Queen Elizabeth, inspecting Swazi Warriors

The Duke of Gloucester returned to London in January after two years as Governor-General of Australia; he was succeeded by the Hon. Mr. W. J. McKell. His Majesty the King, the Queen and the two Princesses started their South African visit in February and returned in May. On April 21 Princess Elizabeth came of age and broadcast to the Commonwealth and Empire. In May that Grand Old Lady, Queen Mary, celebrated her eightieth birthday.

Their Majesties and the Princesses with Field-Marshal Smuts in Drakensberg, National Park

Westminster Abbey: the wedding of Princess Elizabeth and Lieutenant Philip Mountbatten, R.N.

King Michael of Rumania abdicates

Captain Odom flew around the world

Princess Elizabeth's engagement to Lieutenant Philip Mountbatten, R.N., was announced on July 9. The wedding, with all due pomp and popular jubilation, took place on November 20. The bridegroom was created Duke of Edinburgh. Four kings, a queen and two prince-regents attended the glittering ceremony. Throughout the nations, in villages, towns and cities the people rejoiced: this being the first great royal occasion since the war, the British went *en fête*. Americans were no less interested in the royal love story.

The British bacon ration was halved; further food cuts came four days later and no more American tobacco was to be imported. Potatoes were rationed in November; the miners got a raise of fifteen shillings per week. Motoring was further restricted early in December; the Registration for Employment Order came into force. Morrison and Bevin appealed to the nation to support the Government measures; the King's Speech, in October, announced the amendment of the Parliament Act, cut the armed forces, abolished the Poor Law and nationalized the gas industry. Mr. Gary Allighan was expelled from the House of Commons 'for offences against Parliamentary privilege and decorum'. The municipal elections in November brought 625 Conservative gains and 652 Labour losses in the 388 boroughs. Plans for reducing capital expenditure by £200 million were announced in December; a few days later America agreed to unfreeze the balance of the loan to Britain. Labour called for a fight against Communist infiltration into the trade unions; an Anglo-Russian trade agreement was signed. Britain was fighting hard against bankruptcy and austerity seemed worse than the privations of wartime.

The world was shrinking: Captain Odom flew around it in 73 hours and 5 minutes; the first 'automatic' flight over the Atlantic was made in September. A jet-propelled Meteor flew from Edinburgh to London at 617 miles per hour.

In Eastern Europe, Russia and her local representatives continued the systematic elimination of all opposition. The General Election in Hungary brought a victory for the Government bloc; Petkov, the Bulgarian opposition leader was executed in September. The Comintern became the Cominform when the Communist Information Bureau was organized with headquarters in Belgrade; its Far Eastern seat was Harbin, Manchuria. Maniu, the Rumanian Peasant leader was sentenced to life imprisonment; young King Michael was forced to abdicate. Another king—little Victor Emmanuel of the enormous moustachios—died in exile.

Maurice Schuman—French Prime Minister

Senanayake of Ceylon—full responsibility

Marshal Pibul Songgram of Thailand

Ceylon also started on the road to independence with Mr. Senanayake forming the first Cabinet under the new constitution; Mauritius was also given a new form of government. In Malta Labour won the elections. The full responsibility of Ceylon within the Commonwealth was proposed in November. U Saw and seven others responsible for the murder of pro-British U Aung San and his colleagues were sentenced to death in Rangoon.

The Paris municipal elections brought large gains for De Gaulle. Ramadier resigned, only to form a new Coalition Government. This lasted only three weeks as crippling strikes spread in France which did not end until December 9. Schuman became Prime Minister; almost immediately he had to deal with strikes on the railways, the mines and many factories. There were serious strikes, riots and demonstrations in many cities of Italy which went on for ten days; in December a Cabinet reshuffle brought in the Republicans and the Saragat Socialists.

Russia abolished rationing and devalued the rouble. British troops withdrew from Iraq and Italy. There was a *coup d'état* in Thailand by Marshal Pibul Songgram who managed to stay in power for the next nine years. John Cobb established a ground speed world record of 394·196 m.p.h.

> *We are convinced that the best way to prevent future wars is to work for the independence and well being of all nations. This conviction guides our present efforts and will guide our future decisions.*
>
> Nov. 17. TRUMAN on Marshall Aid

John Cobb—fastest man on the earth

John Gunther, explorer at home

André Gide—Nobel Prize for France

Lack of paper and strikes still hampered publishing in Britain. Of the important books of the year Professor Gordon N. Ray's scholarly edition of *The Letters and Private Papers of W. M. Thackeray* was a landmark. John Gunther's *Inside U.S.A.*, Kravchenko's *I Choose Freedom* (its title became quite a slogan), Trevor Roper's *The Last Days of Hitler*, Michael Sadleir's *Forlorn Sunset*, Nigel Balchin's *Lord, I was Afraid*, and Margaret Storm Jameson's *Before the Crossing* were much sought after. André Gide won the Nobel Prize for Literature.

Hugh Trevor-Roper, Hitler's obituarist

Margaret Storm Jameson—much sought after

Jack Kramer—at Wimbledon total victory for the U.S.

Sir Edward Appleton won the Nobel Prize for Physics and the Society of Friends was awarded the Peace Prize. The Derby was won by the French horse 'Pearl Diver'—one of the first of the many French contenders to come; the Grand National by 'Caughoo'. The Davis Cup went to the U.S.; Americans also swept the board at Wimbledon with Jack Kramer winning the men's singles and M. Osborne the women's. There was a deep longing for peace in the world.

Sir Edward Appleton Nobel Prize for Britain

The Derby. In peacetime sunshine Pearl Diver won for France

Dockers struck; ships lay idle

ON NEW YEAR'S DAY 1948, Italy got a new constitution and Britain got the mixed blessing of British Railways. Lord Listowel was appointed Minister of State for the Colonies and the British Governor of Burma handed over his authority to the First President of the new Republic. A treaty of alliance was signed by Britain and Iraq, which was six days later rejected both by the Regent and the Cabinet. Bevin launched his Western Union plan, attacking the Communist design to dominate both East and West. To prove the good intentions of Britain the ban on tourist travel to the Continent was lifted.

The first by-election of the year brought a Conservative victory in Camlachie; in the next two the Conservative vote was considerably increased. A statement was issued on wages and prices which were spiralling away merrily and another on defence which was costing astronomical sums. In March Britain drew the last £25 million of the American Loan and the Economic Survey promised little relief. Though the Iraq Treaty fell through, similar alliances were signed by Britain with Transjordan and Saudi Arabia. Electricity was nationalized on April 1. The budget increased the taxes on beer, whisky and cigarettes, gave a little relief to earned income but introduced a capital levy which rose sharply above £2000. Mr. Dalton came back to the Cabinet in May. Field-Marshal Smuts was installed as Chancellor of Cambridge University; he had been defeated in the South African elections but remained one of the great elder statesmen of the world. The foundation-stone of the new House of Commons was laid. A dockers' strike in London and Liverpool ended after two weeks, having led to a state of emergency in the country.

General Marshall, father of the vast American aid programme to Europe and the underdeveloped countries

Tribute to F.D.R., the statue of President Roosevelt in Grosvenor Square

Nine days later Mrs. Roosevelt unveiled her late husband's statue in London and F.D.R. joined Washington, Lincoln and Franklin as one of the great Americans honoured in the capital.

The U.S. Conscription Bill was passed in June and the Anglo-American Co-operation Agreement within E.R.P. was signed a few days later. Mr. Truman still had a good deal of trouble with the Republican majority in Congress; this was election year which made things worse. Thomas Dewey threw his hat into the ring on the Republican side; Truman was the obvious Democratic candidate.

U.S. Presidential election. Republican H.Q.   *Mr. Dewey's supporters parade with banners*

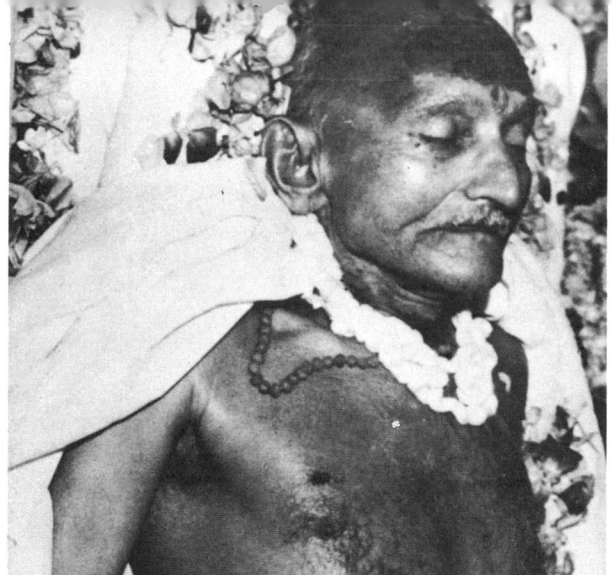

Mahatma Gandhi—the stubborn saint

Rajagopalachari and Nehru—the troops had left

The dispute between the new States of India and Pakistan over Kashmir was submitted to the Security Council. On January 30 one of the most remarkable men of our century, Mahatma Gandhi, a fabulous mixture of naïvety and cunning, of saintliness and political acumen, of meekness and stubbornness, was assassinated by a Hindu extremist, one of the most lunatic acts in human history. The last British troops left India at the end of February. Lord Mountbatten left the new Dominion and Republic in June; Mr. Rajagopalachari was sworn in as Governor-General.

All over Asia the trend was towards independence—and war. The Dutch and the Indonesians signed a cease-fire agreement on board an American warship in January. Malaya's new constitution came into force on February 1. The first Governor-General of Ceylon was installed three days later. In Japan Dr. Ashida became Premier, forming a new Cabinet early in March. The Thai Government resigned in April. Manuel Roxas, the President of the Philippines died; the new independence also brought stubborn civil war to the far-flung islands. Chiang Kai-Shek was elected President of China; the first Legislative Assembly met. There were elections in South Korea and a provisional central government was established in Indo-China. Dr. Wong Wen-hao became Chinese Premier. Viet Nam was recognized as an 'independent associated State within the French Union'. In the Middle East Palestine was the focal point. By May it became evident that nothing but partition could solve the problem. On May 14 the Jewish National Council proclaimed the State of Israel which was promptly recognized by the U.S.A. The British Mandate ended the same night; next day Israel applied for membership in the United Nations. Trying to prevent an Arab-Jewish war, Count Bernadotte was appointed as mediator; the Security Council called on all governments to abstain from hostilities. Bernadotte proposed a four-weeks' truce which started on June 11. A World Jewish Congress opened at Montreux to try and solve the immense problems of the new State; the last British troops left Palestine on June 30.

British troops leave Palestine

Count Bernadotte proposed a truce

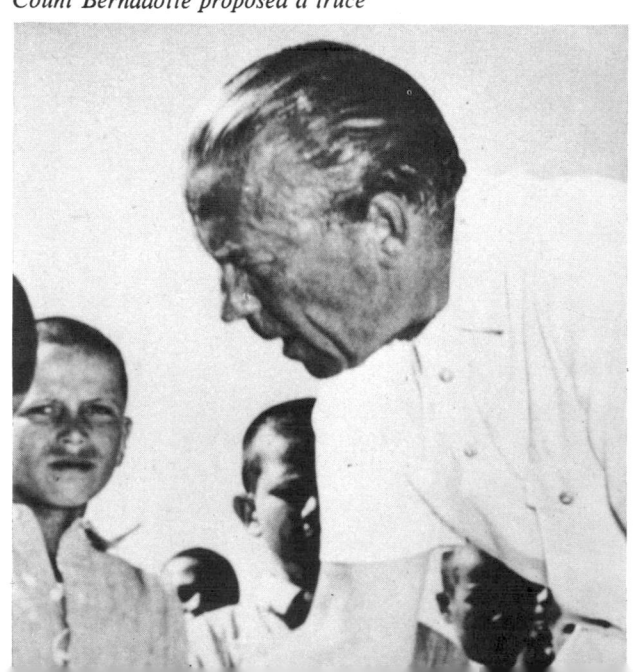

To Berlin by airlift—to deliver the milk

There was a new Cabinet in Iraq where General Elections were held in June; there were similar changes in Persia and Turkey. Britain disbanded the Transjordan Frontier Force, known as the Arab Legion, in February. The real crisis of the year came in Germany. In February Britain and the U.S. introduced their bi-zonal Charter. In April there was a collision over Berlin between a British passenger aircraft and a Soviet fighter; fifteen lives were lost. The London agreement on the Western Zones of Germany was published on June 7; nine days later the Russians walked out of the Allied *Kommandatura* of Berlin. When the French accepted the London agreement and currency reform was introduced into the Western Zones, the Russians banned all traffic between the Russian Zone and the West; all railway traffic was prohibited between Berlin and Helmstedt. The U.S.S.R. had decided to strangle the German capital and force the Berliners into the Soviet camp. By July 10, the blockade by land and water was made absolute. The three Western powers immediately protested to Moscow. They also organized, with little delay, the famous airlift which, for many months, kept the city alive. In spite of Russian threats and interference, the *Luftbrücke* (air bridge) remained unbroken. The West German Constituent Assembly held its first meeting at Bonn, early in September. A huge anti-Communist rally was held nine days later in the beleaguered city. The Western Powers referred the Berlin dispute to the Security Council, which met in October. As usual, when one of the great Powers was involved, there was a good deal of heated talk but no action. By the end of the year the German capital proved that it could survive; in the November elections the Communists were overwhelmingly defeated.

Mrs. Kosenkina—refugee from a third floor in New York City

The anti-Communist sensation of the year was the escape of Mrs. Kosenkina—refugee from a third floor in New York City from the Soviet Consulate in New York; she jumped from the third floor of the building rather than be sent back to her country. The Russians claimed that she was 'abducted' but she made it plain enough what her choice was. Two days after Christmas 1948, Cardinal Mindszenty, the Primate of Hungary was arrested and the systematic persecution of the Catholic Church began. Early in July Count Bernadotte proposed discussions for a settlement in Palestine. Two days later Jewist terrorists abducted five British officials. By August 1 the British withdrawal was complete. On September 17, Count Bernadotte was murdered in Jerusalem by Jewish gangsters—one of the blackest deeds of senseless fanaticism. His report was published three days later, showing the scrupulous fairness and tolerance of its author. The Arabs formed a Palestine Government at Gaza. A cease-fire agreement was signed at the end of November in Jerusalem; next day the representatives of the Arab States met at Jericho and King Abdullah was proclaimed as King of Palestine and Transjordan. How much of the Holy Land he would actually rule, no one could tell.

King Abdullah and Glubb Pasha—how much of the Holy Land?

A tank at Gaza, where the Arabs formed a government

Arabs kill a Jewish sniper on the Mount of Olives

The first post-war Olympic Games opened in London

In Britain the National Insurance Act came into force and everyone started pasting stamps on to their cards. The British Lend-Lease debt to America was settled. Flour and bread rationing ended.

The King and Queen, who had celebrated their Silver Wedding, give a royal welcome to Olympic contenders

Prince Charles—an old kings' name for a new heir to the throne

The heroine of the XIV Olympiad was Mrs. Blankers-Koen of Holland who won almost every event she entered; the 6000 competitors were watched by more than a million people. The Marshall Aid brought a windfall of $310 million to Britain; a very welcome boost for the meagre dollar reserve. Thousands of people queued up at the exhibition of Danish Art Treasures. Millions rejoiced at the birth of Prince Charles on November 14. Nine days later there was sadness and anxiety at the announcement of the King's illness which led to the cancellation of the projected royal visit to Australia.

The Danube Conference opened in Belgrade and the Western Powers were virtually excluded from navigation on the great river. Britain signed a trade agreement with Eire; just before Christmas she became an independent republic, still vaguely tied to the Commonwealth. Another new republic came into being when South Korea proclaimed her statehood with the indestructible Dr. Syngman Rhee as her President. Burma had her violent teething-troubles; martial law was proclaimed in August; in September, U Tin Tut, a staunch friend of Britain, was murdered by Communists in Rangoon. Nokrashy Pasha, Egypt's moderate Prime Minister, shared his fate in December. Mahomed Ali Jinnah, the first Governor-General and main architect of Pakistan died in September. December brought the death of J. Hofmeyr who was General Smuts' chosen successor as leader of the South African United Party.

The two main trouble-spots of the world were Greece and China. Martial law was imposed throughout the Kingdom of the Hellenes in October; the Government resigned next month and a coalition of Liberal and People's Party members followed. There was still bitter fighting in the mountains between Communist guerrillas and Government troops.

In China the Communists occupied Mukden and were in control of all Manchuria; martial law was declared throughout North China and Dr. Sun Fo became Prime Minister. Mao-Tse Tung and his men were pausing to gather forces for a new, powerful attack. The march of the Chinese Red Army from the north—one of the longest in history—was nearing its end, and a new balance of Asiatic and World Power was imperceptibly being struck with unforeseeable consequences to history.

Civil war in Greece—rebel prisoners

This was the year—1948—in which secret documents were hidden in a pumpkin and the tragic Alger Hiss case began, with Whittaker Chambers, an ex-Communist, accusing several ex-Government officials (including Hiss and Harry White) of being members of the Communist underground. White died of a heart attack but Hiss lived to fight the charges, finally going to jail for perjury.

Alger Hiss, the accused

Whittaker Chambers, the accuser

Harry S. Truman—the single-handed winner of a U.S. Presidential Election. In the United States the November elections brought back Mr. Truman as President. The Democrats also swept into power in both Houses of Congress

Again Britain's David Lean brought Dickens to the screen with magnificent vitality with 'Oliver Twist'. Alec Guinness as Fagin and Robert Newton as Bill Sikes

Professor P. M. S. Blackett—Nobel Prize winner

The Nobel Prizes were carried off by Britain (Professor P. M. S. Blackett in Physics and Mr. T. S. Eliot, in Literature—by Sweden (Professor Arne Tiselius, Chemistry) and by Switzerland (Dr. P. Moeller, Medicine). America beat Australia in the Davis Cup; Wimbledon was again an American triumph—and an American horse won the St. Leger. There were notable advances in the cure of malaria and the fight against ocular onchocerciasis which is a blindness caused by a worm in parts of Africa. The Roman City of Canterbury was discovered—and so was a duck-billed dinosaur in a sandpit in New Jersey.

THE FIRST DAYS of the fourth postwar year—1949—promised peace in several trouble-spots. The new State of Israel had won a series of unexpected and spectacular victories over Egypt and a cease-fire was signed in the Negeb between the two countries. Five British military planes were shot down by Israeli fighters near the Palestine-Egyptian border. Transjordan asked for British troops to be sent to the Gulf of Aqaba. The armistice talks between Egypt and Israel opened in Rhodes.

Zoltan Korda and Alan Paton—filmed 'Cry The Beloved Country'

T. S. Eliot—Nobel Prize winner

Eleven days later the first elections for the Constituent Assembly were held in the new Jewish State. By the end of the month the British Government granted her a somewhat grudging *de facto* recognition.

Dr. Chaim Weizmann was elected President of Israel in mid-February. The Egyptian-Israeli armistice was signed shortly afterwards. In May Israel was admitted to the United Nations and established full diplomatic relations with Britain. Israel's victory brought mutual recriminations and protracted political crises in the Middle East. In Iraq General Nuri-as-Said led a new government. The Syrian Government was overthrown by General Husni Zaim who became Prime Minister, Minister for Defence and the Interior. The armistice lines began to harden into frontiers cutting Jerusalem into two and creating many economic and geographical problems.

Hundreds of thousands of Arab refugees were evacuated by UNO from the Holy Land to the neighbouring countries

Sydney Stanley, half comic, half sinister

John Belcher resigned from Parliament

'Three days, seven hours, sixteen minutes. . . . Three days, seven hours, fifteen minutes. . . . Three days, seven hours, fourteen minutes. . . .'

Scramble for toffee—unrationed

There was a cease-fire in Kashmir between India and Pakistan. Nathuram Godse, the assassin of Gandhi was sentenced to death in February and executed nine months later. In April the Commonwealth Conference in London accepted the Indian declaration that she wished to remain in the Commonwealth as an 'independent sovereign republic'. The new Republic had some hard times to face: grave economic difficulties, lack of dollars and of food, the persistent hostility of Pakistan, the need to create a new civil service and an army of her own. Nehru's decision was to steer a course of cautious neutrality between the East and West blocs.

The United States recognized the Republic of Korea (South). In his New Year's Message to Congress, President Truman called for anti-inflation measures, the repeal of the Taft-Hartley labour law and legislation against racial discrimination. Mr. Marshall resigned and was succeeded by Dean Acheson as Secretary of State.

In Britain the Nationality Act came into force on January 1. The Lynskey Tribunal's report was published near the end of the month, disclosing indiscretion in some government offices and leading to the resignation of John Belcher from Parliament. Mr. Sydney Stanley, a half-comic, half-sinister character departed for Israel; George Gibson, the Trade Union leader also retired from his office. In March we were cheered by winning the final Test Match series against South Africa. The Liberal Party met at Hastings in conference. On March 31 Mr. Churchill made his great speech in Boston, declaring that but for the atom bomb in American hands, Europe would have fallen to Communism and London would be under bombardment. War, he said, wasn't inevitable; but the 'fourteen men in the Kremlin were more dangerous than Hitler' because the late Führer had no fundamental idea, no political philosophy.

The budget of Sir Stafford Cripps was called one of 'taxation and tears' by a Liberal; his own party was also bitterly disappointed. Telephones became more expensive; pool betting and large bequests were more heavily taxed. The dollar and gold drain still continued and not much relief was promised before 1952. In spite of the continued austerity, Labour won three by-elections; but the London County Council poll produced an equal number of Conservative and

Labour seats with one Liberal holding the balance. The London dockers went on strike in April; Labour published its election manifesto, calling it 'Labour Believes in Britain'. The Commonwealth Prime Ministers met. Sweet rationing ended on April 24—but the frustrated British sweet tooth was too ravenous and it had to be reintroduced in July.

The municipal elections in England and Wales brought a decided Conservative swing. In May the Avonmouth dockers went on strike; troops had to be introduced at Bristol and Liverpool when the stoppage of labour spread. 'Export or die' being the slogan, a Dollar Export Board was established. There was another dock strike in London in June. Reports on Population and the Press were published with neither resulting in anything revolutionary.

Peron proclaimed his new constitution. A seasonal revolution in Paraguay brought a new President, General Rolon, to power. Four weeks later he was deposed.

There were ugly racial riots in Durban, South Africa, casting the long shadow of worse troubles to come. The Suez Canal Company gave Egypt a greater share in the profits and control of the Canal. Britain released a portion of Egypt's sterling balance. There were violent Communist-inspired riots in Uganda. A conference on Central African transport problems met at Lisbon. The Emir Idris el Senussi proclaimed the independence of Cyrenaica; Transjordan changed its name to Hashemite Kingdom of the Jordan. The ferment in Africa was simmering slowly to a boil.

Relations between the Communist and the free world showed little sign of improvement. British, French and Dutch delegates withdrew from the Communist-dominated World Federation of Trade Unions. When Molotov was replaced by Vyshinsky, the fiery Public Prosecutor of the notorious Moscow trials, in the office of Foreign Minister it was obvious that this did *not* mean a more conciliatory Russian policy. The Western Powers felt the need for unity in defence: the North Atlantic Treaty was signed on April 4 by Great Britain, France, the Benelux countries, Denmark, Italy, Iceland, Norway, Portugal, Canada and the United States.

Race riots in Durban

Andrey Vyshinsky—fiery Prosecutor

The North Atlantic powers closed ranks

Cardinal Mindszenty of Hungary faces Communist judges

In March four Church leaders received life sentences in Bulgaria. The Hungarian Parliament was dissolved in April. The World Congress of Partisans of Peace met in Paris in April; Stalin and his propagandists were busy turning the word 'peace' into a servile instrument of Soviet imperialism. A 20,000 million rouble State loan was launched in the U.S.S.R. in May; soon 'peace-loans' would be used to tax and double-tax every worker and peasant. The General Election in Hungary (the fourth in five years) brought an overwhelming victory' for the Independence Front, i.e. the Communists and their satellites.

General Sir Brian Robertson—June appointee

Rajk—former Foreign Minister arrested

Kostov of Bulgaria: old Communist—new traitor

On June 16, Rajk, the former Foreign Minister of Hungary was arrested and one of the most nauseating tragi-comedies of Communist duplicity began. Nine days later another old Communist leader, Kostov of Bulgaria was arrested in Sofia.

The integration of Europe became more tangible. Norway rejected the Russian offer of a non-aggression pact. The Benelux countries met at the Hague. France and Italy established a Customs Union. A United Nations Conference was held at Annecy on tariffs and trade. The Statute of the Council of Europe was signed in May. An International Socialist Conference was held in Holland. As the prospects of an early German peace treaty receded, the Western Allies took steps to ease the burden of occupation and to create a West German State. A Three-Power agreement for tripartite control machinery was signed in Washington in April and an Occupation Statute, to come into force when the Federal Republic was established, was published a few days later. Britain, France and the U.S. also agreed on the future of restricted and prohibited industries in Western Germany. A Ruhr Authority was established. On the fourth anniversary of VE Day the basic law for a Western German constitution was adopted in Bonn, approved by the three Military Governors. Sir Brian Robertson was appointed British High Commissioner on June 1. Three weeks later the Charter of the Allied High Commission was published and the Federal Republic was within sight. There was some talk about the *Wirtschaftswunder*, the 'economic miracle' of Western Germany's recovery though it was only in its early stages.

The Chinese Communists lost no time in showing their anti-Western attitude. On April 20, Communist batteries opened fire on H.M.S. Amethyst which was proceeding on its 'lawful business' through the Yangtze Gorge to Chungking

The Canadian Parliament was dissolved in April; a month earlier Newfoundland had become part of the great Commonwealth Confederation. The General Elections brought a Liberal victory. There were elections in Belgium and serious riots in the tin-mines of Bolivia. Elections, too, were held in the Trieste Free Territory.

The second half of the year saw the still stronger tightening of the Russian hold on Eastern Europe. Dimitrov, the hero of the Reichstag Fire Trial, died in Moscow, somewhat mysteriously; he was a champion of a Balkan Federation which Moscow disliked. Kolarov, the former Foreign Minister, succeeded him as Premier of Bulgaria. The Socialist Parties of Bulgaria, Czechoslovakia, Hungary, Poland and Yugoslavia met in London and set up a Socialist Union of Central-Eastern Europe.

The prospects of the free world in the Far East were not exactly bright. Bao Dai formed a Viet Nam Government early in July. Chiang Kai-Shek and President Quirino of the Philippines proposed a union of Far Eastern countries—a laudable plan with little chance of success. A People's Government was established in Manchuria. Canton fell to the Communist forces; Chungking was occupied by them at the end of November. On December 10 Chiang Kai-Shek arrived in Formosa, his forces utterly defeated.

The Commonwealth Finance Ministers met in London. In New Zealand there was a referendum on compulsory military training. Australia gave £A10 million to Britain as a free gift. A round table conference on Indonesia opened at The Hague in August. The Fourth Commonwealth Relations Conference took place in Ontario; the NATO Council met for the first time in Washington. The United States of Indonesia were established in November when agreement was reached with the Dutch. President Quirino was re-elected in the Philippines. In Canberra, British, Australian and New Zealand leaders conferred on Commonwealth policy in the Pacific and Asia. An Islamic Economic Conference was held in Karachi. Duncan Stewart, the Governor of Sarawak, was assassinated in December. On December 17 Dr. Soekarno was inaugurated as the first President of Indonesia; Dr. Hatta became the first Premier. The French High Commissioner formally transferred his authority to the State of Viet Nam.

Britain was still struggling with the economic aftermath of the war. Sir Stafford Cripps announced a cut of £100 million a year in dollar imports. Troops were called in to handle food cargoes in the London docks and a state of emergency was declared. The Colonial Development Corporation's groundnut scheme proved a sad failure. The Conservatives published their 'Right Road for Britain' and on July 25 the dock strike ended at long last. Gibraltar was given a new constitution; Malta demanded one firmly.

'*Keep this under your hats. I learned from a very reliable source that Cripps is going to put a hundred per cent purchase tax on aspirins*'

Mr. S. S. Holland—the New Zealand elections brought victory for Mr. Holland and his National Party

Robert Menzies: the Australian elections were won by the Liberal and Country Parties; Mr. Menzies formed a Cabinet

The Earl of Harewood chose an Austrian bride.

In September came the thunderbolt of the devaluation of the pound by 30 per cent—from 4·03 to the dollar to 2·80. The Opposition called it 'one of the most serious economic defeats in history'; the Government defended it as inescapable. The sterling area, reluctantly, followed suit. Thousands of British travellers abroad found themselves in difficulties, with a third of the meagre allowances suddenly disappearing. In October stringent measures to control inflation were announced, aiming at a saving of £250 million. The General Council of the T.U.C. recommended that all claims for higher wages should be postponed. Iron and Steel were nationalized but the enactment of the Bill was postponed until after the General Election. The free trade unions met in conference to set up a rival international organization to the Communist-controlled W.F.T.U. In the Corfu Channel case Britain was adjudged £843,947 damages against Albania by the Hague Court—but, as in some damage suits, the money still remained to be collected. The suspensory veto of the House of Lords was curtailed by a Bill; it turned the Upper House of Parliament into little more than a high-level debating club. Britain and Yugoslavia signed a five-year trade agreement.

The Middle East was still in ferment. In July British diplomats and officials from these territories met in London. The Egyptian Government resigned; Hussein Sirry Pasha formed a new one. Husni Zaim's brief dictatorship in Syria ended with his arrest and execution; Atasi Pasha succeeded him. Nokrashy Pasha's assassin was sentenced to death. Iran became 'Persia' again—at least as far as foreign languages went; Abdul Hossain Hazhir, a former Premier was assassinated in November. Nuri-as-Said, Iraqi Premier, resigned: a new coalition government was formed. UNO favoured the internationalization of Jerusalem—the Arabs and the Jews didn't. There was a military coup in Syria and a new government was formed by Khalid al Azm. The Parliament of Israel met in Jerusalem on Boxing Day.

In July President Truman signed the Atlantic Treaty and called for military aid to free nations. The United States published a White Paper on relations with China; a most unhappy document. Strikes still bedevilled the Union. Bills for Mutual Defence Assistance and Foreign Economic Recovery were signed by the President in October. Near the end of the year the standardization of arms was agreed on by Britain, Canada and the U.S.A.

The great and perhaps salutary shock of the year occured in September when Washington announced that an atomic explosion had taken place in the U.S.S.R. 'The enemy had it too'—Russia had developed her own atomic weapons. How much time she had gained by her vast espionage organization of which the first traces had been discovered in Canada and which was to be gradually tracked to Britain and the U.S., is still an open question. But the entire balance of world power changed again and there were some 'agonizing reappraisals' in the Western World.

The African continent was restless. The South African Citizenship Act was the first step in the establishment of 'apartheid' though in December the government announced the temporary postponement of the segregation measures. A report was published on constitutional reform in the Gold Coast. In November a miners' strike in Nigeria led to heavy clashes with the police at Eingu in which nineteen men were killed; the disorders continued for several days, with looting and fighting at Port Harcourt and Aba. The legislation in South-West Africa was referred by U.N. to the World Court at The Hague.

The two Germanies emerged into statehood during the year. In August there were general elections in Western Germany; a trade agreement was signed between her and the sterling area. The *Bundesrat* and *Bundestag* (Upper and Lower Houses of Federal Parliament) met in Bonn early in September; Professor Theodore Heuss was elected President and doughty Dr. Konrad Adenauer, former Mayor of Cologne, Chancellor of the West German Republic. The first government was formed five days later, the Military Government régime ended formally. The last British plane of the airlift landed at Gatow airport on October 6. In November the Benelux, French and American Foreign Ministers held a conference in Paris to discuss their policy towards Germany. The so-called Petersberg Agreement between the Allied High Commissioners and the German Chancellor was published two weeks later. In December Germany was made a participant in the European Recovery Programme. On December 19 the trial of Field-Marshal von Manstein ended; he was sentenced to eighteen years for war crimes. Russia retorted promptly to the establishment of the Federal German Republic by setting up her régime in Eastern Germany with Wilhelm Pieck as President and Otto Grotewohl as Prime Minister. There were general elections in Austria, where Dr. Figl became Chancellor. In Norway the Socialists gained a large majority at the polls. The civil war ended in Greece and British troops were withdrawn. After nine years the Athens-Salonika railway was reopened. Yugoslavia became a member of the Security Council. Franco made a State visit to Portugal, where the elections did not change Salazar's dictatorship. Mr. Max Petitpierre was elected President of the Swiss Confederation.

The romance of the year was the marriage of the Earl of Harewood and Miss Marion Stein—daughter of an Austrian refugee—the young couple had a strong mutual interest in their love of music. His Holiness the Pope inaugurated the twenty-fifth Holy Year. Professor Einstein announced his 'generalized theory of gravitation', having celebrated his seventieth birthday at Princeton.

George Orwell's sombre *Nineteen Eighty-Four* was the book of the year; Norman Mailer's *The Naked and the Dead* was praised and denounced in equal measure. Nancy Mitford published *Love in a Cold Climate*, Charles Morgan *The River Line*, H. E. Bates *The Jacaranda Tree*, and Elizabeth Bowen *The Heat of the Day*.

Konrad Adenauer: German Chancellor.

Tommy Handley—great clown in sound radio.

British cinema scored a world success with Graham Greene's 'The Third Man'. Orson Welles as Harry Lime

Edith Evans and Peter Finch in 'Daphne Laureola'

The Lady's Not for Burning brought a revival of the verse-play—though it needed the scintillating verbal wit of Christopher Fry to pull it off—with James Bridie's *Daphne Laureola*, T. S. Eliot's *The Cocktail Party* and Lesley Storm's *Black Chiffon* being equal hits. The Edinburgh Festival, in its third year, was a solid success; so was Benjamin Britten's *Let's Make an Opera!* which was performed both at the Aldeburgh and the Cheltenham Festivals. The exhibition of Landscape in French Art, 1550–1900 drew huge crowds to Burlington House. When Tommy Handley died, ITMA and a whole era in broadcasting came to an end.

In science there were developments in the exploration of cosmic rays (by two Russians, working 10,000 ft. up in a mountain laboratory); Harwell separated plutonium from uranium in the 'Gleep' (low energy pile). A second and more powerful pile reached its full power during 1949, producing enough artificial radioactive material to supply all medical, industrial and research needs. The first non-stop flight around the world was made in ninety-four hours by an American B-50 bomber. The Piltdown Man was discovered to have lied about his age—a mere 100,000 years old.

The De Havilland Comet flew in 6½ hours from London to Tripoli

FOR BRITAIN THE most important event in the first months of 1950 was the first post-war General Election (the 1945 poll had taken place between VE and VJ Day). The Labour Party issued its manifesto on January 18; five days later the Conservatives published theirs. The election campaign was comparatively brief but rather acrimonious; Mr. Bevan's unfortunate remark about Tories being 'vermin' was only one example of mutual mud-slinging. The result brought Labour back but with a vastly reduced majority: 315 seats instead of 393 in 1945; the Conservatives won 298, the Liberals 9 and Irish Nationalists 2. With barely a working majority, Mr. Attlee formed his new government on February 28.

A Conservative victory

Old soldiers vote in Chelsea

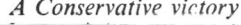

FUCHS GAVE BOMB TO RUSSIA

In Australia the Liberals won the elections, with Labour second and the Country Party third; in Egypt Nahas Pasha's Wafd Party swept the board with 228 seats against the five other parties, barely winning 90; the Wafdist leader formed his government nine days later.

In his traditional 'State of the Union' speech on January 4, Mr. Truman spoke of the 'expanding economy' of America, of quadrupling American production in the next fifty years.

Early in January Britain recognized the Communist Government of China. Mao-Tse Tung established a pro-Communist Government for Tibet in Chinghai. In March Chiang Kai-Shek resumed the Presidency of Nationalist China and took over supreme command of the armed forces, now restricted to Formosa. Russia and Communist China signed a thirty-year treaty and an agreement for the 'joint development of the resources of Sinkiang' which gave the Soviet Union large economic advantages. Peking offered Tibet 'regional autonomy' if she joined the Communist régime; Tibet declined without thanks.

The two traditional enemies, France and Germany, began to draw together. A Franco-German Parliamentary Conference met at Basle. Agreements were signed between the French Government and the Saar Prime Minister. Adenauer advocated full economic union between the two countries. The Schuman Plan about a single international authority for French and German steel and coal production was published in May. The *Bundesrepublik* joined the Council of Europe. The Foreign Ministers' Conference in London issued a statement about the 'reintegration of Germany'. Anglo-French discussions were held on the Schuman Plan and in June there was a six-Power Conference about it in Paris.

British economy badly needed international co-operation. Wage stabilization, the balance of payments were still unsolved problems; so was the high cost of defence. Sir Stafford Cripps's April budget introduced a retrospective surtax of 95 per cent, increased by 10 per cent the strength of beer and restored the 200,000 per year housing programme; it was a cautious budget and he was able to announce an improvement in exports and a slight rise in the dollar reserves. But taxation still swallowed 43·5 per cent of the national income. In two divisions the government scraped home with a majority of five.

Apparently the stronger beer did not impress the London dockers; next day they came out on strike and five days later troops had to be called in to do their work. The strike ended in eleven days. In May petrol rationing ended; but both cars and petrol were heavily taxed and there was not much congestion on the roads.

Klaus Fuchs—the traitor scientist

There were individual shocks in political life; the arrest and sentence of fourteen years imprisonment of German-born Dr. Klaus Fuchs, an atomic scientist who had been a Russian spy.

Afro-Anglo wedding

The Bamangwato chief, Seretse Khama, who married an Englishwoman and who was banned from his country, under not entirely straightforward circumstances.

On March 8 Marshal Voroshilov declared that Russia possessed atom bombs

Until the middle of the year the Middle East and Asia had a comparatively peaceful time. Dr. Rajendra Prasad was elected as the first President of India; the Republic was formally proclaimed on January 26. The first session of the Indonesian Parliament opened. India and Pakistan signed an agreement on their respective minorities. The Arab League members signed a collective security pact. In April the King of Jordan announced the annexation of Arab Palestine; the British Government recognized the union and at the same time gave the State of Israel full *de jure* recognition.

In January a state of emergency had to be declared in the Gold Coast because of strikes and riots. South Africa adopted a Bill to suppress Communism; the aftermath of the Rand riots was bitterness and resentment. More and more the Union's racial policies were developing into a major Commonwealth and world problem, exacerbated by the stubborn Afrikan refusal to follow the British example of recognizing the essential equality of black men with white.

The Soviet Union reintroduced capital punishment; in February the rouble was revalued. It made life much more expensive for foreign diplomats in Moscow.

On June 6 Mr. Trygve Lie, the Secretary-General of UNO, announced his twenty-year peace plan. Nineteen days later the incessant probing of the Soviet Union along the vast perimeter between the totalitarian and the free world, found a weak spot in Korea. The North Koreans invaded at dawn. Two days later the U.N. Security Council recommended all members to help the South Korean Republic to repel the attacks. Truman announced armed 'cover and support'. Within three days the North Koreans had captured Seoul, the South Korean capital. Moscow spoke of 'provocative actions of troops of the puppet government of South Korea' which had 'unleashed military operations'. Not even Stalin could pretend that the South had invaded the North; but he made an unashamed attempt to make the South the aggressor. All over the world people asked whether this meant the beginning of the Third World War?

Wonsan, in North Korea, as the armies roll on

War in Korea—the battles were in mountains

Early in July Gromyko was still accusing the South Koreans of a 'provocative attack'. Britain asked the U.S.S.R. to induce the North Koreans to withdraw; this must have caused hollow laughter in the Kremlin. The Security Council passed the motion that the U.N. forces should be placed under a unified command under the United States; MacArthur was appointed commanding general of these forces in Korea. Nehru also made an attempt at conciliation; the United Nations appealed to fifty-two nations for troops. Stalin gave Nehru a dusty answer. The Australians decided to provide ground troops. The Security Council met in August with Malik of the U.S.S.R. in the chair. The talk did not stop the bullets. On September 1 the North Koreans launched a full-scale attack across the Naktong river. Two weeks later, however, American forces landed at Inchon and established a bridgehead for the U.N. forces. Twelve days later they had recaptured Seoul, handing it over formally to Dr. Syngman Rhee. The 38th parallel—the frontier between South and North— was crossed by South Korean troops on October 1. Pyongyang, the North Korean capital was occupied. The North Korean army was utterly routed though part of it escaped into Manchuria and was reformed to fight again.

The face of retreat—a South Korean soldier

The Glorious Gloucesters hand-fought their way back

Near the end of the month the first reports of the participation of Chinese Communist troops in the Korean fighting were published. On November 5 MacArthur stated that 'alien Communist forces' had moved into Korea from Manchuria, and reported on the new situation to the Security Council. Three weeks later he announced a new offensive 'to end the war in Korea'. This proved to be somewhat optimistic; four Chinese armies poured over the River Yalu and the U.N. forces had to withdraw. On November 30 Truman broadcast about the 'new situation' in the war-torn peninsula and the possible use of the atom bomb by the U.N. forces. Pyongyang was evacuated by the U.N. forces early in December. On December 14 the U.N. Assembly adopted various proposals for a cease-fire; these were rejected by the Chinese Prime Minister. Six days later the Chinese crossed the 38th parallel and the war seemed to go badly for the U.N. forces.

Baudouin—A new King for the Belgians

The Palestine Conciliation Commission announced the failure of mediation between Arabs and Jews. Mediation also failed between India and Pakistan. The Iraq government resigned, Syria had a new constitution and signed a treaty of friendship with Pakistan. An International Islamic Economic Conference was held in Teheran. Turkey joined NATO and was elected a non-permanent member of the Security Council. Colonel Hinnawi, the leader of the Syrian *coup d'état* in August 1949 was assassinated. King Farouk announced in a speech from the throne that he intended to terminate the 1936 Anglo-Egyptian treaty.

In Britain the British Colonial Development Corporation's report proved to be a sad tale of unfulfilled expectations. Mr. Attlee announced that the Portsmouth explosion on July 14 had been due to sabotage. A civil defence pamphlet on atomic warfare made grim reading. In August Stalin closed down *British Ally*, the British magazine published in Moscow. The Trades Union Congress was held at Brighton; in September an emergency session of Parliament opened to adopt new defence measures. National service was extended to two years. Britain's participation in the Korean war demanded men and money. Communist plans to create chaos in British industry were clearly established. The recruitment of volunteers for civil defence got under way.

The Duke of Edinburgh opened the new Legislative Council of Gibraltar. In December Mr. Attlee went to Washington to discuss Anglo-American problems with President Truman. Ten days later it was announced that Marshall Aid to Great Britain would end on January 1, 1951.

The year's death-roll was a grievous one. In July Mr. Mackenzie King, the former Canadian Prime Minister, died. Field-Marshal Smuts passed away in September. Henry L. Stimson, the American statesman and King Gustav V of Sweden died in October. Mr. Peter Fraser, the former Premier of New Zealand and S. V. Patel, the Deputy Prime Minister of India died in December, so did Dr. Renner, the President of Austria.

America signed a series of agreements with Asian countries on 'Point Four' and military aid. There was a nationalist rising in Puerto Rico and on November 1 two Puerto Ricans pumped a score of bullets into the front of Blair House, Truman's temporary residence in Washington. They failed to kill the President and were quickly caught. But the crime was an indication of an emergent Latin-American problem.

In Belgium the royal crisis continued. The Regency ended on July 20; two days later King Leopold returned to Brussels and broadcast an appeal of support to the nation. But next day strikes and riots broke out in the capital and several other cities. At the end of the month a 'March on Brussels' was organized by the King's opponents. Within twenty-four hours he agreed to delegate his powers to Prince Baudouin, his eldest son, who took the oath as Prince Royal. M. van Zeeland formed a Christian Social Government.

'And if you persist in being late for A.R.P. lectures we have means of helping you to be early'

Henry L. Stimson: an American Statesman

150

In November the world mourned the death of George Bernard Shaw, the greatest playwright of modern times

From Picasso—a 'Peace Dove' for the Soviet

Bertrand Russell—Nobel Prize winner

Benjamin Britten—a new symphony

The American elections brought Republican gains in the House of Representatives but still left the Democrats in control. A state of emergency was declared in the States in mid-December. General Eisenhower was appointed Supreme Commander of the Western European Forces and the military side of Western Union was merged in NATO; Germany was to become part of the organization. The United States sent a note to Russia about a peace treaty with Japan; MacArthur warned the Japanese that they would have to 'rearm for self-preservation if international lawlessness continued'. Five years after the end of the war the two main former enemies of the democracies were being recruited for the Western line-up against Soviet aggression.

The Russian Orthodox Church leaders issued peace appeals. In Hungary the Communists forced an agreement upon the Church; a week later all except four religious Orders were dissolved in the country, thousands of monks and priests were thrown into the street. In November the new dogma of the Bodily Assumption of the Blessed Virgin Mary was solemnly promulgated in the framework of the Holy Year.

There were new governments in Denmark and Greece. New Zealand abolished her Legislative Council; Australia got a $100 million loan from the International Bank. The first elections under the new constitution were held in Trinidad. Communist dock strikes led to a state of emergency in New Zealand. Indonesia was admitted to the United Nations. The East German elections brought over 99 per cent support for the National Front's official list; three days earlier the electors of East Berlin demonstrated courageously but futilely against the voting methods. Russia and her satellites held a conference in Prague about the future of Germany. The Chinese, having tried to incorporate Tibet by negotiation, invaded her in October. Tibet appealed to the U.N. Secretariat. Peking delegates made their first appearance at U.N. meetings. The King of Nepal was deposed: his successor was the three-year-old second son of the Crown Prince. The World 'Peace' Congress opened in Warsaw. Poland and East Germany were told by Russia to agree on the Oder-Neisse frontier line and did so. Trygve Lie's term as Secretary-General of UNO was prolonged.

The harvest of books in 1950 was just as ample as before—17,072 new volumes and reprints were published in spite of the long printers' strike. Bertrand Russell won the Nobel Prize for Literature and published his *Unpopular Essays* which proved extremely popular. Thor Heyerdahl's *The Kon-Tiki Expedition*, Cecil Woodham-Smith's *Florence Nightingale*, Richard Aldington's controversial *Portrait of a Genius, But . . .* (D. H. Lawrence), Arthur Bryant's *The Age of Elegance* were the outstanding non-fiction works. Hemingway's clumsily-titled *Across the River and Into the Trees*, C. S. Forester's *Mr. Midshipman Hornblower*, A. J. Cronin's *The Spanish Gardener* and John Hersey's moving *The Wall* were among the most successful novels. The British continued to read more and publish more books than any other English-speaking people. Paper-back publishing was rapidly expanding.

At Stratford John Gielgud and Peggy Ashcroft were a comic Benedick and a beautiful Beatrice in 'Much Ado About Nothing'. Anthony Quayle's directorship was bringing great prestige to the Memorial Theatre

The Stratford season offered the inspired acting of John Gielgud and Peggy Ashcroft under Anthony Quayle's direction. The bi-centenary of Bach's death was commemorated with many concerts and special festivals. There were new symphonies by Alan Rawsthorne and Benjamin Britten. The Music Festivals at Hastings, Bournemouth, Aldeburgh, Cheltenham and Edinburgh were all well patronized—just as the Three Choirs Festival and Gloucester and the Triennial at Leeds.

Pope Pius XII proclaimed the dogma of the Assumption into Heaven of the Mother of God

General MacArthur told the Japanese—'Rearm for self-preservation'

Anna Magnani—Italy's rough-cut grande dame *of cinema—gave greatness to Rossellini's 'The Miracle'*

Juano Fernandez, brilliantly ironic as a half-caste aristocrat in the film of Faulkner's 'Intruder in the Dust'

The bitter war in Korea—the Communist forces broke through

Television was beginning to gain ground over sound broadcasting, with Shakespeare and J. B. Priestley competing with Wimbledon, Lords and Epsom. In broadcasting, Louis MacNeice's new translation of *Faust* was loved by the highbrows; 'Twenty Questions' and 'We Beg to Differ' by the not-so-intellectuals.

In science two new elements were added to the list, there were new discoveries about atomic particles and the speed of light. Colour television made progress. The shadow of the hydrogen bomb was a dark, grim one; cortisone and ACTH promised some relief if not cure of arthritis.

At the half-mark of the century there was no pause; the quest for peace and prosperity was just as arduous, the outcome just as uncertain as before.

> *It cannot be sufficiently stressed that science is not independent of social conditions, class, or party. Science is the product of social work and will remain a means and a weapon of class warfare as long as rival classes exist.*
> ISTVAN RUSZNYAK, President of the Hungarian Academy of Sciences

> *Power is sweet; it is a drug, the desire for which increases with habit. Those who have seized power, even for the noblest of motives, soon persuade themselves that there are good reasons for not relinquishing it.*
> BERTRAND RUSSELL

AT THE BEGINNING of 1951 the Korean War still dominated the headlines. The Communist forces had broken through and the South Korean government had to evacuate the capital again. Early in February the U.N. General Assembly, by forty-four votes to seven, declared China guilty of aggression in Korea. Twelve days later over a 100,000 Red soldiers launched a new massive attack. But by the middle of March American and South Korean forces had recaptured Seoul for the second time. Relations were far from happy between President Truman and General MacArthur; on April 11, the President announced that he had dismissed the Supreme Commander of the Allied forces and Commander-in-Chief of the U.N. Command. Eight days later MacArthur addressed a joint meeting of the U.S. Congress, having landed two days before in San Francisco where he received an enthusiastic welcome. His speech was a vigorous and defiant defence of his conduct and policy, presenting himself as a crusader against Communism in a 'global' war against a 'global' threat. But though the Republicans talked of the President's and Mr. Dean Acheson's 'impeachment' MacArthur stayed 'fired'.

Mr. Bevan was appointed to head the Ministry of Labour and National Service in January. Four months later he resigned over new charges introduced to the National Health Service, his monument as a legislator

Teheran—martial law and a nationalization bill

The rudest shock Britain suffered was in Persia. In January the Shah ordered his own vast estates to be sold to the peasants. In March General Azmara, the Prime Minister, was assassinated; his successor was Hussain Ala. The Majlis unanimously adopted the proposal to nationalize the oil industry on March 15. Two weeks later martial law was declared in Teheran; in April Hussain Ala resigned and was succeeded by Dr. Musaddiq who soon became world-famous for his anti-British speeches and his frequent crying fits. The nationalization Bill was passed unanimously both by the Majlis and the Senate, and the Shah signed the decrees on May 2. Britain decided to appeal to the Court of International Justice; the Persian Government promptly rejected this, evidently unimpressed by the arrival of a British cruiser off Abadan. The British case in the oil dispute was presented at The Hague on the last day of June.

The Arab States (except Jordan) signed a collective security pact in February. The Israeli government was defeated in Parliament and resigned. An agreement was signed between the Sultan of Morocco and the French

The Festival of Britain—on the South Bank an act of faith

Resident-General. There were Cabinet changes in Turkey and Syria; a provisional government was formed in Libya. The Lebanese elections resulted in the victory of the Government Party where Abdullah al-Yafi became Prime Minister.

In May H.M. the King opened the Festival of Britain which was an act of faith and, in the field of arts, a considerable success. The South Bank was given a New Look (which it badly needed) and people argued about the Shot Tower and the new Festival Hall, not to mention the Battersea Park Fun Fair and other improvements.

April saw another large-scale Communist offensive in the war-torn peninsula. This was renewed in May; but the United Nations counter-attack, mounted a week later, forced a general enemy retreat. At the end of June General Matthew Ridgway, MacArthur's successor, offered to send representatives to discuss an armistice. Mr. Malik of the U.S.S.R. had already broadcast a proposal for a cease-fire through the United Nations.

The Korean War: negotiations were resumed in 'a village in no-man's-land'

July opened with the Chinese acceptance of the proposal to discuss a cease-fire in Korea; Kaesong was proposed as the place for armistice negotiations. These opened on July 10 but the end of the year both the fighting and the talks were still going on, having been broken off twice by the U.N. Command and once by the Communists. In October the negotiations were resumed at Panmunjom, a village in no-man's-land. The Chinese and North Koreans proved both tough and shifty bargainers, debating each small point and yielding only after endless talk. They refused to let International Red Cross representatives visit their prisoner-of-war camps.

The World Peace Council met in East Berlin. The French President paid a State visit to Canada. In Peking an agreement was signed for the 'peaceful liberation' of Tibet though the Tibetans didn't know what they had to be liberated from.

Russia transferred all former Japanese property in Manchuria to the Chinese Communist government. Mac-Arthur granted the Japanese government more power. A World Muslim Conference opened in Karachi. There was a new government in Viet Nam. Another anti-government plot was discovered in Thailand; two months later, in an attempted *coup d'état*, the Premier was seized. A provisional central government of the Ryukyu Islands was set up on Okinawa. A new coalition government was formed in Indonesia.

The Dutch government resigned in January, so did the Greek Cabinet. Austria and Yugoslavia restored diplomatic relations. France and Italy agreed on a common defence policy. At the end of February the seasonal resignation of the French government took place; M. Queuille was elected Prime Minister nine days later. There were strikes in Barcelona in protest against the high cost of living; by the last week in April there were 300,000 workers out in Northern Spain. Dr. Dress formed a new Dutch government. French transport was crippled by a wave of strikes in Paris. The two Italian Socialist Parties merged and three Democratic Socialist Party Ministers resigned. Marshal Carmona, the President of Portugal died. Denmark and the U.S.A. signed an agreement for the joint defence of Greenland. The Bill for reforming the French Electoral law was passed in

On guard at Suez—on the Canal trouble brewed

May. General Papagos resigned as C.-in-C. of the Greek armed forces. In the June elections the De Gaullists gained 121 seats, the Socialists 107 and the Communists 106.

Britain and Egypt agreed on the Egyptian sterling balances; but there was trouble brewing up over the Canal. Egypt banned all ships carrying goods to and from Israel though the U.N. Security Council called on her to end these restrictions. In October Egypt abrogated the Condominium Agreements over the Sudan; the Governor-General refused to accept this unilateral step. A few days later British troops occupied Suez and Ismaila; next day they took over all the key installations in the Canal Zone. The Egyptians protested and a lengthy guerrilla war of ambushes and knifings began. (Egypt had rejected the British proposals for a joint Middle East Command.) Britain, the U.S.A., France and Turkey issued a joint statement on the need for organized defence in the Middle East; a White Paper was also issued on the futile Anglo-Egyptian negotiations that had lasted a whole year. A state of emergency was proclaimed in the country; British troops partly demolished a native village in the Canal Zone which had served as a base for repeated attacks. Egypt recalled her Ambassador from London; a long conflict loomed.

Canada was delighted by the State visit of Princess Elizabeth and the Duke of Edinburgh; they went on to Washington as honoured and popular guests.

Princess Elizabeth and the Duke of Edinburgh in Canada. Canada was delighted

Mr. Harriman of New York called on Dr. Musaddiq of Iran, accompanied by Mrs. Harriman and the U.S. Ambassador

The Colombo Plan for economic and technical co-operation within the Commonwealth came into effect early in July. A conference was held in Nairobi on African defence and the future of Tanganyika was the subject of lengthy discussions. Australia, New Zealand and the U.S.A. signed a Pacific Security Agreement. In the New Zealand elections the National Party defeated Labour. An 'Independence of Malaya' Party was formed in Singapore. The Central African Federation Conference opened at Victoria Falls in September. Australia rejected the proposed amendment of the constitution.

The Persian oil dispute went badly for Britain. On July 5 the International Court of Justice ruled that Persia must do nothing to prejudice the case. The Teheran government challenged the competence of the Court. A few days later Mr. Harriman, President Truman's special envoy arrived in Persia, trying to mediate. He had little success. Early in August the Lord Privy Seal, Mr. Stokes, led a mission to Teheran; proposals for settlement were published eleven days later but the talks were suspended before the end of the month. Britain withdrew the financial and trade facilities enjoyed by Persia. Persia replied with an ultimatum; on September 23 she ordered all British staff of the Anglo-Iranian Oil Company to leave Persia within seven days; this was extended but by October 3 all but eleven British technicians and administrators had left. Britain submitted the dispute to the Security Council which ruled, by nine votes to two, that it was competent to deal with it. On October 8 Musaddiq arrived in America for the Security Council meeting. Two days later the Council decided, with only Russia voting against, to await the International Court's findings. Musaddiq thereupon changed front and

Uncle Sam was embroidered on the banners of anti-U.S. Persian rioters—the U.S., too, was 'imperialist'

appointed the Persian Minister at The Hague to represent his government at the hearings. When the date for presenting Persia's answer to the British complaint arrived, she asked for an extra thirty days so that the dispute was still undecided by the end of the year. In the meantime Musaddiq visited Cairo to enlist Egyptian support, reconstructed his government to obtain more personal power and held a General Election.

It seemed in this disturbed year as if the Old Man of the Mountain had come to grim life again and was sending his assassins all over the world. In July Riad as-Sulh, the former Premier of the Lebanon was murdered; four days later King Abdullah became a killer's victim; before the end of the month the Governor of South Viet Nam and General Chanson, the French Commissioner, were also shot dead. In October Sir Henry Gurney, the High Commissioner for the Malayan Federation, and Liaquat Ali Khan, the Prime Minister of Pakistan came to a violent end. Natural death claimed Admiral Sherman, Chief of the U.S. Naval Operations, the ninety-five-year-old Marshal Pétain who had outlived both his glory and his shame, and M. Litvinov, the Soviet Foreign Commissar from 1930 to 1939.

There were new governments in Greece, Malta, Finland, Japan—and of course, France. The Italian, Spanish, Jordan, Israeli, Czech, Syrian, Swedish, Norwegian, Siamese Cabinets were also reconstituted—some of them more than once within six months. A provisional peace treaty with Japan was published in July; in the same month the state of war between Britain and Germany was formally terminated. In September a conference opened in San Francisco for the conclusion and signature of the Japanese peace treaty; it was signed by forty-nine countries and America concluded a security agreement with her ex-enemy. The German Occupation Statute was replaced by new agreements in the three Western Zones. Greece and Turkey were invited to join NATO; the Congress of the European Movement which met in Hamburg approved the inclusion of Germany in the European community. The state of war was terminated between the U.S.A. and Germany in mid-October. Britain, France and the U.S. submitted disarmament proposals to the U.N. Assembly in November. The NATO Council met in Rome. Dr. Adenauer visited London in December. Twelve days later forty-five German war criminals were released by the British and U.S. authorities. The International Refugee Organization closed down at the end of the year.

There was a World Youth Festival in the Soviet sector of Berlin and a Communist Youth Rally in the Eastern half of the city. The World Peace Council met in Vienna—exactly five days after China contributed to 'world peace' by the occupation of Lhasa, the capital of Tibet.

In Woodford—his own constituency

A True Blue in Fleet Street

In September the largest oil refinery in Europe was opened at Fawley, Hampshire. In the last week of the month Britain and the world were shocked by the news that H.M. King George VI had to undergo a serious lung operation which was later reported to have been completely successful.

In October Mr. Attlee decided to go to the polls again. The result was a shock for Labour; the Conservatives won 321 seats to Labour's 295, with 6 Liberals and 3 'others'. Mr. Churchill once again formed a Conservative government with Mr. Anthony Eden as his Foreign Secretary and Mr. R. A. Butler as Chancellor of the Exchequer. The new government faced another economic crisis and Mr. Churchill and Mr. Eden left for the United States on the last day of the year to discuss Anglo-American co-operation. After twelve years, trading in foreign exchange started again in London. But the road to solvency was still a long and uphill one.

The two great ladies of the English stage, Dame Edith Evans and Dame Sybil Thorndike in 'Waters of the Moon'

The Festival of Britain commemorated the centenary of the Great Exhibition; it was also designed to show the world what the British had achieved in the last few decades in every branch of the creative spirit. Twenty-two centres were chosen in England, Scotland and Wales to organize local festivals of the arts—which they did with varying success but with equal enthusiasm.

No less than seven new English operas were presented during the year and over a dozen were revived. Benjamin Britten's *Billy Budd* and Vaughan Williams's *The Pilgrim's Progress* were equally successful. There was a brilliant season at Covent Garden, Glyndebourne and Sadler's Wells; the Americans brought Gian Carlo Menotti's moving *Consul* to London. Half a dozen new ballets were commissioned during the year including two by Constant Lambert and Arthur Benjamin.

All the leading stars of the stage were on show during the Festival months—Laurence Olivier and Vivien Leigh, Alec Guinness and Peggy Ashcroft, Ralph Richardson and Peter Ustinov, John Clements and Kay Hammond. The hits of the year included Giraudoux's *The Madwoman of Chaillot*, N. C. Hunter's *Waters of the Moon*, Peter Ustinov's *The Love of Four Colonels* and Christopher Fry's *A Sleep of Prisoners*, staged in St. Thomas's Church, Regent Street. America sent two 'sensational' musicals, *Kiss me, Kate* and *South Pacific*, both of which settled down to long and profitable runs.

Eric Shipton: tracks on the slopes of Everest

The books of the year included Priestley's topical *Festival at Fairbridge*, the rowdy and robust *Boswell's London Journal 1762–63*, the memoirs of the Duke of Windsor and Leslie Paul's autobiography *Angry Young Man*, the title of which became the name if not of a movement, of a very vocal group of young intellectuals. E. M. Forster's brilliant *Two Cheers for Democracy*, Jacquetta Hawkes's remarkable *A Land*, S. Runciman's *History of the Crusades* were also published in 1951. In fiction C. P. Snow's *The Masters*, Graham Greene's *The End of the Affair*, I. Compton Burnett's *Darkness and Day* were among the memorable English novels; Colette's books were hailed by thousands in the English translations.

Chemists succeeded in evolving synthetic cortisone and a chemical called krillium which was supposed to revolutionize agriculture. Britain produced the first useful heat, America the first useful electricity, from atomic energy. A 'flying spot' microscope was invented by Professor J. Z. Young and Mr. F. Roberts of University College, London, which promised tremendous advantages in research. Mr. Eric Shipton brought back photographs of the tracks of 'the Abominable Snowman' from the high slopes of Mount Everest though no one had yet seen the creature.

For the third year in succession Britain gathered the Nobel Prize for Physics: the laureates were Sir John Cockcroft, the director of Harwell and Professor E. T. S. Walton of Trinity College, Dublin, the first men to split atomic nuclei with artificially achieved high tensions.

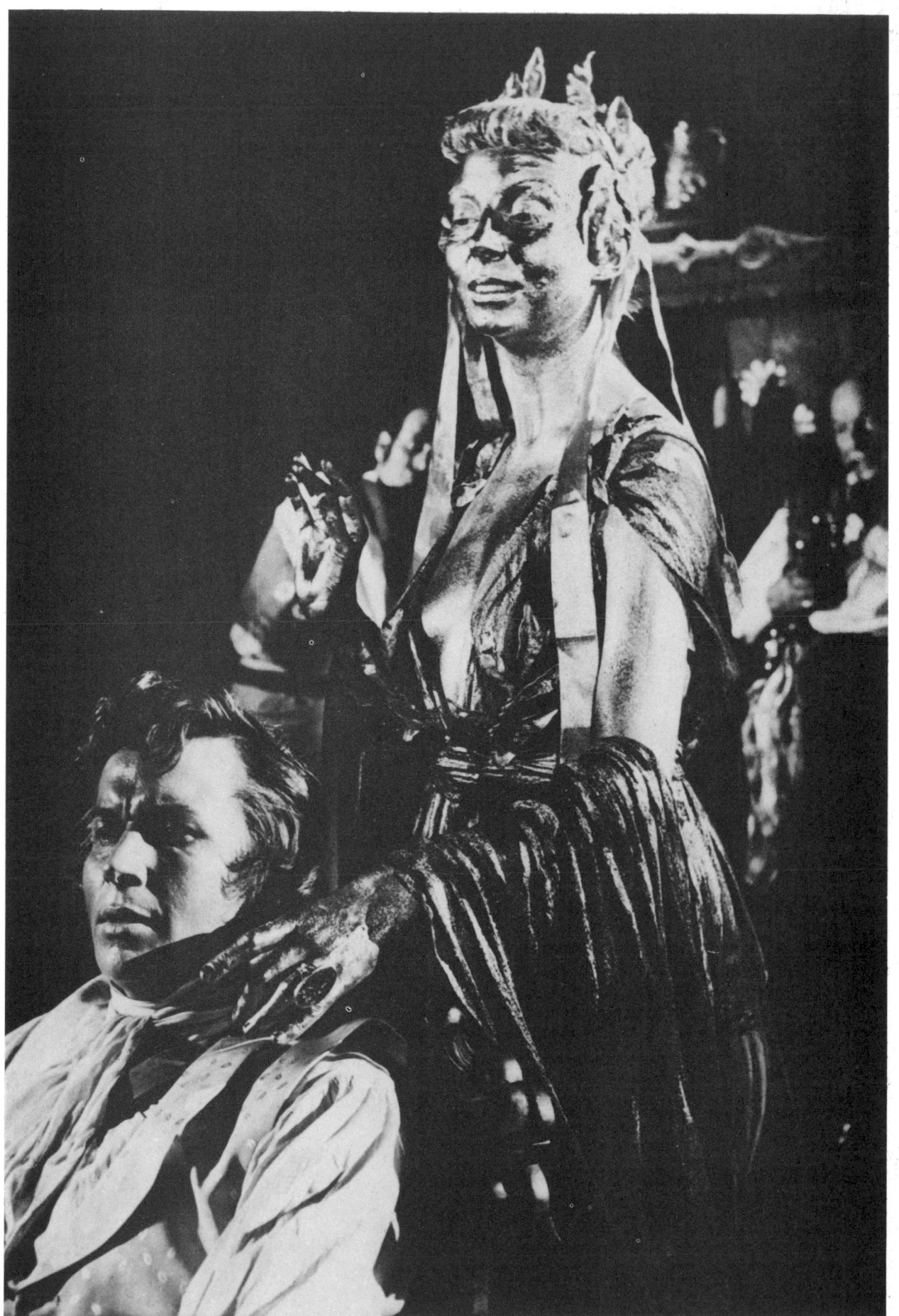

Pamela Browne and Robert Rounseville in 'Tales of Hoffman', a British tour de force *in film*

King George VI—a beloved monarch waves good-bye to Princess Elizabeth and her husband

Three Queens mourn a Father, Son, Husband and King

At the end of January 1952, Princess Elizabeth and the Duke of Edinburgh left for their Australian tour; their first stop was Kenya. Six days later Britain and the world were shocked by the death of King George VI at the early age of fifty-six; His Majesty died in his sleep. Two days later Queen Elizabeth II's accession was solemnly proclaimed. The royal funeral took place at Windsor; it was attended by the four royal dukes, the Duke of Edinburgh, the Duke of Gloucester, the Duke of Windsor (who hurried to Britain from America) and the young Duke of Kent, representatives of every part of the Commonwealth and many foreign countries. The King's character and self-sacrificing life were described in a warm tribute Mr. Churchill paid to him. His people mourned a very lovable and modest, heroic man.

Mr. Butler—the budget was early

The budget was early; Mr. Butler's text was 'solvency, security and incentive'. Food subsidies were reduced, family allowances raised, income tax was eased for many; but petrol became more expensive and an excess profit levy was also introduced. Britain had to husband her dollar reserves and in April tried to explain to America why imports from the dollar area had to be restricted.

The young Queen had the sympathy, affection and good wishes of her people. She was the first British monarch to be styled 'Head of the Commonwealth' and many began to speak of a new, proud and prosperous Elizabethan Age. Like her father she, in her private life, symbolized the family affection and moral qualities of her people. Her youth and beauty rejuvenated the idea of the Commonwealth as a 'Family of Nations'. Utterly feminine, yet her dignity was kingly.

Prosperity was still something to toil and hope for. The annual Defence statement, presented to Parliament in February, showed still greater burdens; it was Field-Marshal Viscount Alexander's task, as the new Minister of Defence, to create modern armed forces and supply them with the right weapons. At least Britons could rejoice in the ending of one wartime restriction—identity cards were abolished.

In June, Mr. Churchill, addressing the Press Association, warned the country of further economic difficulties.

In America it was election year again. 'I Like Ike' became the Republican slogan when General Eisenhower agreed to run for President; his main rival was Senator Taft. Adlai Stevenson, dubbed an 'egghead' was the choice of the Democrats after Truman had withdrawn and Senator Kefauver ran into considerable opposition both in the South and in the big cities. A large Foreign Aid Bill was signed by President Truman in June and there were further discussions in London between Mr. Acheson, Mr. Eden and M. Schuman on Western foreign policy.

General de Lattre de Tassigny who led the liberation forces into Paris died in January; Mr. Senanayake, the Prime Minister of Ceylon passed away in March; in April Sir Stafford Cripps died in a Zurich clinic.

Dr. Nkrumah was elected the first Prime Minister of the Gold Coast

In Cairo violence erupted and buildings were bombed and set alight by terrorists

The British position in Egypt became more and more unpleasant. On January 26 there was a 'black day' in Cairo with riots, looting and the murder of ten British residents. Next day, the King dismissed Nahas Pasha from the Premiership; Aly Maher Pasha succeeded him. British troops had disarmed and expelled Egyptian police from Ismailia, which was the immediate cause of the disorders. The Egyptian government resigned on March 1; Ahmed Nagib al Hilaly formed a new one next day; three weeks later King Farouk dissolved Parliament. The Sudan Legislative Assembly adopted the draft constitution in April. At the end of June there was another Cabinet crisis in Cairo; Hilaly Pasha was succeeded by Hussein Siry Pasha.

The Mutual Security Agency took over the functions of the Marshall Plan Organization. A conference opened in Paris on the setting-up of a European Army. Greece and Turkey were admitted to NATO; Mr. Eden proposed that the Council of Europe, the Schuman Plan and the European Defence Community should form an integrated co-operative.

Libya applied for United Nations membership and held its first General Election. The first Parliament opened in Nigeria. The South African Supreme Court decided that it was unconstitutional for the government to separate white and coloured people by two electoral lists. The Government, to destroy the authority of the Supreme Court, introduced a bill to create a High Court of Parliament. The British scheme for a Central African Federation was published in June.

In the Pacific Korea was still the festering sore. The truce talks continued all year; so did the fighting which was sometimes very fierce. The Communists were grimly dug-in, and, holding fast to UNO protocol, the West did not unleash their full forces on land or in the air. Korea was split between two stalemated armies.

The armistice talks almost foundered on one point: the repatriation of prisoners. More than half of those in U.N. hands refused to be handed back; and, as Mr. Eden put it, 'it would clearly be repugnant to the sense of values of the free world to send these men home by force'. In May, however, the same free world was shocked by the events in the vast prison camp on Koje Island, off the south shore of the Korean peninsula. Here the prisoners had gained control over their weak guards; the American general commanding the garrison was kidnapped and his successor obtained his release at the cost of some rather excessive concessions. A third commander, General Boatner, was appointed to restore order. It became evident that a small and ferocious group of Communists had tried to turn the prison camp into a new battlefront behind the U.N. lines.

Jungle War in Malaya

In January Sir Gerald Templer had been appointed High Commissioner for the Federation of Malaya: his main task was to try to bring to a close the costly and still inconclusive war which Communists and other terrorists conducted in the teeming jungles.

The new Commander speaks—his young aide, Nasser, listens, thoughtfully

The government of Hussein Siry Pasha in Egypt lasted only three weeks. A day after Hilaly Pasha became Prime Minister again, General Mohammed Naguib seized power and was proclaimed Commander-in-Chief.

In March Britain restored Heligoland (the island had been used as a target for bombing practice) to the Federal Republic. Russia proposed terms for a German peace treaty which were unacceptable to the Western Powers and apart from an endless but futile exchange of notes nothing much happened. Twice a minor international crisis arose when Soviet planes attacked a French civilian plane near Berlin and when Soviet fighters shot down a Swedish aircraft over the Baltic. The Russians denied responsibility on both occasions; the Western Powers could do little except protest.

If the first six months of the year were disturbed and uneasy violence and conflict were the keynotes of the second half.

The Stalinist grip tightened on the satellites. Even such an old, trusted Communist as Ana Pauker the formidable female Foreign Minister of Rumania had to be purged. In Hungary, Rakosi, who had until now preferred the role of the power behind the throne, became Prime Minister. Chou En-lai led a Chinese delegation to Moscow; a Sino-Soviet agreement was signed about Port Arthur and the Changchun Railway. Finland completed her reparations deliveries to the U.S.S.R. Rumania was given a new constitution and a new electoral law to assure the one-party system. The XIX Congress of the Communist Party opened in Moscow on October 5. The new Five Year Plan was enthusiastically adopted, a new Central Committee was elected (except for one member it was the same as before). Malenkov was given the honour of delivering the Central Committee's report and a Comrade N. S. Khrushchev introduced the amendments to the party statutes,

Farouk—the Egyptian king abdicated to become a familiar figure on Mediterranean beaches and in Roman night clubs

The Olympic Games were held at Helsinki where sixty-eight countries were represented; Hungary won sixteen gold, ten silver and sixteen bronze medals, ending in third place behind the U.S.A. and the U.S.S.R. Athletics, on the world scene, unobtrusively were becoming a Soviet propaganda force.

The Arab-Jewish 'cold war' continued with no lessening of tension and hate. King Talal of Jordan was forced to abdicate in favour of Crown Prince Hussein. Eritrea became part of the Federation of Ethiopia. West Germany signed an agreement for compensation with Israel; the Arab League protested violently against it.

Evita Peron whom many considered the true ruler of Argentine died of cancer in July. General Ibanez won the presidential election in Chile. Throughout Latin America social unrest was becoming manifest. The Monroe Doctrine placed no embargo on ideas and a new and immense centre of world political unrest was coming into being.

The European Coal and Steel Community was finally established; its High Authority held its inaugural meeting in August; the Council of Ministers met in September. The Duchess of Kent and her son visited Singapore. In October there was an Asian and Pacific Peace Conference in Peking. Communist China signed a ten-year agreement with Mongolia.

In Korea Dr. Syngman Rhee had himself re-elected President by the simple method of locking up the members of his Parliament until they agreed to his second term. Mr. Yoshida was re-elected Prime Minister of Japan. In December General Eisenhower visited Korea where the negotiations and the desultory fighting seemed equally endless. The U.N. Assembly adopted the Indian proposals for an armistice; twelve days later China turned them down.

Mau Mau savagery under martial law

There was trouble in Kenya where the President of
the African Union was arrested; the ugly menace
of Mau-Mau led to a state of emergency.

*A Mau Mau poster—Africans too cowered
before the menace*

Kenya—rifles and spears—the enemy was bestial

The H-bomb: the bomb that destroyed Hiroshima was 'old-fashioned'

Reports on the Central African Federation were published. Riots broke out in French Morocco.

The Trieste Free Territory was given a new administration. Dr. Schumacher, leader of the German Social Democrats, died; so did Count Sforza, the former Italian Foreign Minister, Benedetto Croce, the eminent historian and philosopher, and Signor Orlando, the Italian Premier of World War I. Dr. Drees, a Labour leader, formed a coalition government in Holland. There was still no progress on the Austrian Peace Treaty. In Sweden the elections brought Conservative and Liberal gains.

Changes, bickerings, moves and counter-moves were overshadowed by the grim realities of the atom. The Russian atom tests were unheralded and unpublicized though there was no doubt about their regular progress. On October 3, 1952, the first British atom bomb was exploded in Monte Bello Islands, Australia. Mr. Churchill stated in Parliament that the ship on which the bomb was exploded 'completely vaporized at a temperature of nearly one million degrees'.

On November 1, 1952, the first hydrogen bomb was exploded at Eniwetok and three weeks later President Truman confirmed the reports. The new bomb had made the atom bomb practically obsolete—certainly its destructive force, the power of 'thermo-nuclear reaction' was many times the multiple of the 'old-fashioned' bombs that fell upon Hiroshima and Nagasaki.

More than an era ended; the civilized world was now in the position to be able to destroy itself, at vast expenditure but in a short time and with little actual effort.

Mr. Eisenhower—after twenty years a Republican in the White House

Mr. Nixon and family—from California a young Vice-President for the U.S.A.

On November 4, 1952, the people of the United States went to the polls and elected General Eisenhower by a majority of 6½ million votes, their thirty-third President. 'Peace' was the President-Elect's declared foreign policy, and the defeated Democrats promised support of *that*—with reservations on his home policy. The Soviet Union took stock, quietly, of the soldier turned statesman.

Young Richard Nixon of California became Vice-President and after twenty years the Republican Party returned to power.

There was no ebb in the flood of books in 1952: 18,741 new titles and reprints rolled from the presses. In biography Sir Harold Nicolson's *King George the Fifth* was both the most distinguished and the most successful; Viscount Simon's *Retrospect* and Alan Moorehead's *The Traitors* also drew glowing notices. The *Collected Poems* of eighteen years established Dylan Thomas as one of the most important modern poets of Britain. Arthur Koestler's *Arrow in the Blue* was a striking record of a rebellious life and spirit. Edward Young's *One of our Submarines* was considered as one of the best books written about the Royal Navy. In fiction Evelyn Waugh's *Men at Arms*, Henry Green's strongly individual *Doting* and Angus Wilson's *Hemlock and After* were in the great tradition of social criticism mixed with brilliant satire.

Berg's strange and haunting opera *Wozzeck* had its first performance at Covent Garden. Flora Robson scored a personal triumph in *The Innocents* (the stage version of Henry James's *The Turn of the Screw*). The musicals *Call Me Madam* and *Porgy and Bess* (with an all Negro cast) both had long runs.

Japan erupted on to the screens of the world with the savagely moving 'Rashoman'

There was a magnificent Leonardo da Vinci exhibition at the Royal Academy and a collection of Dutch Pictures (1450–1750) also drew large crowds. Great controversy was aroused by the international sculpture competition of which 'The Unknown Political Prisoner' was the subject; the winner, Reg Butler, was assailed by the traditionalists and fervently defended by the cohorts of modern art.

The film industry received considerable help from the Eady Plan under which part of the cinema tax was channelled into a Film Production Fund. The most striking and successful pictures of the year included John Huston's *The African Queen*, Sir Carol Reed's *The Outcast of the Islands*, David Lean's *The Sound Barrier*, Anthony Asquith's *The Importance of Being Earnest*, Zoltan Korda's *Cry The Beloved Country* and Alexander Mackendrick's *Mandy*. From America the mammoth *Quo Vadis*, *A Streetcar Named Desire*, *Death of a*

In Tennessee Williams's 'A Streetcar Named Desire', Vivien Leigh played Blanche Dubois, and won an Oscar

Salesman, The Quiet Man brought spectacle and some new ideas. Japan shocked and delighted cinema-goers with *Rashomon* and India puzzled us with *Aan*. The French sent *Casque D'Or, Seven Deadly Sins* and *The Strange Ones*; Italy, De Sica's *Miracle in Milan* and *Due Soldi di Speranza*. Walt Disney acquired a rival in the U.P.A. cartoon-makers whose *Gerald McBoing Boing* was a brilliant innovation.

Commercial television began to rear its head—whether ugly or charming depended on your views—when thirty-four large commercial organizations applied for licences that would provide 'some element of competition'. None was granted but the Associated Broadcasting Development Company was formed and Mr. Norman Collins forecast a fifty-station network.

EMPTY SHOES

Beria—he shared power

The first jet-propelled airliner, the Comet, gave Britain a lead in aviation. The total eclipse on February 25 was observed by about sixty astronomers in the Sudan. Uranium was being discovered all over the world—some of it, as in Australia, by specially equipped aircraft. Germ warfare became a hotly debated political issue when the Chinese Communists charged the U.S. with dropping infected insects from airplanes; some Communist scientists obediently backed the charge, but no one produced a clear and unbiased report. It took a long time before Russia and her allies abandoned this line of propaganda.

THE DREAM OF 'One World' was as far from fulfilment in 1953 as at any time since the beginning of the twentieth century. The play was more or less the same but the cast underwent important changes.

In America the Eighty-third Congress was convened for January 3; the first Republican Congress in almost a quarter of a century. On January 20, sixty-two-year-old Dwight D. Eisenhower took the Constitutional oath as President. Soon enough it became evident that at least in foreign affairs the Eisenhower Administration wouldn't depart radically from the line of its predecessors. As a soldier, 'Ike' was only too aware of the abomination of war; deeply concerned about the hydrogen bomb, he said: 'This horror must not be.' It was announced

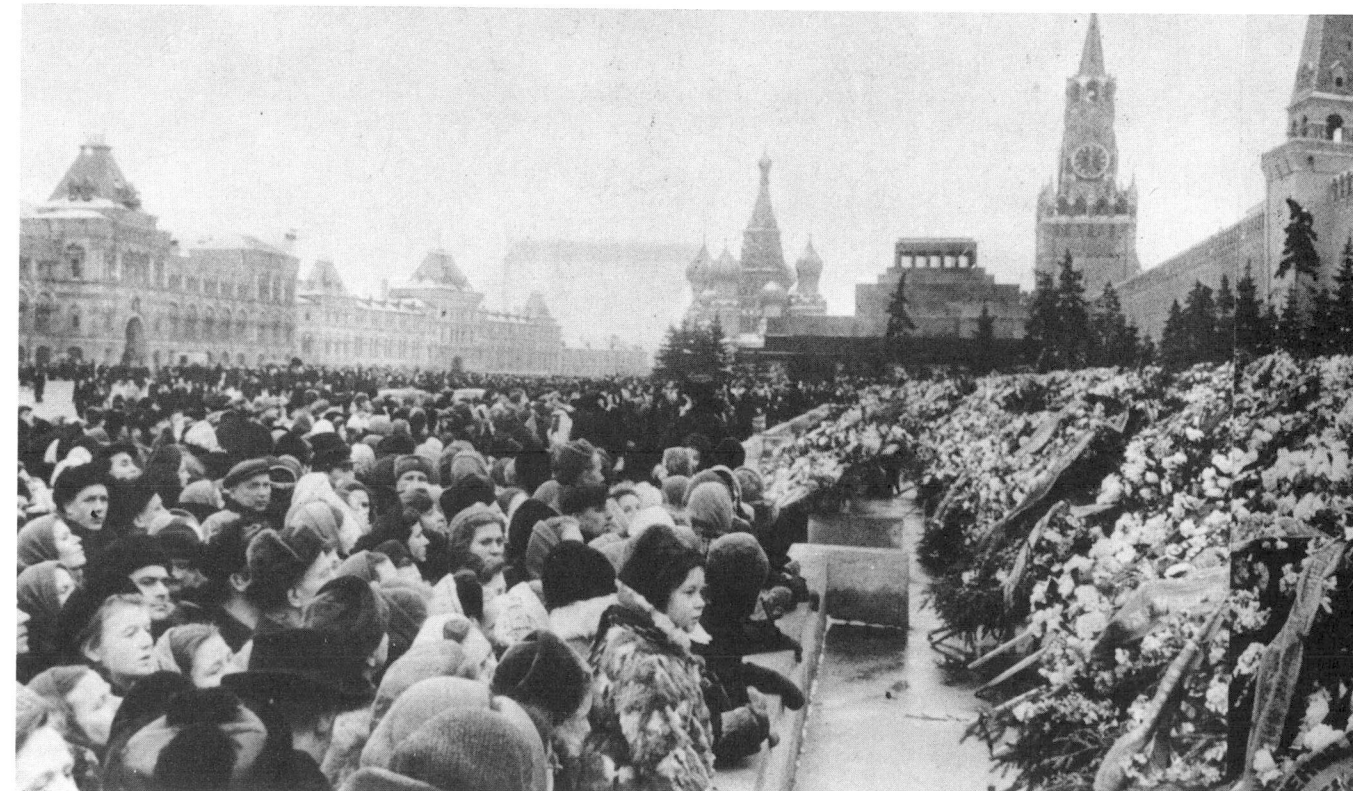

Wreaths for Stalin along the Kremlin walls—inside the fortress the struggle for power quietly began

Stalin: his genius and strength were apparent—his inhuman policies and evil deeds were denied by none

in Congress that Formosa was to be 'deneutralized' and become a base in the struggle against Communism. The external challenge was fully realized; where the President and his associates disagreed with the Right wing was over the largely imaginary Communist danger within America. This danger was stridently publicized by Senator McCarthy, one of the strangest figures in the controversial gallery of American politicians.

The most dramatic upheaval came in the Soviet Union. On January 13 Moscow announced a 'doctors' plot' which involved the top physicians of Russia and was also made an occasion of an anti-Jewish purge. Less than three months later, at dawn on March 6, Moscow radio announced: 'The heart of comrade and inspired continuer of Lenin's will . . Joseph Vissarionovich Stalin has stopped beating. . . .'

A colossus had toppled, a nightmare had ended. No one could deny Stalin's genius; no one could deny his evil and inhuman policies. For twenty-nine years he had ruled Russia; and now the world watched the struggle to fill his place.

His immediate successor was Georgi M. Malenkov who had been for many years Stalin's associate. He shared power with Beria, for long head of the dreaded Soviet Secret Police and V. M. Molotov, the veteran Foreign Secretary. Nine days after his accession Malenkov made a conciliatory statement, declaring that international disputes could be settled by 'peaceful means'. Two weeks later there was proof of the seriousness of the 'peace offensive'; the truce talks long suspended, got under way again and the Communists made some concessions on the moot point of what should happen to prisoners-of-war who did not want to be repatriated. In April Eisenhower called for Russian 'deeds' to show their peaceful intentions; in May Churchill proposed high-level discussions with Malenkov 'as soon as possible'. The 'thaw' was on in various directions.

In mid-May the Czechs released William Oatis, an American journalist whom they had imprisoned on trumped-up espionage charges.

The great upheaval caused by Stalin's death was not over yet. On June 17 the East Germans rose against the Communist rule. It was a heroic and forlorn attempt; the West could not intervene except at the risk of unleashing a general conflict and the rising was squashed by the Russians and German Communist troops. Nor did the unrest in other satellites bring any relief in the iron-hard totalitarian rule.

On July 10 Lavrenti P. Beria, the powerful head of the Secret Police Army was purged. He was denounced as a traitor and, some time in December, shot. He served as a handy scape-goat for the grave economic difficulties which Russia and her orbit were experiencing. Four days after Beria and his 'apparatus' fell, the West proposed that the Four Power negotiations on Germany and Austria should be restarted.

In the Far East Communist China was consolidating her position and leaving little doubt that she wanted to dominate Asia. The West, under American leadership, was lining up the Japanese, Chinese Nationalists and Filipinos to stop the Communist expansion. At long last a truce was signed in Korea where military action ended at 10 p.m. on July 27. Syngman Rhee had released 27,000 North Korean prisoners six weeks before which may have speeded up the negotiations. Now an intricate procedure was set up under which the P.O.W.s were held in Indian custody while both sides were given a chance to 'explain' to their soldiers why they should return home. This ended the day before Christmas, 1953: 22,217 prisoners in U.N. hands still refused repatriation; on

East Germany: a heroic attempt—the people rebelled against Communist rule—and were crushed by Soviet armour

the Communist side there were 350, including 22 Americans, who preferred the Red brand of 'freedom'. Their future was still unsettled; it was to be decided at a later political conference but the conference itself had run into a dead-end. The U.N. insisted that Russia should attend it on the Communist side if at all; the Communists wanted Russia invited as a 'neutral'. In December Arthur H. Dean, the U.S. envoy who tried to solve the problem, gave up and went home.

Another Far Eastern war was still dragging on—the Indo-Chinese conflict was in its eighth year. The French were unable to finish off the Chinese-backed Vietminh forces; French economy was being bled white by the cost. The U.S. finally underwrote 60 per cent of the military budget.

India was still insisting on representing the 'Third Force', a neutral barrier between East and West. The Kashmir dispute was still festering between Pakistan and India; and when the U.S. sent military aid to Pakistan, Nehru protested violently.

East Germany: for dead rebels—a wooden cross

War in Indo-China—by elephant and with mortars in the jungle

France was weary of the struggle; and
in December when René Coty was elected to succeed Vincent Auriol as President of the Fourth Republic, there was
some relief at the news that Vietminh
was willing to start peace talks.

President Coty

In Britain the outstanding event of the year was the Coronation with
all its pomp and circumstance, with rain and the miracle of television
for once balancing the sins of the 'idiot box', with peers hiding
sandwiches in their coronets.

In Westminster Abb[ey]
Prince Philip does [ ]
homage to the Quee[n]
after the Coronation

ey,

n,

189

Edmund Hillary and Sherpa Tensing: Everest a gift for a Queen

John Hunt, Edmund Hillary and Sherpa Tensing, a Nepalese guide, conquered Everest five days before the great ceremony in Westminster Abbey as a truly magnificent gift to the young Queen.

Life was easier for most of us. Only butter remained on the ration; chocolates, nylons and cars were in plentiful or at least adequate supply. Mr. Butler took sixpence off income tax and kept the cost of living fairly steady. Mr. Churchill became Sir Winston; he was still dominating the British and the world political scene. Mr. Eden's illness kept him out of politics for a while; Mr. Attlee was still firmly in control of the Opposition. When the North Sea gales burst through the coastal defences not only of England but of Holland and Belgium as well, there was speedy and generous response to aid the flood victims.

Sherpa Tensing—this was how we did it

The great flood—Walcheren—speedy and generous aid

The dikes break in Holland

—and Putney—the trees on the Embankment were awash

In the U.S., the Rosenberg, husband and wife spy-team, were executed for passing hydrogen bomb secrets to the Soviet

Late in June Sir Winston's illness led to the postponement of the Big Three meeting in Bermuda; finally they met in December. NATO was now four years old. Though the military leaders protested, it was decided to keep the armed forces in the Western alliance at its present level without further increase—mainly for economic reasons. In May the first atomic artillery shell was fired successfully in Nevada.

In August Malenkov announced that Russia also had the hydrogen bomb. It was a shock for the West and there seemed little prospect of the atomic race slowing down. In December Eisenhower proposed a world pool of atomic materials for peaceful use and the Soviet Union agreed to discuss it.

An unexpected change-over occurred in Iran. Musaddiq, the anti-Western Premier, had brought his country to the brink of economic disaster by the nationalization and shut-down of the oil industry. In order to override his Parliamentary opposition, he had allied himself with the Communist Tudeh party. But in August the eccentric Premier overreached himself.

Senator McCarthy was on the war-path. He denounced Mr. Harry S. Truman. He was angry with Britain for trading with Communist China and with Mr. Eisenhower for not forcing America's allies to take a line approved by Senator McCarthy

193

He forced the Shah into exile and was promptly over-thrown by rebellious soldiers and arrested. At his trial he wept and orated; he was sentenced to three years' solitary confinement. In December, after a thirteen-month break, Britain and Persia resumed diplomatic relations. In October the Israelis retaliated against Arab raiding by destroying a Jordanian village. It was a massacre and U.N. censured Israel for it; this time the U.S.A. supported the vote.

The Schuman Plan for European coal and steel integration started to operate in February. In April Dag Hammarskjold became U.N. Secretary-General.

Senator Robert Taft, the defeated candidate for Presidential nomination died at the end of July of cancer. Ramon Magsaysay was elected President of the Philippines.

In the United States President Eisenhower, as a 'new boy' was still feeling his way and some of his followers were disappointed by his conception of his high office—for he saw himself more as a mediator than as a leader. But prosperity was high and the 'boys' were coming home from Korea. The off-shore oil rights—a much-debated issue—were turned over to the States and not to Federal control. But the main issue was not legislation—it was investigation. Subversion was supposed to be rife in the government, the schools, the trade unions, the churches.

Until this attack, Eisenhower had never challenged McCarthy squarely. He had merely said: 'Don't join the book-burners' but this was a somewhat equivocal reply. Now, as McCarthy questioned the President's leadership in foreign policy, Eisenhower replied quickly. The urgency of allied unity, he said, overrode relatively minor differences. He declared that Communism would be a dead issue by next year—something which McCarthy, whose prestige and even survival depended on the witch-hunt, most indignantly refused to accept. But in the meantime hundreds of people lost their jobs and thousands were afraid that they would lose them.

In literature the public's taste seemed to run to travel and adventure. The book of the year, it was generally agreed, was Sir John Hunt's (he had been knighted for his great exploit) *The Ascent of Everest*; Heinrich Harrer's *Seven Years in Tibet* and Cecil Woodham Smith's brave debunking of the Crimean War both sold extremely well. Among the novelists L. P. Hartley achieved general acclaim with his *The Go-Between*.

In the theatre Mr. T. S. Eliot's *The Confidential Clerk* was a serious play based on farcical premises. Wynyard Brown's *A Question of Fact* and Graham Greene's *The Living Room* also drew big audiences. Benjamin Britten's Coronation piece, *Gloriana* was accounted the most important musical event of the year though not the most popular.

T. S. Eliot's 'The Confidential Clerk'—a serious farce

Christie—an old tradition

Bentley—arguments raged

Cohen and Schine—the senator sent his sleuths

The 'sensations' were provided by the Old Bailey. Christie's gruesome murders in Rillington Place revived the traditions of Jack the Ripper; they also raised the disturbing question whether Evans, who had been executed a few years before, had been guilty or innocent—for at his trial Christie had been the star witness of the prosecution. Argument raged about the hanging of Derek Bentley, a minor, whose younger accomplice had killed a policeman. Teddy boys, take-over bids and homosexuality provided the leader-writers with inexhaustible topics.

There were many distinguished guests at the Coronation. During the rest of the year London's visitors included Marshal Tito (who was found to have manners which few Communist leaders cultivated before Krushchev changed it all), Mr. Adlai Stevenson and Signor De Gasperi. Senator McCarthy's two special investigators, Mr. Cohn and Mr. Schine also arrived but didn't stay long and were received more like a music-hall team than a double menace.

The Queen watches Fijian dancers during the Commonwealth tour

Dr. Jagan: large audiences, little support

They said in 1953

In the final choice a soldier's pack is not so heavy as a prisoner's chains. PRESIDENT EISENHOWER

It requires not only courage but mental resilience for those whose youth lay in the calmer and more slowly moving times in order that they may adjust themselves to the giant outlines and harsh structures of the twentieth century. SIR WINSTON CHURCHILL

I don't see so much of Alfred any more since he got so interested in sex. MRS. ALFRED KINSEY

H.M. Queen Mary, here seen holding her great-grandson, H.R.H. Prince Charles, did not long survive her beloved son King George VI. The nation mourned a gracious lady, who had not lived quite long enough to see her granddaughter crowned

Marlon Brando as Antony in a masterly American Production, in black and white, of Shakespeare's 'Julius Caesar'

The loss of Queen Mary, the Queen's dearly-beloved and indefatigable grandmother, was deeply felt by millions. It was a personal tragedy that she did not live long enough to see her granddaughter crowned. The obituary list included Sir Edward Marsh, the discerning patron of painting and poetry, Sir Muirhead Bone, the artist and Sir Godfrey Tearle, the actor, Miss Margaret Bondfield who was the first woman Cabinet Minister, and Hilaire Belloc, a writer of passionate beliefs and great gifts.

Among the films of the year the most noteworthy foreign imports were *Les Jeux Interdits*, *Les Belles de Nuit*, *Fanfan La Tulipe* and *M. Hulot's Holiday* from France. *The Sinner* from Germany, *Sadko* from Russia, *Rome 11 O'clock* from Italy. Britain produced *The Cruel Sea*, *The Titfield Thunderbolt*, *The Oracle*, the delightful *Genevieve*, *The Beggar's Opera*, *The Captain's Paradise*, *The Man Between* and the documentary *The Conquest of Everest*. From America came *Shane*, *Moulin Rouge*, *Roman Holiday*, *I Confess*, *Lilli*, *The War of the Worlds*, *Julius Caesar* and Disney's remarkable *Nature's Half Acre*.

Nasser—success on the second try

THE BEGINNING OF 1954 focused the spotlight on the Middle East and Africa. The first Parliament of the Sudan opened. Two months later there were riots in Khartoum. Tribesmen ran amuck, over thirty people were killed and the Parliamentary session had to be postponed.

Late in February came the overthrow of General Neguib by his colleague and deputy, Colonel Nasser; Neguib was forced to resign all his offices and was put under house arrest. Two days later he came back to power; but in March Nasser tried again and this time he succeeded. It soon became evident that the new master of Egypt would pursue a far more belligerent and uncompromising anti-Western policy than his predecessor. In Syria an army revolt ejected President Chichekli; the new government of Sabri el Assali lasted only three months; there were similar though less violent changes in the Lebanon and Iraq. Political stability seemed to be a hopeless dream in the Arab countries. Nor was there much more of it in Europe. The Italian Government resigned early in January. The fiftieth anniversary of the *Entente Cordiale* was celebrated with more nostalgia than enthusiasm on April 7. In Belgium the Christian Socialist Party lost its majority in both Houses. In Ireland *Fianna Fail* fared rather badly at the General Election; Mr John Costello of *Fine Gaël* headed a Coalition Government. The French Government was defeated in June and Pierre Mendés-France, a forceful and original personality, became Prime Minister.

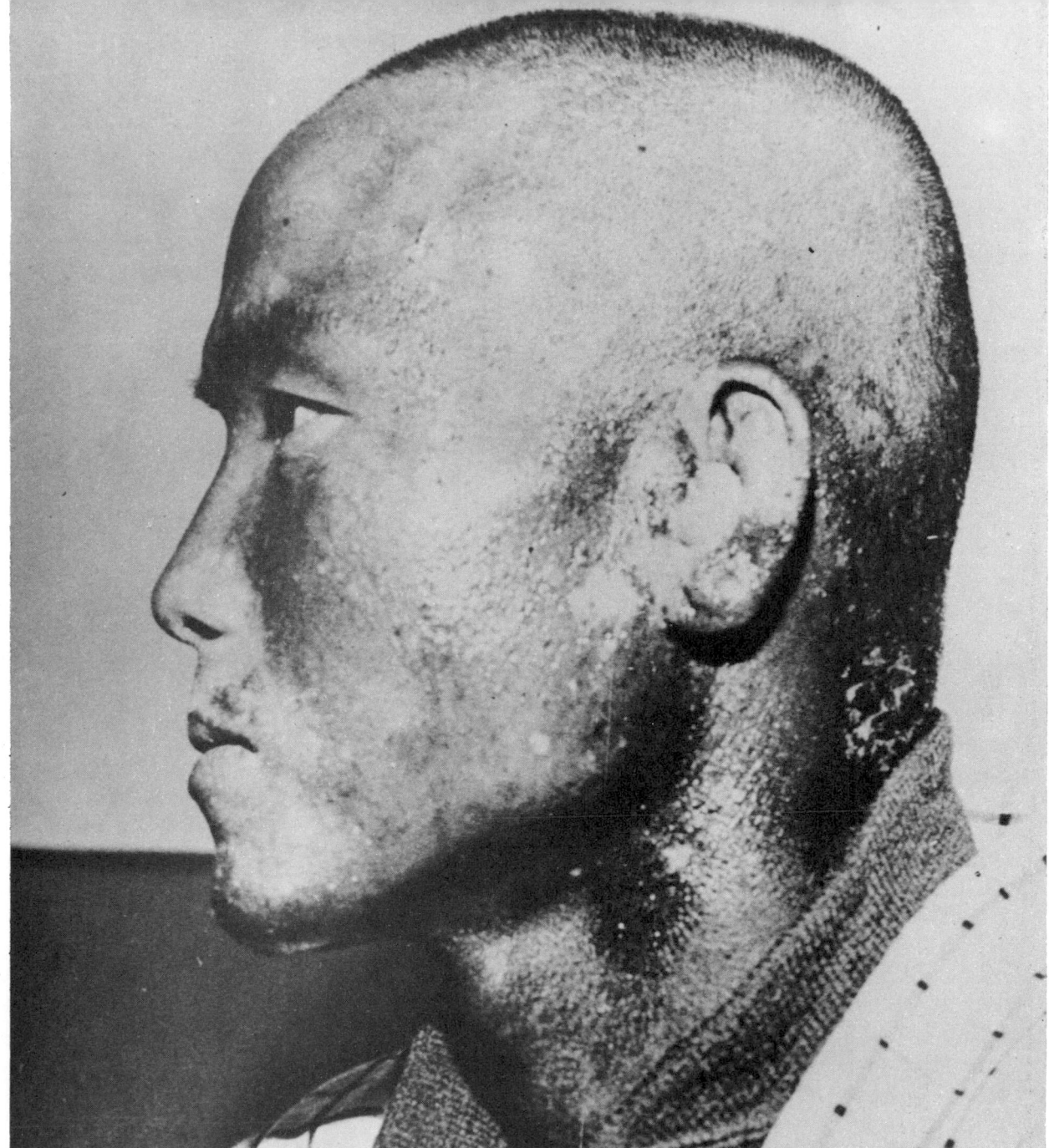

White ash on the deck—·Japanese fisherman suffering from H-bomb injuries

The most vexing and distressing French problem was Indo-China. In January Prince Buu Loc had formed a new government in Vietnam; in April there were a series of decrees setting up a War Cabinet and reorganizing the armed forces. The French guaranteed the independence of the country; but this guarantee had only limited value as the pressure of the Communist forces from Vietminh increased. After a heroic last stand, Dien Bien Phu fell, and it became evident that the fragmentation of Indo-China, its division into a Communist and non-Communist orbit could not be avoided. It was a heavy blow for French prestige and it encouraged other nations under French rule to fight for complete independence. The Geneva Conference on Indo-China which began on May 8 dragged on for many weary weeks until on July 20 an agreement for a cease-fire was signed followed by three armistice agreements; these, in effect, recognized the partition of still another country as a result of Communist aggression.

In March another hydrogen bomb test took place in the Marshall Islands. It was the equal to 'five hundred Hiroshimas' and it frightened America's allies perhaps even more than her potential enemies. In April Eisenhower declared that the biggest hydrogen bomb had 2000 times the power of the first atom bomb. The fall-out at Bikini drifted as a fine white ash on the deck of a Japanese fishing vessel; twenty-three of the crew were affected, two of them critically, by the delayed effects of radiation injury.

Dulles, Churchill, Eisenhower and Eden; the policies were joint

Dulles and Eden met for lengthy talks in April. In May the President signed the long-delayed St. Lawrence Seaway Bill which was to link Canada and the United States. Late in June Sir Winston and Mr. Eden travelled to Washington for talks with the President. On June 29 the 'Potomac Charter', a six-point declaration was issued by the President and the Prime Minister which reaffirmed the joint policies of Britain and America.

Australia was shaken by the Petrov affair. Vladimir Petrov, the Third Secretary of the Russian Embassy in Canberra, asked and was given political asylum in April. He disclosed the existence of a widespread Russian espionage system. A Royal Commission was appointed. Petrov's wife was rescued from the hands of the M.V.D. officials who were forcibly taking her back to Russia.

This led to violent Russian protests and the two countries broke off diplomatic relations on April 23. The Royal Commission's inquiry established the existence of an espionage organization; it also proved that most of the Russians in charge of it were both timid and incompetent. About the same time another Russian M.V.D. agent —Captain Khokhlov—defected to the West in Bonn.

1954 was a critical year for Senator McCarthy who was given bigger headlines than ever before but also suffered his Waterloo. He had already confused and bedevilled the State Department; but now he took on the Army over the honourable discharge of a Major Peress who was a dentist and who had turned out to be a Communist. The conflict ended with McCarthy's temporary triumph but the hearings that lasted from April 22 to June 17, involving McCarthy's special assistants, Messrs. Cohn and Schine (the latter was now a private in the Army) turned the public against him. His strange antics, his overweening egotism, his disregard for the truth, led to a vote in the Senate which censured him. His decline began and accelerated rapidly as he indiscriminately flailed at Republicans and Democrats, his own colleagues and even the President. The strange nightmare was nearing its end by December.

Queen Elizabeth and the Duke of Edinburgh arrived in Australia on the first visit of a reigning British sovereign to the Dominion on February 3. The royal couple toured the whole country, visiting each Federal State, mingling with thousands of people. They left Australia on April 1 and on their way back to Britain visited Ceylon, Libya, Malta and Gibraltar. The tour was an unqualified success.

The Foreign Ministers of the Big Four met in Berlin; the result of the long conference was summed up by a headline: 'The Success of a Failure'. All the Western Powers discovered was that Stalin's death hadn't made Russia more co-operative and that the peace treaties with Germany and Austria were still as far off as ever. At the end of March the U.S.S.R., with a vast tongue in a vast cheek proposed that she should join NATO. This was as near to clowning as a world Power could ever get. In Poland Cyrankiewicz succeeded Bierut as Premier; the Russian Communist Party was drastically reorganized in April. Russia joined the International Labour Organization. Malenkov was elected Prime Minister.

Mrs. Vladimir Petrov: homeward-bound with the M.V.D. as escort

Chiang Kai-Shek was elected for a second six-year term as President of Nationalist China. Asian Prime Ministers met in Colombo.

In Britain widespread strikes marked the almost constant state of industrial and economic restlessness. The Communist-controlled Electrical Trades Union's strike was described as a 'full implementation of Communist doctrine and methods'; they could have just as easily achieved their wage increases by arbitration. In February Mr. Macleod, Minister of Health, announced that cancer of the lung and smoking had an 'established relation'. Television licence fees were increased by 50 per cent; in March the Bill introducing commercial television was introduced and led to bitter argument. In the end the government's views prevailed and Independent Television Authority came into being.

It was a cold winter, with much snow and frost and a record number of burst pipes. The budget brought few changes, encouraging capital expenditure in private industry, reducing entertainment duty for cinemas, theatres and sporting events and giving some concessions in the post-war credits scheme.

On May 6 Dr. Roger Bannister broke the world record by running the mile in less than 4 minutes

Mr. Attlee visited Peking and was given a guided tour

The Mau-Mau threat continued to trouble Kenya where the European settlers felt that the British government's measures were not sufficiently energetic while the police were accused of maltreating suspects. In July Mr. Lyttelton, the British Colonial Secretary resigned and was succeeded by Mr. Lennox-Boyd. A full report on the anti-Mau-Mau operations was issued in October.

Nehru reaffirmed the 'five principles' of peaceful co-existence which he and Chou En-lai had worked out for the two huge Asiatic countries. In July the Chinese Communist leader visited East Berlin; the same day Chinese fighter planes shot down a British Skymaster plane near Hainan Island; the Chinese government apologized promptly. This apology was made less convincing by the fact that American rescue planes were also attacked while trying to save the survivors of the Skymaster.

In September the Manila Conference on South-East Asia defence opened with British, French, American, Australian, New Zealand, Pakistani, Thai and Filipino delegates; two days later the South-East Asia Defence Treaty and the Pacific Charter were signed. A week later the All-China People's Congress began in Peking; Mao-Tse-tung was re-elected Chairman of the Government Council and Chou En-lai his deputy.

There was friction on the Aden-Yemen frontier; but Anglo-Egyptian relations improved with the Suez Canal agreement, approved by Parliament at the end of July. France offered autonomy to Tunisia. There was also an agreement between the Persian government and the Western oil companies to resume work at Abadan and elsewhere. Britain lifted the embargo on arms export to Egypt in August. Libya granted the U.S. airbases. There were new governments in Iraq (Nuri-as-Said), Lebanon (Samy es-Solh), Syria (Fares el Khoury) and Jordan (Tawfiq Abul-Huda). In November General Neguib was formally removed from the Presidency of Egypt; Nasser assumed the offices of Head of State and President of the Revolution Council. In South Africa Mr. Strijdom, a Nationalist, became Premier.

They said in 1954

How are we going to bury nine million corpses?

MR. VAL PETERSEN, U.S. CIVIL DEFENCE ADMINISTRATOR

I am fully and properly worried about the future of mankind.

SIR WINSTON CHURCHILL

How on earth a classless society can afford four classes of railway travel and three classes of waiting-rooms would even defy Karl Marx, never mind a simple Methodist like myself.

SAM WATSON, ON SOVIET RAILWAYS

The flights, landings and take-offs of airships called 'flying saucers' and 'flying cigars' of any nationality are forbidden on the territory of the community of Château-neuf-du-Pape.

DECREE ISSUED BY THE MAYOR

'*Troilus and Cressida*'—*a warm welcome for Walton's opera*

As the prospect of a German peace treaty receded, the Western Powers decided to draw the Federal Republic into the European Defence Community. The *Bundestag* approved Dr. Adenauer's declaration of Western Germany's desire to contribute to Western defence. Nine years after the end of the war both Germanies were being rearmed purely because of the East-West conflict. In Eastern Germany the October elections produced the usual 'unanimous support' for the National Front. As soon as German sovereignty was restored formally Russia proposed a Four-Power Conference for November 29. This was rejected by the Western Powers. Russia threatened Britain with annulling the Anglo-Soviet Treaty of 1942 if the Paris Agreements were ratified; this did not seem a very effective threat. By the end of the year the Federal Republic was firmly established in the Western camp.

Once again it was a record year for publishers—19,188 new titles and reprints were produced. Among them even the shortest list must include Arthur Toynbee's *A Study of History* (the final four volumes), Roy Jenkins's *Mr. Balfour's Poodle*, the best-selling *Madame de Pompadour* by Nancy Mitford and Lord David Cecil's *Lord M*. Clement Attlee's *As It Happened*, Vyvyan Holland's *Son of Oscar Wilde* and Arthur Koestler's *The Invisible Writing* were among the most striking autobiographies. In fiction, C. P. Snow's *The New Men*, John Masters's panoramic *Bhowani Junction*, Kingsley Amis's *Lucky Jim* and William Golding's *Lord of the Flies* proved that the great traditions of the novel were both continued and revived. The American best-seller, *The Adventures of Augie March* by Saul Bellow was equally successful in Britain.

At Covent Garden Sir William Walton's *Troilus and Cressida* was warmly received.

Television was poised on the threshold of commercial programmes, but the B.B.C. was still alone in the field. Orwell's *1984* made brilliant and provocative viewing; on sound radio Dylan Thomas's dramatic poem, *Under Milk Wood* was the event of the year.

Britten's *The Turn of the Screw* had its première at the Teatro la Fenice during the Venice *Biennale*. Sadler's Wells and Glyndebourne both had their successful seasons. Honegger's *Jeanne d'Arc au bûcher* starred Ingrid Bergman and was produced by Roberto Rossellini; it wasn't the triumph such a combination of talents promised. The Diaghilev Exhibition at the Edinburgh Festival (later transferred to London) was a rich feast for ballet fans. In the theatre Sandy Wilson's immensely successful *The Boy Friend*, started its marathon run, with *Salad Days* an equally triumphant hit. Christopher Fry's *The Dark is Light Enough* was warmly received in spite of its obscurity. So was Terence Rattigan's *Separate Tables*. Bridget Boland's *The Prisoner* (a moving dramatization of the Mindszenty case), John Whiting's *Marching Song* and William Douglas Home's *The Manor of Northstead*. From America came *The Tea-House of the August Moon*, John van Druten's *I am a Camera* and *Bell, Book and Candle*, followed by Cole Porter's *Can-Can* and Thornton Wilder's *The Matchmaker*. Anouilh's *Time Remembered* was the only continental play that made an impact.

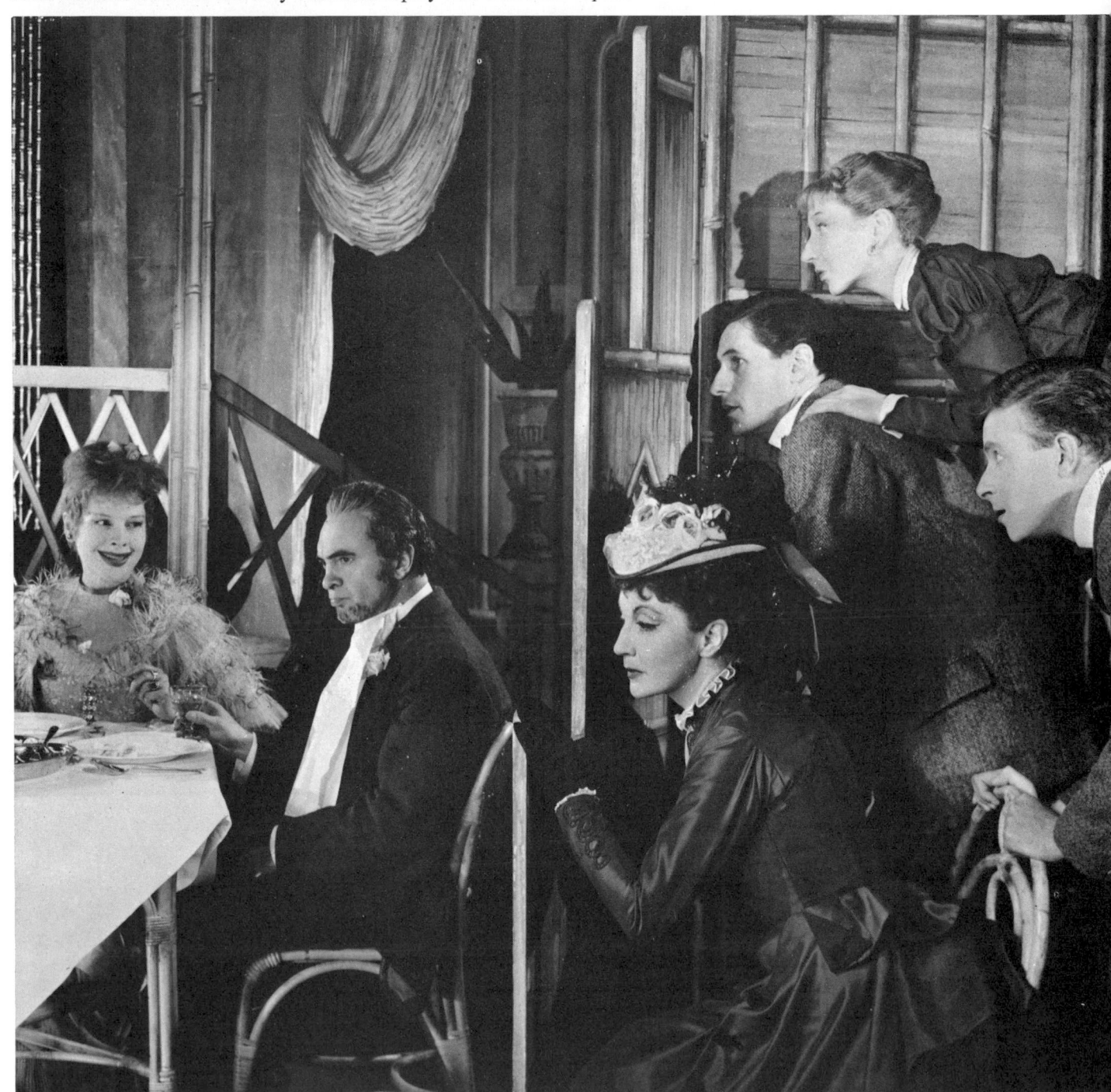

'The Matchmaker'—*an Anglo-American cast in a sparkling American comedy*

Eartha Kitt in 'New Faces'—the singer stole the show

There were storms in the art world around the British Museum where several collections suffered from lack of space and care and around Professor A. E. Richardson's inaugural speech as President of the Royal Academy —the famous architect declared that art critics were 'absolutely useless'. Promenade concerts reached their sixtieth season; York, Aldeburgh and Cheltenham all had successful music festivals.

In the cinema the wide screen challenged television—Cinerama, Cinemascope and Vistavision tried to provide bigger pictures though not necessarily good ones. British Lion, the biggest distributor for independent producers, was put in the charge of an Official Receiver. The outstanding pictures included Castellani's *Romeo and Juliet*, Charles Crichton's *The Hasty Heart*, Ralph Thomas's *Doctor in the House*, David Lean's *Hobson's*

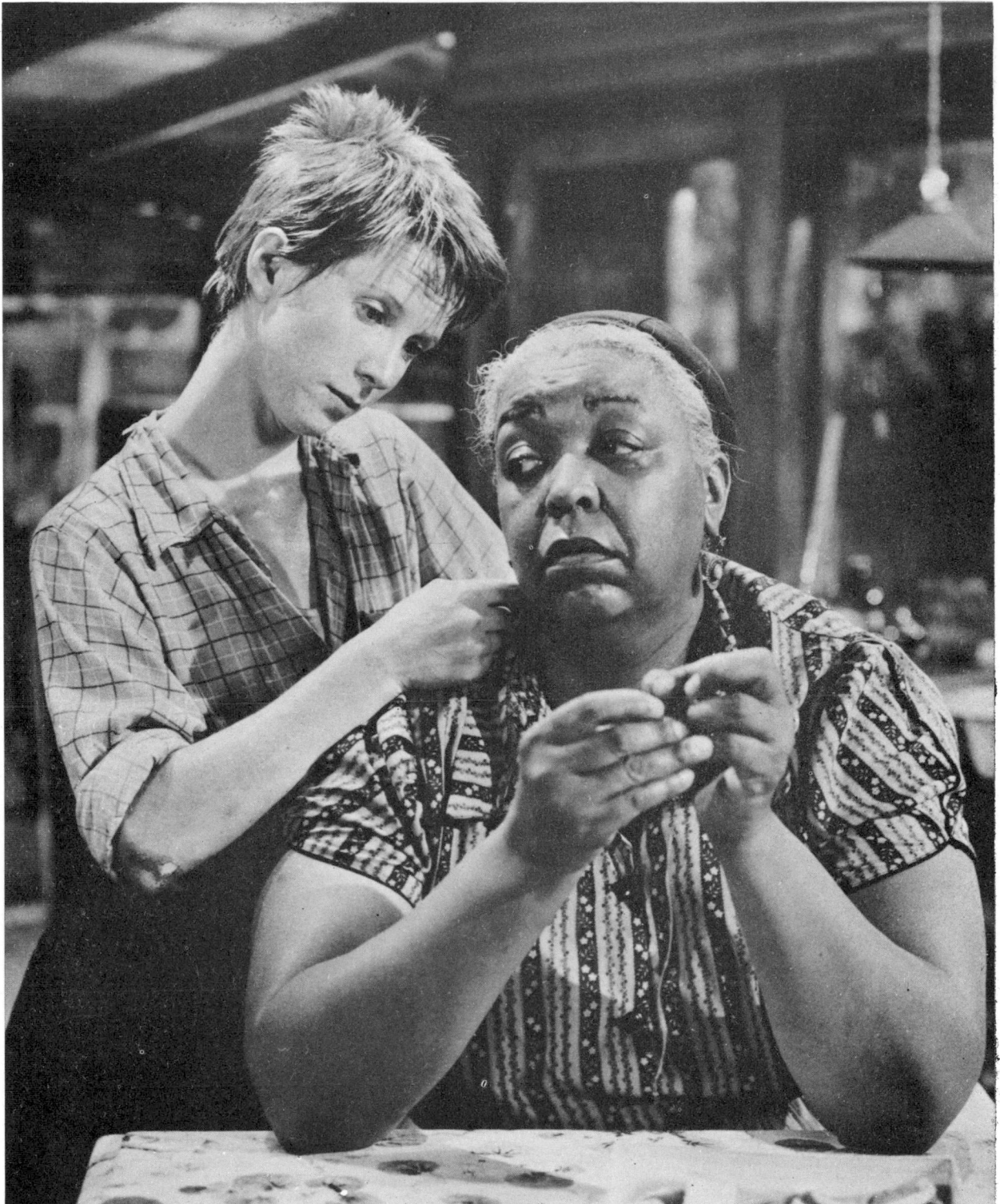

Julie Harris and Ethel Waters in ' The Member of the Wedding'—no segregation in the kitchen

Choice and Frank Launder's very funny *The Belles of Saint Trinians*. Hollywood sent us *The Member of the Wedding*, *The Pearl*, *The Caine Mutiny*, *Rear Window*, *New Faces* and *Seven Brides for Seven Brothers* to pick a short list from a very ample one. France contributed the brilliant *Wages of Fear*, Japan *Gate of Hell*, India *Pamposh* and Italy *Bread, Love and Dreams*.

Lung-cancer and tobacco were the main preoccupations of medicine; a total eclipse of the sun, a new solar telescope, the Zephyr reactor at Harwell and the problems of radio-active waste provided the main headlines for the progress of science.

Khrushchev and Bulganin with Tito in Belgrade: the breach was healed but the reception was cool

1955 WAS AN uneasy year, a prologue to the 1956, which was to be the 'year of miracles', a time of glory and shame. The early flashpoints were provided by South America. President Rámon of Panama was assassinated on January 2. Chile had a new government and joined with Ecuador and Peru in claiming a 200-mile limit for territorial waters—mainly to establish sovereignty over large tracts of the Antarctic. Costa Rica was invaded by rebels from Nicaragua. The Communist Party was outlawed in Cuba; there was a state of siege in Guatemala. Panama and the U.S.A. signed a new agreement about the Canal Zone. Uruguay got a new government in March.

The Soviet-Yugoslav breach was partly healed by a trade agreement; in May, Bulganin and Khrushchev visited Belgrade and Khrushchev's airport speech, blaming Beria for the past difficulties, was received in icy silence by Tito.

The integration of European defence and economic co-operation was making good progress. France proposed a European arms pool in January; a conference was held to consider a West European Arms Production Agency. The Paris Agreements were gradually ratified by all the countries involved: by Germany, Italy, France and Holland in March, by Luxembourg and Belgium in April.

Britain signed trade agreements with Finland and Turkey. In January the bank-rate was raised to $3\frac{1}{2}$ per cent; a month later came the shock of another rise, this time to $4\frac{1}{2}$ per cent. The Commonwealth Prime Ministers met for their regular conference. Important White Papers included nuclear power, military aircraft, the treatment of the Korean prisoners of war and defence among their subjects. Britain's adherence to the Baghdad Pact was approved on April 4.

Next day a whole era seemed to have come to an end when Sir Winston Churchill announced his resignation as Prime Minister. A man of innumerable parts, he was for long periods the very embodiment of British ideals and ambitions. Without him, Britain might well have wavered in the darkest days of the war; and his opponents and friends alike paid tribute to his great qualities. He was succeeded by Sir Anthony Eden; Mr. Harold Macmillan became Foreign Secretary. Mr. Butler's fourth budget reduced income tax and purchase tax on many goods, increased allowances, using the £282 million surplus to good effect. Parliament was dissolved on May 6 and the General Election took place twenty days later. The campaign was mostly conducted by radio and television; the result was an increased Conservative majority with the Tories and their 'Associates' gaining 345 seats and Labour 277 (instead of the 293 in the previous Parliament). The Liberals still had their six.

Sir Winston Churchill: Britain's Man of the Century left Downing Street—a gallant era had ended

The Newspaper Strike over—she couldn't wait to go home to read the news

Mrs. Bessie Braddock, M.P.—The housewives' choice was sick of unofficial strikes and strikers

Princess Margaret—Youth and Beauty

Strikes seemed to become endemic. For four weeks London was without newspapers in March and April; there were strikes by miners, busmen, tugmen, bargemen, dockers and footplate men of varying duration and inconvenience to the public. Mrs. Braddock the Socialist M.P. spoke for the vast majority when she told an audience of strikers that British housewives were sick of unofficial strikes. Certainly, as Mr. Gaitskell said, these were a contributory cause to Labour's defeat in the General Election.

In Africa the first Federal Council of Ministers was formed under the new Nigerian constitution; the United Nations mission to Tanganyika issued its report, calling for self-government within twenty-five years. The British Government had different views and the Trusteeship Council of UNO did not set a target-date for Tanganyikan independence. New terms of surrender for Mau-Mau men were announced by the Kenya Government; by July 10 a thousand terrorists took advantage of them. The South African government increased the number of Appeal Court judges from six to eleven—in order to carry through its apartheid policies which the Court's decisions had blocked. Libya had a new government; a report on the use of land in East Africa was published. East Germany and the Sudan signed a financial agreement. A French Parliamentary mission visited Algeria.

Princess Margaret began her tour of the West Indies at the end of January and won many hearts with her youth and beauty.

Adenauer in Moscow—the Soviets greet an 'imperialist lackey'

In January the Supreme Soviet issued a decree ending the state of war with Germany. In February came Malenkov's resignation as Prime Minister; he was succeeded by Bulganin. The 'collective leadership' was preserved for the time being. Mr. Molotov issued an invitation to the Big Three to meet and discuss the Austrian Treaty. This was accepted though in the meantime the Soviet Government carried out its threat and annulled its wartime treaties with France and Britain. On May 15, almost exactly ten years after the end of the war, the Austrian State Treaty was signed and Austria's independence restored. Dr. Adenauer, after being abused as an 'imperialist lackey' was invited to Moscow and a Four-Power Conference was set at Geneva.

As the Occupation régime ended in Western Germany and she was formally admitted to NATO, Russia summoned the Prime Ministers and Foreign Ministers of her satellites to Warsaw where an Eastern Security Treaty was signed by the U.S.S.R. and her 'protégés'. This was to be known as the Warsaw Pact. The line-up of East and West was now both formal and complete. But people in many countries were still hopeful about a miracle which the 'Geneva spirit' might work.

The Geneva Conference of the Four Great Powers opened on July 18 after Sir Anthony Eden and the Soviet statesmen had made preliminary statements of what they hoped to achieve—mainly about the reunification of Germany and European security.

Geneva Conference: Germany reunited—Europe secure?

Eisenhower pleaded for the removal of 'curtains', Sir Anthony Eden for a security pact between the Four Powers and a reunited Germany and a demilitarized 'safety zone' between East and West. On July 21 the President made the dramatic offer that the U.S. and Russia should exchange complete blueprints of their military establishments. This was later turned down by the Russians. The conference was held in a spirit of amiability; as for practical results, it achieved nothing, least of all a German peace treaty.

The 'thaw' was spotty, at the best. Russia offered her usual 'technical aid' to North Vietnam. On July 27 the Austrian State Treaty came into force. In August the Peking government released the eleven American airmen who had been held prisoner since 1953. The U.S. Ambassador to Prague and the Chinese Ambassador to Warsaw began conversations in Geneva. Another conference met in the city of Calvin discussing the peaceful uses of atomic energy. Moscow announced the reduction of the armed forces by 640,000. Britain offered an amnesty to the Communists in Malaya. Finland was given back the base of Porkkala in exchange for extending the Finno-Russian Treaty for twenty years. Bulganin started his long correspondence with President Eisenhower about disarmament. British and Soviet naval squadrons exchanged goodwill visits to Leningrad and Portsmouth. The Foreign Ministers of the Big Four met at Geneva late in October; their final communiqué, issued after more than three weeks of talks, admitted failure once again—for Mr. Molotov would not discuss German unification nor free elections in Eastern Germany. Ten days after the conference ended Russia announced the explosion of new types of atomic and hydrogen bombs. On November 29 the East German Government was formally recognized by the U.S.S.R. as a sovereign State with East Berlin as its capital.

In the market place at Saigon, 40,000 shouted 'Down with Bao Dai, the traitor'

Nicosia—the price of freedom

Within the Commonwealth and Empire stresses and upheavals showed no sign of lessening. Britain and South Africa signed defence agreements. Mr. Marshall, the Chief Minister of the Singapore government resigned. The Malayan Legislature demanded complete independence; the elections brought victory for the Alliance Party. A new central government was set up in Uganda and a report issued on the Federal system for the Gold Coast. In the Sudan all government services were 'sudanized'. India and Portugal clashed over Goa. The conference of British, Greek and Turkish Foreign Ministers on the Eastern Mediterranean (including Cyprus) opened in London. As the British proposals for Cyprus were submitted to the tripartite conference, there were violent anti-Greek riots in Istanbul and Izmir.

The Turkish Government apologized to Greece but this did not settle the campaign for *enosis*, the return of Cyprus to Greece. There was another vexing dispute over the Buraimi oasis between Britain and Saudi Arabia; in September the British member of the arbitration tribunal resigned and in October the oasis was occupied by the Sultan of Muscat. A round-table conference on Malta opened in London. Sir John Harding was appointed Governor of Cyprus. Mutesa II, the Kabaka, returned to Buganda in October. In November the South African delegation withdrew from the General Assembly rather than submit to international censure of its apartheid policies.

By November the situation had become so bad in Cyprus that a state of emergency had to be declared; a full-scale guerrilla war was going on with Colonel Grivas directing a well-organized force of Greek and Cypriot 'resistance-groups' who terrorized the villages, killed British Service men and civilians and were impossible to corner.

Grivas and friends—civilians and soldiers were killed

Cyprus—in Nicosia, bombs for shopping crowds

213

Mr. Hugh Gaitskell—exit Attlee—a new leader for Labour

In July President Eisenhower signed the U.S. Foreign Aid Bill. Later that month the U.S. announced its plans of launching satellites into space within three years. There were talks between Mr. Dulles and the Japanese Foreign Minister in August; the U.S. signed a trade agreement with the Philippines. In September the country was shaken by Eisenhower's heart attack. He had been on holiday at Denver and the first news was very grave. But he rallied and by November he could return to Washington. By December he was again showing 'signs of fatigue' and the Republican Party was much troubled as to whether he was fit enough to run for another term. A week before Christmas, however, he was pronounced to be out of danger though he postponed his decision about running for a second term until the following February.

In August the I.R.A. made a successful raid on an army training centre in Berkshire. In September Britain proved her 'imperialistic tendencies' by formally annexing the uninhabitable Atlantic eyrie of Rockall. President Lopes of Portugal visited London in October; a supplementary budget was introduced by Mr. Butler, increasing purchase tax and the tax on distributed profits, curtailing public expenditure, raising the cost of telephones. At the Guildhall Sir Anthony Eden spoke of the Middle East and warned about the dangers inherent in the Israeli-Egyptian tension. In December Mr. Attlee followed Sir Winston's example and resigned as leader of the Opposition; Mr. Hugh Gaitskell was elected as his successor. A reorganization of the government resulted in Mr. Macmillan becoming Chancellor of the Exchequer, Mr. Selwyn Lloyd Foreign Secretary and Mr. Butler Lord Privy Seal. Britain and India concluded an agreement for co-operating in the peaceful development of atomic energy.

France was having constant and increasing trouble in North Africa. There was a state of siege in Casablanca, following a series of anti-European outrages; in August there were serious disorders in Morocco and a massacre of Europeans. The Tunisian government resigned in September; the following month the French government decided to withdraw from the U.N. General Assembly owing to what it called 'hostile interference' in regard to Algeria. The Moroccan crisis was solved, at least temporarily, when the French gave in to the demand for the return of the former Sultan who was welcomed back to Rabat by tremendous acclaim; on December 7 Si Bekkai formed the first representative all-Moroccan government.

Ngo Dinh Diem, in Vietnam a new dictator in business

The Rif rebellion, tying down more than a hundred thousand French soldiers, still continued. Edgar Faure's government was defeated on November 29, Parliament was dissolved and the year left France in considerable confusion.

There was much restless discontent in Vietnam; in July the International Armistice Commission's headquarters were sacked in the Saigon riots. In October there was a referendum which advocated the deposition of the Emperor Bao Dai and Ngo Dinh Diem proclaimed a Republic as President and Head of State. A new dictator set up in business—while across the world, in the Argentine, a long-established one lost his power. Juan Peron, the Strong Man of South America was toppled from his luxurious perch and had to flee the country. His opponents fought over the succession for some months until, in November, General Aramburu was installed as provisional President. The world was regaled for weeks with tales of Peron's mistresses, cruelties and the rich loot he left behind.

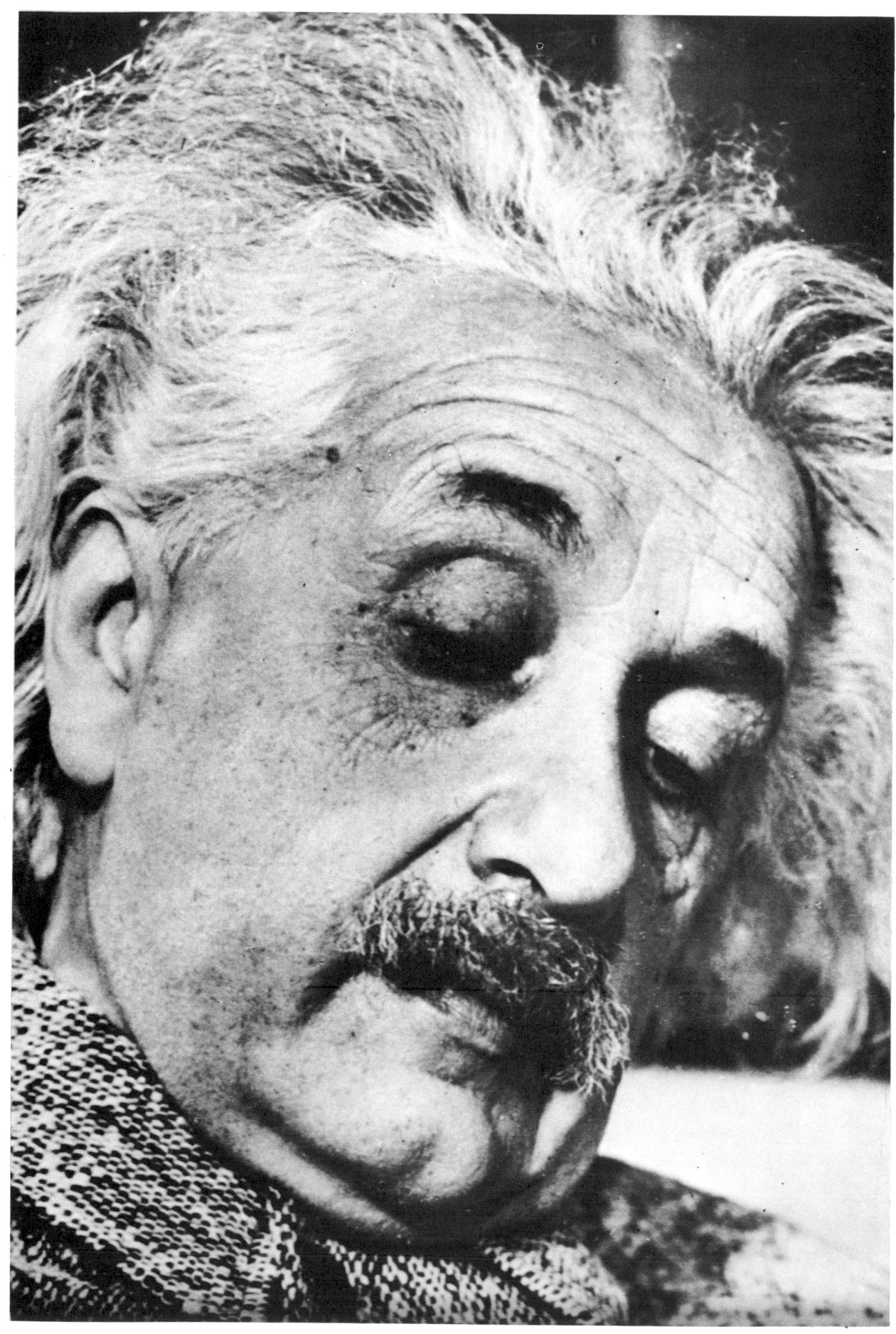

Albert Einstein—the unique genius of the twentieth century

Dr. Salk—towards defeat of the polio menace to humanity

1955 deprived the world of the shrewd courage of the Right Hon. Leopold Amery, of the doughty Labour politician, the Right Hon. Arthur Deakin, of the brilliant, unique brain of Albert Einstein, of Sir Alexander Fleming, who gave mankind the great boon of penicillin, of Dr. Garbett, the Archbishop of York, of the great American statesman, Cordell Hull, and of the greatest modern German novelist, Thomas Mann. The Nobel Peace Prize was given to the International Refugee Organization; Professor Hugo Thorell, the Swedish bio-chemist, won the Medicine and Physiology award; that of Physics was shared by Professor W. E. Lamb of California and Professor P. Kusch of New York; another American, Professor Vincent de Vigneaud of Cornell University, was awarded the Prize for Chemistry.

The Salk anti-polio vaccine, after a difficult start, proved its immense value.

Preparations began for the International Geophysical Year; new polar expeditions were planned and carried out. Automation aroused equal enthusiasm and anxiety.

On September 22 the British public saw its first 'commercial'—something reasonably innocuous about tooth-paste. Associated Rediffusion and Associated TeleVision Ltd. went on the air first but soon A.B.C. and Granada were to follow and we became familiar with the miracles of *I Love Lucy*, *Dragnet* and all the other products of American know-how. It took time for I.T.A. to find its feet and not more than half of Britain was able to look in at commercial TV—but even so it made its impact soon enough, justifying both its most severe critics and its most enthusiastic partisans. It was neither as bad nor as good as either claimed. There was much argument about the '14-day rule' which banned all discussion of any political issue debated in Parliament for a fortnight before; the B.B.C. insisted that this should be made a formal directive by the Postmaster-General, instead of the 'gentleman's agreement' of 1947–8.

British films reached a triumph with Olivier's splendid *Richard III*.

With Julie Harris in 'East of Eden', James Dean, mercurial symbol of resentful and puzzled youth

Zoltan Korda made the fourth version of *The Four Feathers*; *Doctor at Sea*, *Geordie*, *Cockleshell Heroes*, *A Kid For Two Farthings*, *The Prisoner*, *The Dam-Busters*, *The Bespoke Overcoat* represented a consistently high level. From America *To Catch a Thief*, *Mister Roberts*, *Carmen Jones*, *Bad Day at Black Rock*, *20,000 Leagues under the Sea*, *East of Eden* and *A Star is Born* brought a widely-varying selection of Hollywood's offerings, Italy sent *La Strada* and *The Overcoat*, France *Les Diaboliques*, *Rififi* and *French Can-Can*, Spain *Marcelino* and Japan *The Seven Samurai*. The Edinburgh Festival showed 172 films from twenty-eight countries.

In the theatre there was a large foreign invasion. Beckett's *Waiting for Godot* brought large crowds to the Arts Theatre, Fritz Hochwalder's *The Strong Are Lonely*, Giraudoux's *Tiger at the Gates*, Anouilh's *The Lark* scored strongly. *Sailor Beware!* was a very funny comedy; Sandy Wilson's *The Buccaneer* was a highly successful musical. Angus Wilson's *The Mulberry Bush* staged at the Bristol Old Vic; William Douglas Home's *The Reluctant Debutante* proved very acceptable satire.

Dorothy Tutin, rising star of the English theatre, gave life to Anouilh's brilliant, but oddly lifeless, 'The Lark'

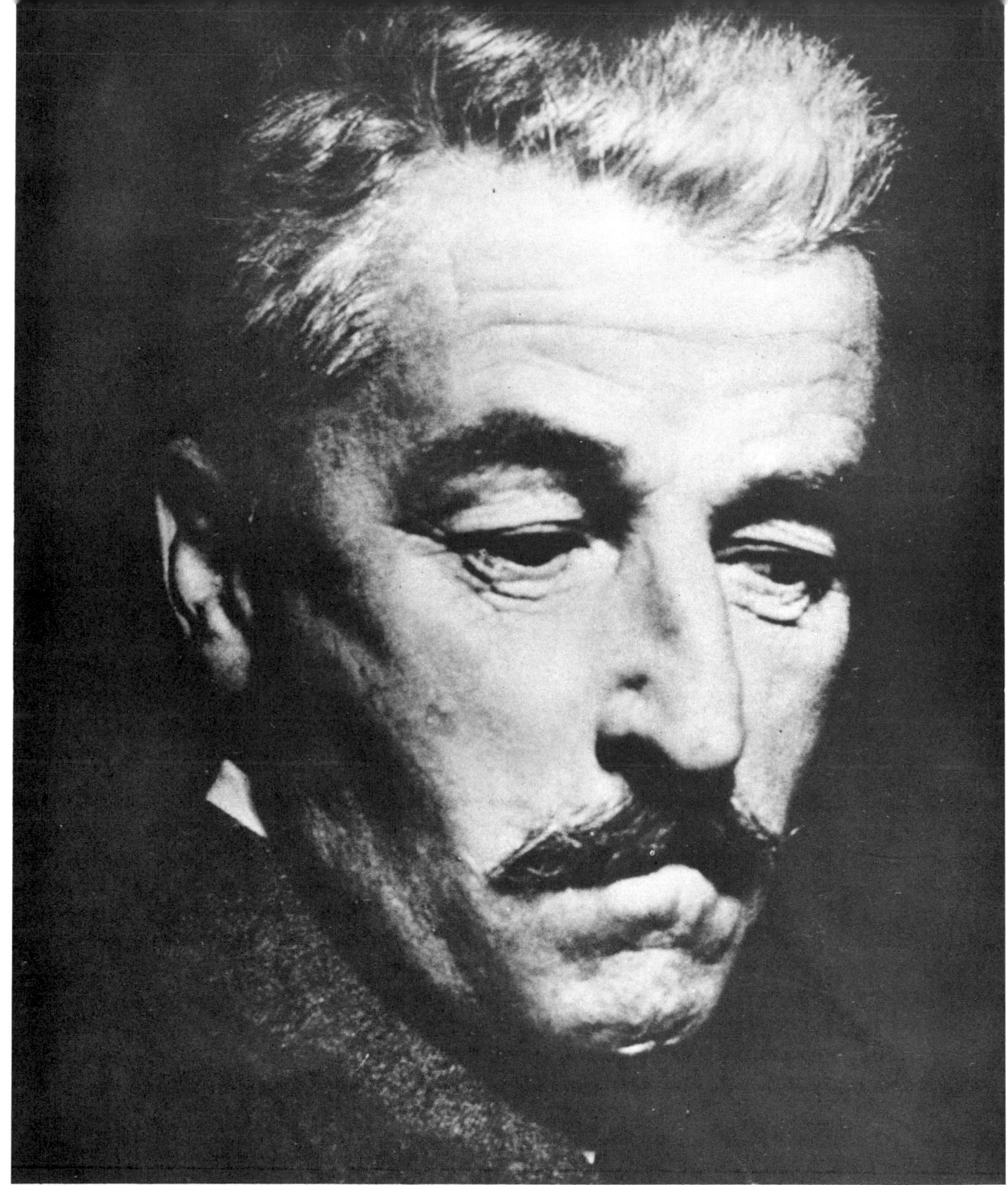

William Faulkner: the American Nobel Prize winner's 'A Fable', engaged the attention of critics

Another record was set by publishers with almost 20,000 books appearing during the year; fiction led with educational and children's books following. Richard Aldington's *Lawrence of Arabia* was a most controversial attack on Lawrence's reputation. In fiction Nigel Dennis's *Cards of Identity*, Joyce Cary's powerful *Not Honour More*, Robert Graves's *Homer's Daughter*, William Faulkner's *A Fable*, and Graham Greene's *The Quiet American* were only few of a rich and varied list.

They said in 1955

An appeaser is one who feeds a crocodile—hoping it will eat him last.

SIR WINSTON CHURCHILL

It is a paradox that every dictator has climbed to power on the ladder of free speech. Immediately on attaining power each dictator has suppressed all free speech except his own.

HERBERT HOOVER

Khrushchev speaks: Stalin was denounced, a myth destroyed

THREE EVENTS DOMINATED 1956, dwarfing everything else; three definite turning-points in twentieth-century history: the Khrushchev speech at the XXth Congress of the Soviet Communist Party; the Hungarian Revolution; and the Suez war. The story of 1956 could be told entirely around these three dramatic and, in many ways, fantastic episodes. The chain-reactions created by them have not yet come to an end.

In the first months of the year it seemed that Russia was making important gains in the diplomatic and economic field. She signed an agreement on atomic co-operation with Yugoslavia, extended her technical assistance to China, opened the new trans-Mongolian railway, sent ambassadors to Libya, Liberia and Western Germany, proposed a twenty-year friendship pact to America, returned the Porkkala naval base to Finland and held a meeting of the Warsaw Pact Powers at Prague. In February she signed an economic aid agreement with Bulgaria and lodged a strong protest with the U.S. against the launching of balloons which contained pamphlets, photographic and other equipment and which were sent over Russian and other Communist territory. She warned America and Britain that any dispatch of their troops to the Middle East would violate the U.N. Charter and constitute a threat to peace.

Then, on February 14, the XXth Congress opened in Moscow. Eleven days later Nikita Khrushchev delivered what must have been one of the most momentous speeches in history—a denunciation of Stalin, a devastating attack on the 'cult of the individual', an exposure of the crimes and mistakes the dead dictator had committed throughout the years of his monolithic rule. The speech was supposed to be secret but it was published by the U.S. State Department. It shook Russia, it shattered the foreign Communist Parties. In vain *Pravda* called Stalin 'one of the greatest Marxists', in vain the Party organizations tried to minimize the significance of Khrushchev's speech. A myth had been destroyed and the myth-makers themselves were in headlong retreat. For a short time there was even a danger of civil war or at least fratricidal conflict between the 'Stalinists' and the 'revisionists'. In Russia the revolts could be suppressed; but in the free world and the satellites the XXth Congress killed the faith in Russian leadership of millions and led directly to the upheavals of the autumn.

But though the shock was immediate, the reaction was somewhat delayed. In the meantime Austria and the U.S.S.R. agreed on Danube navigation problems and Canada signed a trade agreement with Russia, showing that the tension of the original spy trials had been relieved. Afghanistan accepted Soviet aid; the correspondence of Eisenhower and Bulganin continued with lengthening intervals. In March the Danish Premier visited Moscow and the first ambassador of the *Bundesrepublik* arrived. Huge deposits of diamonds, coal, gold, silver and iron-ore were discovered in Northern Siberia; the working week was reduced to forty-six hours.

Burck in 'The Chicago Sun-Times'
DESTALINIZATION
'*Latest Moscow purge*'

Commander Crabbe: while Khrushchev and Bulganin were in Britain, the frogman investigated their navy, and disappeared. Killed or kidnapped? The question remains unanswered, the frogman mystery, unsolved

Mr. Eden welcomes the Soviet 'peripatetic twins'

Malenkov, the deposed Soviet Premier, paid a three-week visit to Britain—studying electrical installations. Russia and the Sudan established diplomatic relations. Mikoyan toured Pakistan, India, Afghanistan and Burma. On March 21 another 'nuclear device' was exploded in the U.S.S.R.; the sixth in eight months was announced on April 2. Various economic and shipping agreements were signed with China and India. The U.S.S.R. announced her readiness to 'aid U.N. efforts for peace in the Middle East'; the Cominform was dissolved.

On April 10 the 'peripatetic twins', Khrushchev and Bulganin, arrived in Britain for a ten-day official visit. This was marked by a somewhat inhospitable quizzing on the part of some Labour leaders to which Mr. Khrushchev took great exception.

In May Russia protested to the U.S. for alleged violation of her airspace; on the same day she announced that another 1,200,000 men would be demobilized by 1957. The French Premier and Foreign Minister visited Moscow; a two-year trade agreement was signed between Russia and the U.K.

On June 1 Molotov followed Malenkov into comparative oblivion and was succeeded by D. M. Shepilov.

In Poznan a tragic and heroic rising

King Hussein dismissed Glubb Pasha who had served for many years as Commander of the Arab Legion

Tito arrived in Moscow on a three-week visit (which was one reason why the veteran Foreign Minister had to go) to patch up the old quarrel. Bulganin wrote another letter, asking the West to match the Russian disarmament; the Crown Prince of Yemen visited Moscow. Shepilov continued the courting of the Arabs, making a tour of Cairo, Damascus, Beirut and Athens. Over 30,000 Russian troops were withdrawn from Eastern Germany. Then, on June 28, came the heroic and tragic revolt at Poznan where the workers rose against the inhuman norms, the lack of food and unbearable living conditions. Tanks and flame-throwers soon crushed the revolt with over 50 dead, 300 wounded and another 323 arrested. Two days later Poles and Russians signed an agreement on 'cultural co-operation' and on the same day, the Central Committee of the Soviet Communist Party, docilely following Khrushchev's lead adopted a resolution to end 'the cult of personality'.

Italy agreed to pay £5·8 million reparations to Ethiopia. There was a meeting in Cairo between Colonel Nasser, the President of Syria and King Ibn Saud; King Hussein of Jordan declined the invitation.

Iraq granted Jordan a £1 million loan for a superphosphate project. An earthquake devastated large areas in southern Lebanon. Egypt gave Jordan a grant for her National Guard. France recognized Tunisia as an independent State. On March 23 Britain announced that Egyptian officers and others were being trained in Poland and Czech 'experts' were training the military in Egypt. The first Tunis election brought complete victory for the National Front. The rulers of the Aden Protectorate States met to discuss the projected federation.

Early in June the Egyptian representative on the Suez Canal Company Board declared that Egypt would not extend the ninety-nine-year concession due to expire in 1968; the Company agreed to transfer over £20 million to the Egyptian government during the next eight years. Two Russian-built destroyers joined the Egyptian Navy. The Moroccan government suspended the emigration of Moroccan Jews to Israel. On July 13 the last British troops left the Suez Canal base. Mrs. Golda Meir, succeeding Mr. Moshe Sharett, became the first woman Foreign Minister in the free world.

Communist China was emerging more and more as a world Power. On January 1 the Chinese newspapers appeared with characters printed horizontally, reading from left to right; in February the government announced a thirty-letter Latin alphabet to replace the 30,000 ideographic characters, with both scripts to be used for a transitory period.

Early in March France recognized the independence of Morocco.

In February the President of the U.S. and Sir Anthony Eden issued 'The Declaration of Washington', a high-minded manifesto on the fight against Communism, which had no appreciable effect on the Communist Powers.

A leader of the Istiqlal Party in a Tangier speech demanded that large portions of Algeria, French West Africa and Spanish Rio de Oro should be incorporated in Morocco. Britain handed two destroyers to Israel. Nasser was elected President of Egypt and the new constitution was approved by plebiscite. Except for Sinai and the Red Sea areas, martial law was ended in the country; the new Cabinet was sworn in by President Nasser.

France's General Election (which excluded Algeria) brought gains for the Communists and for the strange, Right-wing Poujadist Party. The first French atomic power plant started operation at Marcoule. In February M. Guy Mollet became Prime Minister. His gravest problem was Algeria where the Arab nationalists and the French *colons* were engaged in a bloody, merciless war.

Divided Germany was rearming. In January the first of the new West German recruits reported for duty. East Germany created a 'National People's Army', and signed commercial agreements with Norway and Sweden. The three Western Ambassadors in Bonn protested against the increase of East German military activity in Berlin. America and Western Germany agreed on atomic co-operation. In March the Bonn *Bundestag* changed the constitution to allow the introduction of conscription. In June Dr. Adenauer visited America and was given honorary degrees by two universities.

President Eisenhower was still convalescing early in the year and his State of the Union message was delivered by proxy. A scheme called 'a soil bank' was proposed to help the American farmer and the U.S. continued to buy up and store vast quantities of agricultural surplus products; some of it went to Yugoslavia, Austria, Burma, Japan, Indonesia, South Korea and Chile.

King Hussein: dismissed the Commander

Mrs. Meir: first woman Foreign Minister

225

In Monaco, a marriage between Prince Rainier and a 'typical American girl', Miss Grace Kelly

The age-long dream of alchemists was realized when the General Electric Company produced the first synthetic diamonds. 40,000 kgs. of Uranium-235 were released for research and development, half made available in the U.S. and half abroad. On the last day of February Eisenhower declared his readiness to run for a second term. In March Mr. Dulles made a ten-day tour of Asian capitals. The American Ambassador expressed his government's 'sympathetic concern' over Cyprus to the Greek Foreign Minister. Atomic co-operation agreements were signed with Thailand, Canada, New Zealand, the U.K., Australia, Switzerland, Holland and the Irish Republic; the Philippines were chosen as the Asian Nuclear Centre and America undertook to provide aid to Persia for the development of Khuzistan. Eisenhower met the Canadian and Mexican Premiers at White Sulphur Springs. In April America—and most of the world—were thrilled by the 'marriage of the year', the glittering wedding of Prince Rainier of Monaco and Miss Grace Kelly. U.S. controls on exports to the U.S.S.R. and her satellites were much simplified on non-strategic materials.

In May the first hydrogen bomb to be dropped from the air exploded over Namu Island. In June there was another setback in the President's health; he was operated for ileitis, an abdominal complaint, but made an excellent recovery. The joint Anglo-American guided missile ranges in the Caribbean were considerably extended. In Britain full employment and an orgy of hire purchase buying created special problems. In January Europe's largest blast furnace went into operation in Wales; two new research reactors—Zeus and Zeta—started work at Harwell. The Queen and the Duke of Edinburgh flew to Nigeria on a three weeks' visit.

```
HAD TO LEAVE UNEXPECTEDLY    SORRY DARLING    I LOVE
YOU    PLEASE DO NOT STOP LOVING ME
                        DONALD
```

```
I AM QUITE ALL RIGHT    DO NOT WORRY    LOVE TO ALL
```

Burgess—temporary Civil Servant

The Burgess-Maclean case filled the front pages—these two ex-civil servants had disappeared from England and turned up in Moscow. For every person who made the West to East 'switch' there were at least a thousand refugees fleeing from the Communist paradise; just because of this contrast, the former cases always meant big news. A Conference of Privy Councillors was appointed on Security in the Public Services and there was much speculation about the motives and importance of the two men, what 'secrets' they took with them and what would be their fate in the Soviet Union.

Maclean—not very permanent Civil·Servant

Mrs. Maclean—she also disappeared behind 'the curtain'

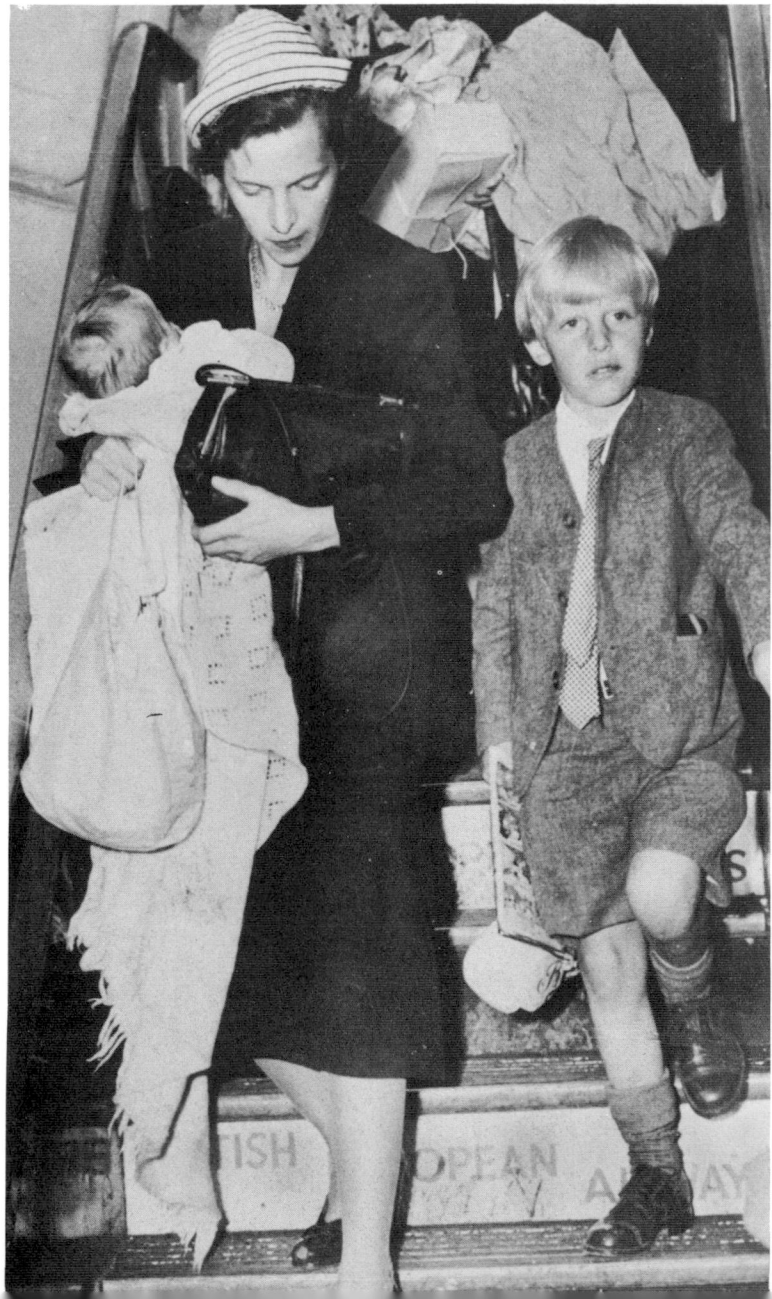

Mr. James Griffith became deputy leader of the Labour Party.

In February the bank rate went up to $5\frac{1}{2}$ per cent, the highest since 1932; Mr. Macmillan announced new anti-inflation measures. Food subsidies were cut and hire purchase was further restricted. In March Mr. Selwyn Lloyd, the Foreign Secretary, visited the Middle and Far East on his way to the SEATO Council meeting at Karachi. The festering sore of Cyprus became more and more dangerous. Sir John Harding and Archbishop Makarios exchanged a futile correspondence; Britain began to jam the Athens broadcasts to Cyprus.

Sir John Harding—more and more dangerous

Archbishop Makarios—the Prelate was deported to the Seychelles

Calder Hall—the first atomic power station

In March the grimly unyielding Archbishop was deported to the Seychelles. The Greek government demanded that the dispute should be put on the U.N. agenda.

Calder Hall, the first atomic power station in the world, went into operation in May. In June the glory of Scapa Flow came to an end with the closing of the great naval establishment. The Queen and her Consort visited Stockholm where the Equestrian Olympic Games were held.

Two British nuclear tests took place at Monte Bello Islands. Her Majesty reviewed a hundred holders of the Victoria Cross in Hyde Park to mark the centenary of the Order. The seventh post-war Conference of the Commonwealth Prime Ministers was held in London.

At Stockholm: the Equestrian Olympic Games

As the second half of the year opened, it seemed that world tension would be relieved—but there were signs of growing discontent in the Communist world. East Germany reduced her army by 25 per cent. The Hungarian Communist leaders warned the workers not to criticize the government and party. The Supreme Soviet met in Moscow and abolished the Finno-Karelian Republic. An Eastern Institute for Nuclear Research was established with the U.S.S.R., China and the European satellites participating. Both Russia and Finland protested against the flights of American aircraft over their territories. When Dr. Grotewohl and an East German delegation visited Moscow, the Russians agreed to halve the cost of the occupation. The first of four new nuclear tests was carried out in the U.S.S.R.; the first boarding schools were opened. Russia and Poland signed an agreement for 'large-scale Soviet aid to Polish economy'. In September Khrushchev followed Mikoyan to Yugoslavia to talk to Tito. The Polish General Election was set for December but postponed by a month. Tito flew with Khrushchev to the Crimea to continue their talks.

Early in October the Bolshoi Ballet came to London. On October 6 the body of Laszlo Rajk and three others executed with him were given a State Funeral at Budapest. His murderers stood at the graveside; thousands of people thronged the cemetery. Imre Nagy, the former Premier, was readmitted to the Communist Party. Khrushchev, Molotov and Mikoyan attended the session of the Polish Communist Party; Gomulka was elected First Secretary and Marshal Rokossovsky, the Polish-born Russian Minister of Defence, was dropped. Two days later, in sympathy with the Polish events, there were mass demonstrations in Budapest, demands for withdrawal of Soviet troops, for the release of Cardinal Mindszenty and return of Imre Nagy to political power. On October 23 the peaceful demonstration turned into a revolution as the A.V.O., the Secret Police, fired at the crowds outside the Broadcasting Station. The insurrection spread; the Hungarian Army, with few exceptions, joined the revolution. Imre Nagy was appointed Premier but Gerö was still First Secretary of the Central Committee. The Soviet troops intervened; there was a massacre in Parliament Square. Gerö was dismissed and succeeded by Janos Kadar, an Old Guard Communist who, however, had been tortured in prison and had been responsible for persuading the late Laszlo Rajk to 'confess'. For ten days it seemed that a miracle would happen —that Hungary would regain her independence and that the Russians would withdraw. Nagy's government included non-Communists. Britain, France and the U.S.A. tabled a resolution at the emergency session of the Security Council indicting the Soviet Union for repressing the rights of the Hungarians by military action. This

Budapest: for Stalin's statue, sledge-hammers, axes and crowbars

was adopted by nine votes to one—but votes could not help the Hungarians. At Györ, an Insurgents' Committee was demanding 'democracy on a Western model'; Cardinal Mindszenty was released and returned to Budapest.

On November 1 the Hungarian Government renounced the Warsaw Treaty and appealed to the world to guarantee the country's permanent neutrality. Soviet troops seemed to have withdrawn from the capital—but the same day they were reported to be pouring across the frontier. Russia vetoed the Western request that the Security Council should consider the critical situation in Hungary but the General Assembly accepted it by fifty votes against eight with fifteen abstentions.

At dawn on November 4 the Soviet troops attacked Budapest; General Maléter, leader of the freedom fighters, was kidnapped with his colleagues while negotiating with the Russians. Premier Nagy fled to the Yugoslav Legation; Kadar, who a couple of days ago had denounced the Russian occupation, turned up at Szolnok, a town forty miles from the capital and announced that he had formed a government.
The Hungarians fought on for another few days; but there was no help the West could send without sparking off a Third World War and Suez, in any case, had fatally divided the free world. The last call for help remained unanswered. Tens of thousands of refugees began to pour across the still open Austrian frontier. Nagy, having been given a safe conduct by Kadar, left the Yugoslav Embassy with a handful of his followers, was promptly kidnapped by the Russians and dragged off to Rumania.

The sorry tale of the short Suez war began in July when Britain and America informed Nasser that they would not finance the Aswan High Dam project. Earlier that month an Egyptian trade mission had started negotiations in London and Nasser had talks in Yugoslavia with Tito and Nehru. On July 26 Nasser seized the Suez Canal, nationalizing the Canal Company. Britain and France protested; Egyptian assets in Britain were frozen.

Budapest: after the rising—the free world stood aghast and helpless

British, American and French discussions opened in London; the French also took financial measures. The export of war materials to Egypt was banned. The American freezing of Egyptian assets was relaxed after five days. 'Precautionary military measures' were taken early in August; the principal maritime Powers, the Soviet Union and Egypt were invited to a conference in London. British and French nationals were advised to leave Egypt. Some army reservists were called up in Britain and Egypt. The Suez Company gave its non-Egyptian employees the choice between their contract with the Company and co-operation with the Egyptian authorities; Nasser decreed the formation of an 'army of national liberation'. British wives and children were flown out of the Canal Zone; two oil company officials were expelled by the Egyptians. Eisenhower appointed a Middle East Emergency Committee to deal with European oil supplies. On August 12 Nasser rejected the invitation to the London Conference and proposed an alternative meeting. The Conference opened, anyhow. Eighteen nations accepted an amended form of a plan put forward by Mr. Dulles; the Soviet Union, India, Indonesia and Ceylon supported an alternative Indian plan. Australia, Ethiopia, Persia, Sweden and the U.S. were asked to 'explain' the eighteen Nations plan to Nasser; Mr. Menzies was chosen to head this committee. Egypt expelled two British correspondents and a Canadian; but Nasser was ready to see Menzies. Two members of the Cairo British Embassy were also told to leave; an 'alleged spy ring' was 'unmasked' and four British nationals were arrested. French troops were sent to Cyprus.

Pál Maléter: freedom fighter

Ben Gurion goes to War—the Israeli victory was complete

The talks between President Nasser and the Menzies Committee began on September 3; six days later Nasser rejected the eighteen Nation proposals. On the 12th Sir Anthony Eden announced the setting up of a 'Suez Canal Users' Association'. A second conference was called for the September 19; Nasser rejected, the U.S.S.R. denounced the Association. The Conference opened with eighteen Nations present; three days later it issued a general declaration which formally established the proposed body.

Early in October Mr. Dulles admitted that there were 'serious differences' between the U.S. and her European allies over Suez. The Security Council adopted the Anglo-French resolution, establishing six principles under which the Canal would be operated; the second half of the resolution was vetoed by Russia. Israel demanded equal rights. A joint military command of Egypt, Jordan and Syria was set up two days after the Hungarian Revolution. Israel mobilized her reserves; on October 29 she invaded the Sinai Peninsula, after assuring Britain that she would not attack Jordan. British ships sailed from Malta. American and British citizens were advised to leave the Arab countries. Next day the Security Council debated an American resolution calling on Israel to withdraw; this was vetoed by France and Britain who, on the same day, sent an ultimatum to Egypt and Israel, calling to end the fighting, withdraw ten miles from the Canal so that Anglo-French forces could move temporarily into Port Said, Ismailia and Suez. This was accepted by Israel and rejected by Egypt.

Within three days the Egyptian Army was in full retreat and Gaza had fallen. The Israeli victory was complete. On November 5 British and French paratroops landed at Port Said. U.N. called on them to withdraw; Canada proposed a U.N. force to take over. There were days of emergency sessions, much diplomatic haggling and violent anti-British and anti-French action in the Arab States. The Anglo-French forces did not advance very far. American pressure became decisive. The strange adventure ended in December. The Canal was blocked by

It was a short war . . . the withdrawal was not delayed

sunken ships and took several weeks to clear. The Israelis unable to stand up to international pressure, withdrew to the original armistice line.

The debate over the Suez episode still continues after four years. It ended Sir Anthony Eden's political career; it upset Anglo-American relations; it drove, temporarily, some of the Arab States into closer relations with Russia. There were some who said that the Anglo-French action should never have been started; others maintained that if they had advanced to Cairo, the U.S. and the rest of the world would have accepted the accomplished fact. The damage to British prestige was considerable; perhaps the whole affair was, in Talleyrand's words, 'worse than a crime, a mistake'.

No traffic on the canal

The Swedish liner 'Stockholm' collided with the Italian 'Andrea Doria' which sank with the loss of fifty lives

The Communists exploited it to the full for their propaganda; and there were voices claiming that it robbed the free world of the moral authority to intervene in the Hungarian tragedy. Today we know that this, at least, is nonsense; the Russians were moving their troops into Hungary long before the Suez conflict exploded and they never had any intention to let one of their satellites escape from their stranglehold, knowing very well that if Hungary went, Poland, Czechoslovakia and the Balkan satellites would also defect before long. When the dust settled and the shouting died down, things seemed to be pretty much as they were before—except for the huge cost, the ruined reputations and a deep feeling of shame and frustration.

Compared to the headline events of these months, the rest of the news seemed tame indeed: in July Dr. Nkrumah's party won the Gold Coast elections. Morocco and Tunisia were admitted to U.N. and Spain handed over her zone to Moroccan rule. The first guided missile ship was commissioned in Britain.

In September Italy and Switzerland agreed to build a road tunnel under the Great St. Bernard Pass; a Vickers Valiant V-bomber flew the Atlantic non-stop. The Convention on the Abolition of Slavery was accepted unanimously by U.N.; British and French electricity grids were to be linked by submarine cable.

Donald Campbell set up a new world water speed record in his *Bluebird*.

Mr. Grimond succeeded Mr. Clement Davies as the Liberal leader.

The anti-neutron was discovered at the University of California. Seretse Khama was allowed to return to Bechuanaland as a private citizen. 'Operation Buffalo' tested a British atomic device in South Australia. The British bread subsidy ended after fifteen years. Admiral Dönitz was released from Spandau Prison.

In October the first British nuclear weapon to be dropped from the air was tested. 200,000 'untouchables' in India became Buddhists. The Duke of Edinburgh left London on a four-month world tour.

France arrested (the Arabs said 'kidnapped') some Algerian rebel leaders on their way to meet the Sultan of Morocco. Cardinal Wyszynski, the Primate of Poland, was released and returned to Warsaw.

Eisenhower was re-elected President of the United States.

The Olympic Games were opened by the Duke of Edinburgh in Melbourne; over thirty of the competitors from Iron Curtain countries refused to go back.

Mr. Jo Grimond: a young leader for an old political party

The first British large heavy water reactor—Dido—was inaugurated at Harwell. Britain and Iceland settled their fisheries dispute. Djilas was arrested in Yugoslavia for 'spreading hostile propaganda'. General Norstad took over the Supreme Command of NATO.

One hundred and forty people were arrested in December on charges of treason in South Africa. Christian Herter was appointed U.S. Under-Secretary of State. M. Spaak became the Secretary-General of NATO. I.R.A. started terrorist raids in Northern Ireland. Milovan Djilas was sentenced to three years imprisonment. Japan was admitted to U.N. There was a revolt in Sumatra against the central Indonesian Government. Yugoslavia announced that it would no longer need foreign military aid. A new method of producing atomic energy—without uranium or excessive heat—was discovered in California. And on the last day of the year Adolf Hitler was officially declared to be dead.

They said in 1956

The two most ridiculous statements I know are 'Liquor doesn't affect me' and 'I understand the Russians.'
CHARLES BOHLEN, U.S. AMBASSADOR TO THE U.S.S.R.

It should be the writer's prerogative to tell the truth. To criticize anybody and anything. To be sad. To be in love. To think of death. Not to ponder whether light and shadow are in balance in his work. To believe in the omnipotence of God. To deny the existence of God.
JULIUS HAY (JUNE)

Sorry, but the Children's Hour has been cancelled. Do not be angry, children, that you have to go to sleep tonight without your bedtime stories. . . .
RADIO KOSSUTH, BUDAPEST, OCTOBER 24

'Look after our children we stay to fight to the last. . . .'
LABELS AROUND THE NECKS OF UNACCOMPANIED HUNGARIAN REFUGEE CHILDREN

Those who know the truth find it easiest to lie.
WARSAW RADIO, NOVEMBER 25

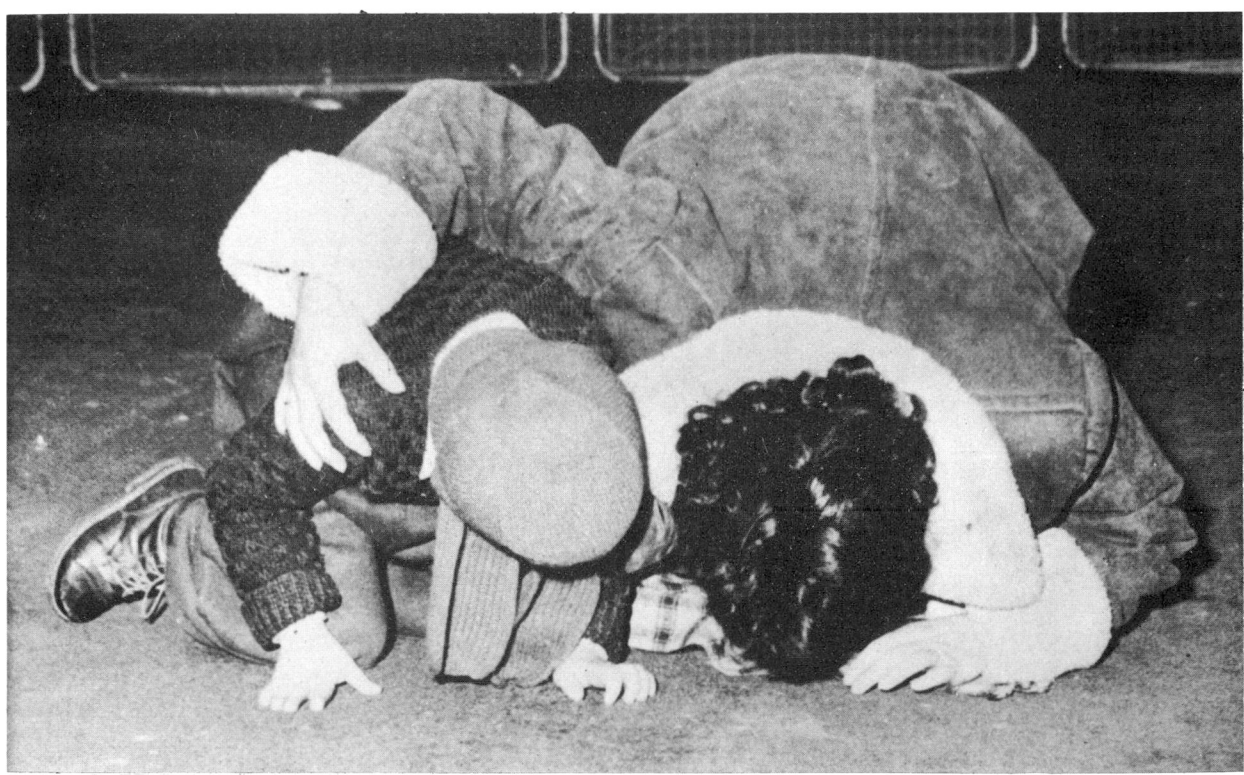

Hungarian refugees kiss the soil of free England

THE AFTERMATH OF Hungary and Suez still dominated the first months of 1957. Before the Curtain clamped down again, almost 250,000 Hungarians had fled to the West and Yugoslavia. The bridge at Andau became world famous. The conscience of the free world was shaken and the Hungarian refugees found a warm welcome everywhere—except by some British Trade Unions.

Suez—ships still blocked the canal—the Treaty was abrogated

Yardley in 'The Baltimore Sun'

WAR IN EGYPT:
'I've great hopes for you, sonny boy'

In 1957, in May, the Soviet adopted a resolution appealing to the Anglo-Saxon countries for an agreement on the immediate cessation of all nuclear tests. Five days later Britain announced the explosion in the Central Pacific of the first British thermo-nuclear bomb 'in the megaton range'; there were two others within the next month and the Japanese protested loudly but in vain. At the end of June Russia inaugurated a man-made 'sea' of almost 400 square miles in the Novosibirsk region of Siberia, created by 'atomic power'.

In January President Nasser abrogated the Anglo-Egyptian Treaty of 1954. Eisenhower proclaimed the 'Eisenhower doctrine', expressing U.S. interest in the Middle East—intended to fill the vacuum which the virtual destruction of British and French influence in this area had created. The Saar joined the German Federal Republic, the French having failed for the second time since 1918 to detach it from the Reich. On January 9 Sir Anthony Eden resigned as Prime Minister; next day Mr. Harold Macmillan was appointed his successor. Mr. Thorneycroft became Chancellor of the Exchequer and Mr. Butler took over the Home Office; Major Lloyd-George and Sir Walter Monckton left the government. Sir Anthony's resignation was partly due to his state of health; on January 18 he left for New Zealand to recuperate.

237

Chou En-lai made a world tour. Three American Stratojets flew round the world, non-stop, in 45 hours 19 minutes, covering 24,325 miles. By the third week of January Egypt and Israel had agreed to repatriate prisoners—the Israelis returned 5881 while the Egyptians freed the four they held. Except for the Gaza strip, Israel gave up conquests in Sinai. Nasser signed three decrees expropriating foreign banks, insurance companies and sales agencies. Early in March Israel told the U.N. General Assembly that she was ready to withdraw from the Gaza strip 'on certain assumptions'; six days later she handed over the Gaza administration to the U.N. Expeditionary Force; a week later Ben Gurion gave a warning that military force would be used if the guerrilla raids of *fedayeen* were resumed. On March 29 the first convoy to enter the Suez Canal left for Port Said; in mid-April the Canal was reopened to ships of maximum draught.

Arab unity, temporarily strengthened by the Suez events, did not last very long. In April there was a violent clash between Jordan and Egypt; King Hussein accused the Egyptian Press and radio of spreading untrue propaganda about him. Martial law was proclaimed in Jordan, the political parties were dissolved, the frontiers sealed and air services to Egypt, Syria and Lebanon suspended. The young King was determined that his country should not pass into the Soviet camp which apparently (and temporarily) Egypt and her allies seemed to have chosen. The Suez Canal Company, having lost the Canal, decided to try and replace it by a tunnel; in May the seventy-sixth annual general meeting of the Channel Tunnel Co. was held in London and the long-dead project was revived. In June the espionage trial in Cairo ended; one Egyptian was sentenced to death, Mr. James Zarb, a Maltese subject, to ten years and Mr. James Swinburn an Englishman, to five years.

The U.N. General Assembly called upon South Africa to reconsider her apartheid policies; the South Africans walked out. The U.S. Ambassador in Prague and the Chinese Ambassador in Warsaw had their sixty-fifth meeting in Geneva since August 1955 to discuss the release of American prisoners in China and the admission of U.S. journalists. In March Ghana achieved her independence within the Commonwealth. President Magsaysay, the beloved leader of the Filipinos was killed in an air-crash. The Canadian General Elections in June brought back the Progressive Conservative Party and Mr. John Diefenbaker as Premier.

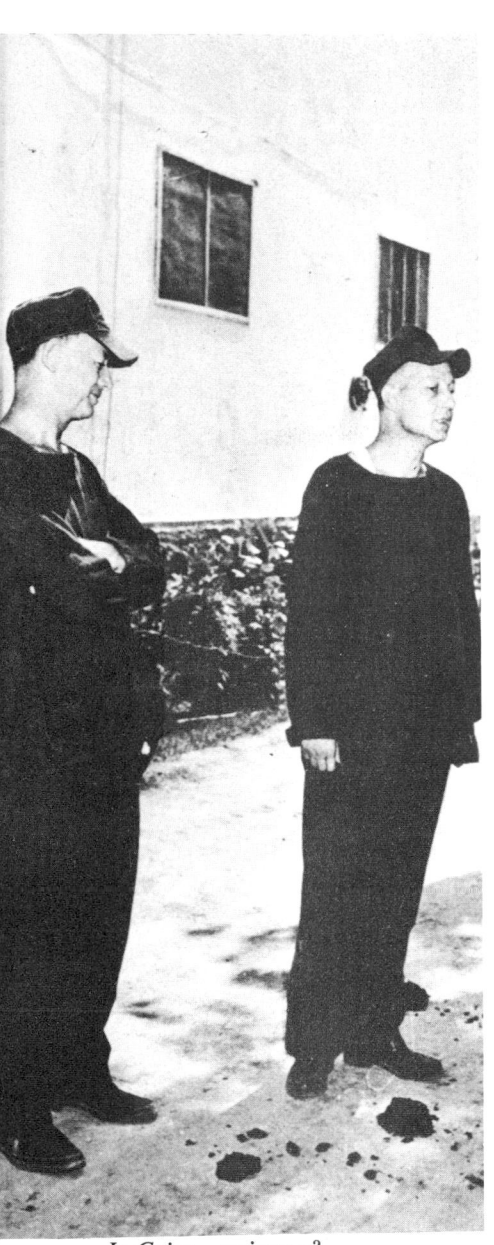

In Cairo—espionage?

Magsaysay: the beloved Filipino

Mr. Diefenbaker: Canadian Prime Minister

Mr. Harold Macmillan—in March he met Mr. Eisenhower and mended the Suez rift

Though the critics of the Suez adventure forecast dire economic consequences for Britain, these somehow failed to materialize. In February the bank rate was reduced by half per cent; in June the ordinary travel allowance was extended to the dollar area and there was a general increase in business allowances. Mr. Thorneycroft was able to grant tax reliefs amounting to over £130 million.

Cyprus, however, was still a difficult problem. In March EOKA offered to suspend its activities if Archbishop Makarios were released. Two weeks later the British government decided to free him—but not allow his return to Cyprus; Grivas and other 'foreign nationals of EOKA' were offered safe conduct to Greece. The Greek Ambassador returned to London. But the Turkish Cypriots would have nothing less than partition. On April 17 Makarios arrived in Athens; late in June he proposed that he should return to the island and that bilateral negotiations should be opened between him and the British government. Both suggestions were rejected by Whitehall.

By May Kadar felt safe enough to summon his Parliament which extended its own life by two years, postponing the General Election that was already overdue. Two weeks later the Soviet Union and Hungary signed an agreement for the 'temporary stationing' of Soviet forces in the country.

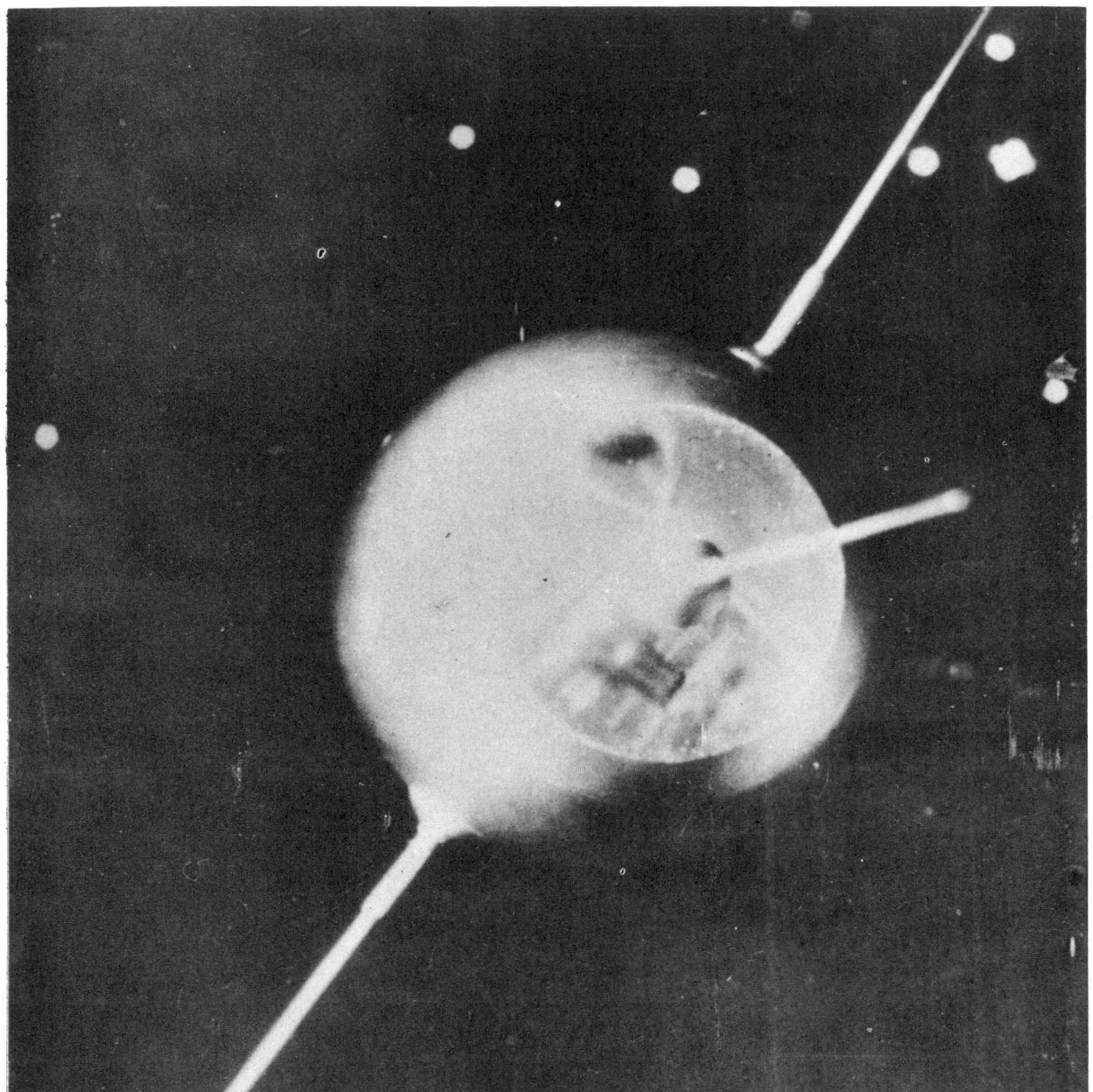

Sputnik I: the Soviets invade space

In February the *London Gazette* announced that the Queen had granted her consort 'the style and titular dignity of a Prince of the United Kingdom' and that he would be henceforth known as 'Prince Philip, Duke of Edinburgh'. In April came another State visit—this time to France. The French government fell in May when M. Guy Mollet resigned; his resignation wasn't accepted by the President for three weeks when M. Maurice Bourges-Maunoury succeeded in forming a Cabinet.

Sputnik I gave Amercian complacency a bad jolt and proved that in the developments of rocket and space technology the Soviet Union had stolen more than a march on them. A new kind of hydrogen bomb was exploded in Russia two days later. In November the second Sputnik was launched by Russia, weighing half a ton and carrying a dog whose fate became the concern of all animal lovers. (It died.) Russia also announced the building of the world's largest and fastest airliner, the turbo-prop-engined T.U.114; in November there was news of the world's most powerful radio telescope having been completed, and in December the atomic icebreaker, *Lenin*, was launched in the Neva. Bulganin sent a series of letters to U.N. member States and to Switzerland, proposing Summit talks, the banning of nuclear tests and the creation of a security zone in Central Europe. The answers were not very enthusiastic.

There was a violent series of earthquakes in Persia which killed more than fifteen hundred people.

The Aga Khan, head of the great Ishmaili sect, staunch friend of Britain, man-of-the-world and owner of famous horses, died and was succeeded by his grandson, Prince Karim.

In February, the 'Lenin', an ice-breaker, on the Neva

Franco and Salazar met at Ciudad Rodrigo to discuss Spanish-Portuguese co-operation. British, Swedish and American scientists discovered Element 102 at the Nobel Institute, Stockholm.

Franco told his Parliament that when he died or retired, the monarchy would be restored. Tunisia abolished the monarchy and invested Habib Bourguiba as Head of State and President of the Republic. The British Home Guard which was revived in 1950 and maintained on a reserve basis, was disbanded.

As the nuclear tests continued and East and West seemed to be unable to agree on the terms of disarmament, Canada and America integrated their air defence and set up DEW (Distant Early Warning) that would give, perhaps, an hour's grace for the big cities of the North American continent before the hydrogen bombs fell. France devalued the franc and tried out four Prime Ministers before thirty-eight-year-old M. Gaillard formed a Cabinet in November. In the British Guiana General Elections Dr. Cheddi Jagan's Left-wing party won nine out of the fourteen elective seats and Dr. Jagan formed a government. An American Air Force doctor established a world record when his balloon carried him to 100,000 feet. An R.A.F. Valiant bomber crossed the Atlantic in just over six hours; a British Canberra set up a new world altitude record of 70,000 feet over the Channel. Benito Mussolini's battered body was reinterred in the family tomb at Predappio.

Haakon, the beloved King of Norway died and Prince Olaf succeeded him as King Olaf V. The West German training ship *Pamir* went down about 600 miles south-west of the Azores; only six of her eighty-six young crew could be saved.

Mr. Hammarskjöld was unanimously re-elected Secretary-General of U.N. for another five years. An American airline inaugurated a direct service from Los Angeles to London over the Polar route.

There was a dangerous accident at the Windscale Atomic Energy Plant; the sale of milk was banned over an area of 200 square miles but no dangerous after-effects followed. Her Majesty and Prince Philip paid a five-day State visit to Canada and then went on to the United States where the Queen addressed the U.N. Assembly. Nasser, contrary to Russian expectations, would not allow Communism in his own country; on October 19 a trial *in camera* opened in Cairo and eighteen members of the outlawed Communist Party were sentenced to prison; the property of all Party organizations was confiscated. On October 23 Mr. Macmillan arrived in Washington for discussions with President Eisenhower; the Suez breach was now almost completely healed. Britain and the U.S.A. began to supply arms to some of the Arab countries, notably Tunisia. This upset France badly and the French delegation walked out of the NATO Parliamentary Conference. On November 25 Eisenhower suffered a mild stroke and for a few days he was in some danger; but he recovered remarkably well and three weeks after his illness was able to attend the NATO Atlantic Council meeting in Paris.

The Jodrell Bank radio telescope went into operation in October

Dr. Ralph Vaughan Williams: his eighty-fifth birthday was celebrated throughout the world by all lovers of music

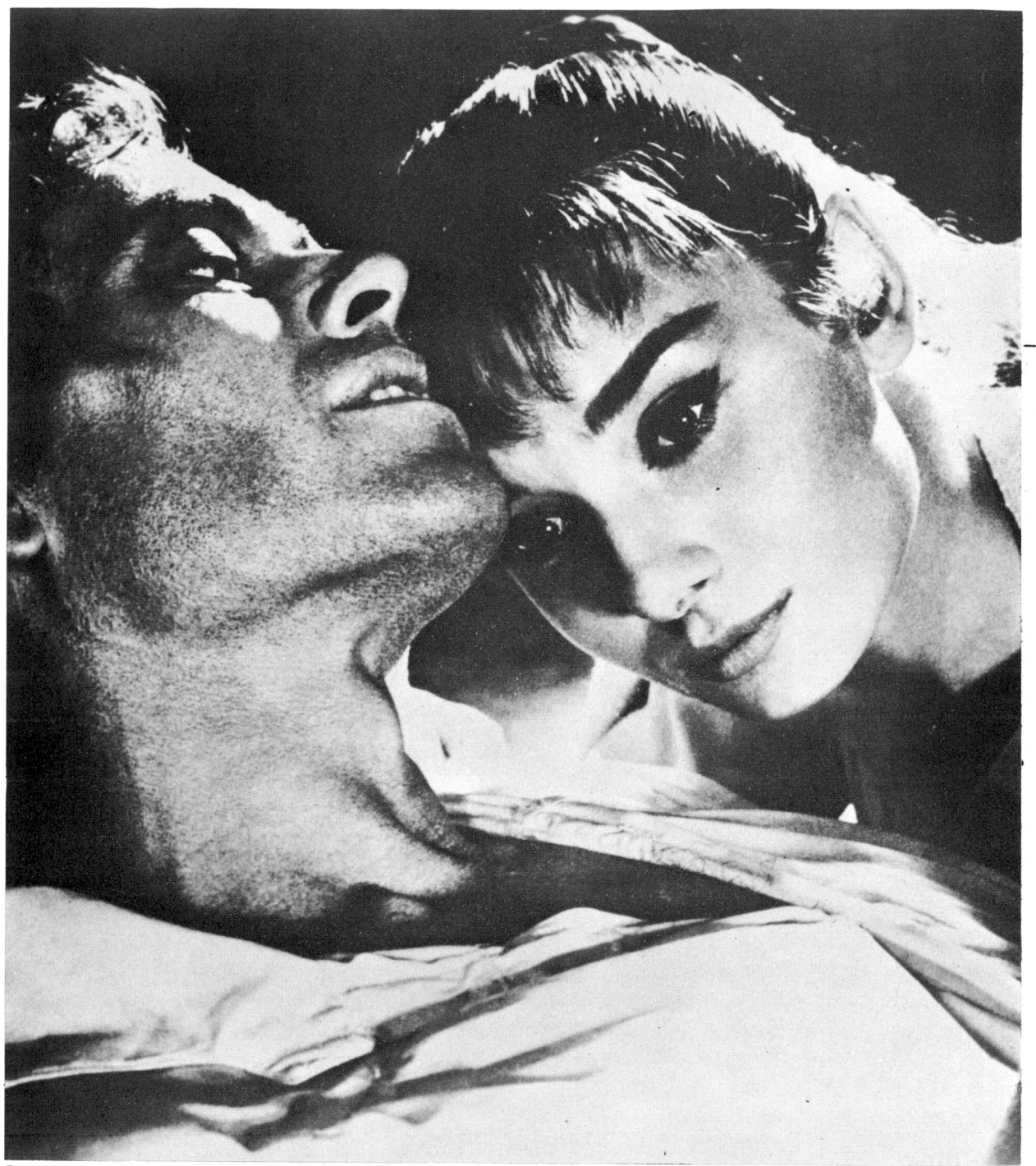

Lovers in Russia, early nineteenth century: Mel Ferrer and Audrey Hepburn in 'War and Peace'

In the theatre long runs were causing quite a queue of new plays. *The Boy Friend, Salad Days, Sailor Beware, The Mousetrap* and *Dry Rot* all continued their triumphant careers. Among the new-comers Nöel Coward's *Nude with Violin*, the brassy, good-humoured *Grab Me a Gondola* competed with Enid Bagnold's unusual and moving *The Chalk Garden*, Robert Bolt's (a most promising new-comer) *Flowering Cherry*, a personal triumph for Sir Ralph Richardson; John Osborne's *The Entertainer* was a true *tour de force* by Sir Laurence Olivier. Ionesco's *The Chairs*, Benn Levy's *The Rape of the Belt* and Jack Popplewell's *Dear Delinquent* were other successful arrivals.

In films the British producers were feeling keenly the loss of that prince of artist-businessmen, Sir Alexander Korda (who had died, of a heart-attack, in January 1956). Many cinemas had to close. The Eady levy became obligatory instead of voluntary as before. Among the British pictures *Across the Bridge*, Chaplin's *A King in New York*, the Anglo-American *The Bridge on the River Kwai* were outstanding; *Brothers-in-Law* and *Lucky Jim* brought success to the Boulting brothers and to Ian Carmichael. *Ill Met by Moonlight* and *The Yangtse*

Lovers in Mayfair, early twentieth century: Marilyn Monroe and Laurence Olivier in 'The Prince and the Showgirl'

Incident were the best war films. Sir Laurence Olivier's and Marilyn Monroe's partnership in *The Prince and the Showgirl* didn't quite come off. From America, apart from the super-colossals like *Around the World in 80 Days*, *War and Peace* and *Cinerama Holiday*, there came a group of strikingly original and sensational films, among them *A Man is Ten Feet Tall*, *Twelve Angry Men*, *A Face in the Crowd*, *Sweet Smell of Success*, *Baby Doll* and *The Bachelor Party*. The new National Film Theatre was opened by Princess Margaret in October, followed by the first London Film Festival.

The Third Programme, the refuge of 'eggheads' was cut by two hours and Network Three went on the air, a 'specialized interests' programme. Commercial television was competing with the B.B.C. where both were available; but the B.B.C. was fighting back. By the end of October there were 7½ million TV licences in Britain. 'Tonight', and 'Free Speech' were the best documentary programmes; I.T.A. was constantly attacked for the low-level offerings but people still looked in. Sir Ivone Kirkpatrick succeeded Sir Kenneth Clark as Chairman of the Authority. The first World Commercial TV Congress was held in London.

Chaplin's return: the great comedian in 'A King in New York'

'An unprecedented figure' of 20,719 titles was achieved in 1957 by the publishers; of these 5921 were reprints. Fiction, biography and travel decreased; naval and military, medical and surgical, trade and industry, law and Parliamentary books were on the increase.

Hugh Dalton's *The Fateful Years*, E. E. Reynolds's *Baden-Powell*, Caitlin Thomas's *Left-over Life to Kill*, Nancy Mitford's *Voltaire in Love* were among the most outstanding biographies and autobiographies; P. G. Wodehouse's *Over Seventy* and Sir Robert Bruce Lockhart's *Friends, Foes and Foreigners* were equally well received. In fiction there were new and welcome books by Anthony Powell, Iris Murdoch, H. E. Bates, Elspeth Huxley, John Braine (a discovery), Lawrence Durrell, Evelyn Waugh, William Sansom and Angus Wilson, Patrick White's *Voss* was singled out for almost universal praise. There were many books about the Hungarian Revolution among which a documentary volume edited by M. J. Laski and George Mikes's *The Hungarian Revolution* stood out.

The International Geophysical Year started on July 1 and produced valuable co-operation between scientists of many lands. Laika, the space dog circled the earth for more than a million miles before she died; the Americans promised to launch their 'Project Vanguard' by the spring of 1958. Zeta raised high hopes for producing electricity by thermonuclear (fusion) reactions. Tuberculosis was gradually being mastered. The Salk vaccine, in spite of some setbacks, was proving increasingly effective.

They said in 1957

All ordinary violence produces its own limitations, for it calls forth an answering violence which sooner or later becomes its equal or its superior.

ALBERT SCHWEITZER

The point to remember is that what the government gives, it must first take away.

J. S. COLEMAN

If you consider the personalities of the great tyrants of this century, it will be plain, I think, that they were unhappy people, above all embittered and envious; and in their supposed dedication to the vague mass of mankind they revealed an apathy or contempt towards the worth of any one man.

ALISTAIR COOKE

In the Communist system insecurity is the way of life for the individual.

MILOVAN DJILAS

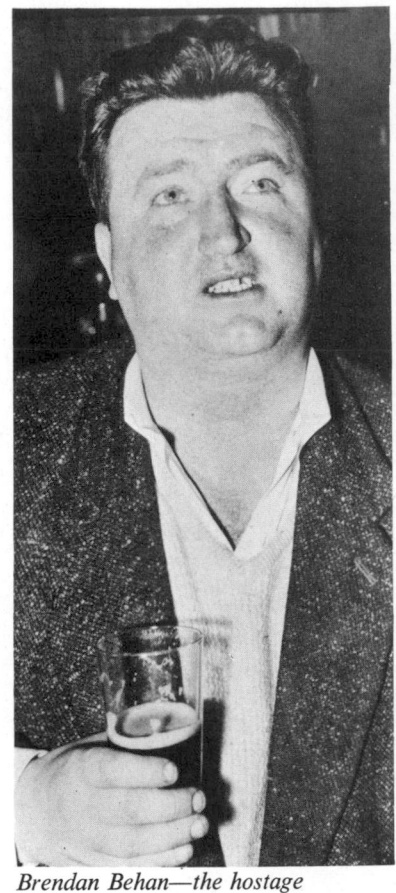

Brendan Behan—the hostage

Anthony Powell—time was music

P. G. Wodehouse—the Anglo-American literary comedian of the century published 'Over Seventy'

Imre Nagy: Free Hungary's short-lived Prime Minister—'Safe Conduct' led to execution

WHILE THE FIRST, tentative attempts were made to explore space, the West was trying to strengthen its unity and Russia continued her 'peace-offensive'. On January 1, 1958, the European Common Market and Euratom came into being. West German forces—two armoured divisions, some transport aircraft and torpedo boats—joined NATO. Mr. Macmillan left on a six-week goodwill tour of the Commonwealth. Mr. Bulganin sent the first of his letters to nineteen States, proposing a Summit Conference. America accepted and proposed an agenda, suggesting that the Foreign Ministers should have a preliminary meeting. This was rejected by Bulganin early in February but at the same time he sent a list of subjects to be discussed. Mr. Rapacki elaborated his plan for a nuclear-free zone; the Communist countries accepted it but it was rejected by the Western Union, Britain, America and Canada. By the end of February it was Mr. Bulganin who proposed a Foreign Minister's meeting; in March he wrote to Mr. Macmillan, denouncing the agreement on Anglo-American missile bases in the United Kingdom; Russia also accused the Western Powers of 'trying to distract attention from a Summit Conference by resuming disarmament negotiations through the U.N.'. The Americans replied that they were not willing to bypass the United Nations. A four-point peace plan was next put forward by Russia, banning the use of outer space for military purposes, eliminate military bases on foreign territories and to create international co-operation in the study of space. A fortnight later Mr. Bulganin's letter-writing came to an abrupt end; he was sacked from his Premiership and Khrushchev took over the chairmanship of the Council of Ministers. Stalin's real successor had emerged at last. Bulganin was given the job of Chairman of the State Bank. After six months he was exiled to the Stavropol region; in September he was dismissed from the Party Presidium and in November he was accused by Khrushchev as an 'oppositionist'. He made an abject 'confession' to the Central Committee in December. On the last day of March the Supreme Soviet resolved to terminate the atomic and hydrogen weapon tests. America merely 'observed' that this came at the end of an intensive series of secret experiments and explosions. Mikoyan and Kozlov became first Deputy Prime Ministers.

In January the West Indies Federation came into being and Lord Hailes, the first Governor-General, took the oath of office.

John Foster Dulles: the U.S. would defend Berlin

The Queen and Prince Philip paid a three-day State visit to Amsterdam.

In April Russia called a meeting of the Security Council, demanding 'urgent measures' to put an end to the flights by American military planes carrying atomic and hydrogen bombs across the Arctic 'towards the frontiers of the Soviet Union'. The Security Council met on April 21 but the Russian resolution was withdrawn in protest because the Council decided to take a vote on the same day. Another crisis blew up over Berlin in May when Mr. Dulles repeated the Allied guarantee that they would treat any attack on the German capital from whatever quarter as one upon themselves. Soviet-Yugoslav relations worsened again when Russia withdrew the credit of £100 million which it had offered the Yugoslavs in 1956; Tito replied that he wouldn't even negotiate on the proposal and would claim compensation if Russia insisted. After twenty years East Germany ended food rationing.

Mr. Macmillan and President Eisenhower conferred in Washington for two days in June; the Prime Minister went on to Ottawa. Mr. Khrushchev, in still another letter, asked the British and the Americans if they really wanted a Summit meeting, saying that their wish to talk about Eastern Europe and the reunification of Germany would 'kill the conference in the bud'. In mid-June there came an announcement that, after a secret trial, the Hungarians had executed Imre Nagy, the former Prime Minister, General Pál Maléter and two other leaders of the October revolution. Zoltan Tidy, the former President of the Republic and several others received long prison sentences. The murder of the kidnapped Hungarian politician again caused world-wide indignation of which the Hungarians, feeling secure under the Soviet wing, took little notice.

The Canadian General Election brought a second victory for the Conservatives under Mr. Diefenbaker.

The Parker Tribunal decided that there had been no leak on the increase of the Bank Rate in September 1957.

At Rochdale Mr. Ludovic Kennedy, the Liberal candidate, lost the election but polled twice as many votes as the Conservative; at the Torrington by-election the Liberals took the seat from the government by a majority of 219.

Spring meeting at the South Pole: Sir Edmund Hillary and Dr. Vivian Fuchs

Artificial insemination (A.I.D.) was condemned by the Church but the government refused to make it illegal. The by-elections of May and June did not change the balance of the parties. A railway workers' dispute was settled in June but London busmen came out on strike on May 5. People had to walk and discovered that they liked it. Subsequently the London Transport Board had to start a campaign of 'Hop on a Bus' to cure them of this newly-acquired habit. The strike ended on June 21; about the same time there was an unofficial dockers' strike which led to a shortage of meat as Smithfield also became involved.

Sir Edmund Hillary, heading the New Zealand section of the Commonwealth Trans-Antarctic Expedition, reached the South Pole with his companions. Seventeen days later the British section, led by Dr. Vivian Fuchs, arrived at the same goal. By March 2 Dr. Fuchs and the united expedition had completed the first land crossing of the Antarctic continent from Shackleton Base to Scott Base, covering 2200 miles in ninety-nine days.

Britain's economy was booming though the shock of Mr. Thorneycroft's resignation (the Chancellor of the Exchequer left the Cabinet because he wouldn't approve of higher spending than the year before) caused some anxiety. He was succeeded by Mr. Heathcoat Amory who received a warm welcome.

Mr. Amory's first budget simplified and reduced purchase tax, raised the exemption limits of income tax, made 'dividend stripping' illegal and gave some relief on estate duty and initial capital expenditure.

The Brighton Police trial shocked the public—because it revealed misbehaviour in the force.

The Algerian war was a terrible financial and man-power-drain on France; yet there seemed to be no end in sight. On February 8 French aircraft from Algeria raided a Tunisian village which was alleged to be a base for the 'National Liberation Forces'. The Tunisians reacted strongly; they banned French warships from Bizerta and abrogated the extra-territorial status of the important harbour. The dispute became acrimonious and in April M. Gaillard's Government was defeated on its African policy. In May came the revolt of Europeans in Algiers, overwhelming the police and occupying the government headquarters. General Massu, the grim and slightly sinister French parachute commander formed a committee of public safety.

The 'bombardment' of space continued almost uninterrupted. On January 10 the Americans fired successfully their Atlas inter-continental ballistic missile from Cape Canaveral. On the last day of the month they launched their first artificial earth satellite named Explorer or Alpha 1958; this was tiny compared to the first two Sputniks but was still up there after many months while the Russian satellites had disintegrated after four and five months respectively. In March the Vanguard I test satellite was launched, even smaller than the Explorer—but the small sphere, destined to test solar cells, was expected to stay up for 200 years. It was followed by Explorer III, slightly larger, on March 26, and by Sputnik III (May 15, with a payload of 600 lbs.).

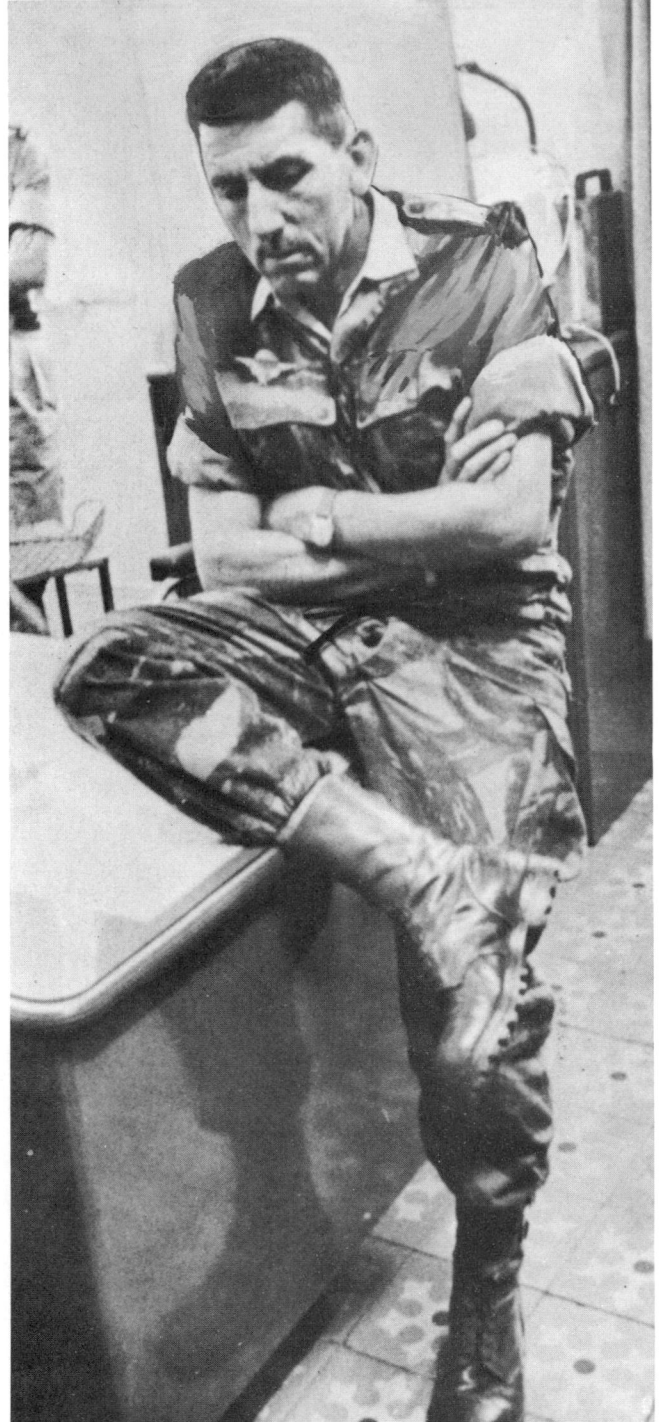

General Jacques Massu; 'public safety' was the issue

The Arab world was still in ferment and provided the most violent headlines with its internal dissessions, and with its see-sawing attitudes between East and West. In February Egypt and Sudan had a clash over frontier areas along the Red Sea with Nasser protesting loudly against these territories being included in the Sudanese elections. Sudan rejected the protest and a compromise proposal and sent a protest to U.N.; Egypt climbed down, postponing the dispute until after the elections. On February 1 Egypt and Syria proclaimed the 'United Arab Republic'; the two countries had no contiguous frontiers and the Syrians discovered before long that in this partnership Egypt was to be dominant; but the Union was approved by a plebiscite in both countries.

De Gaulle and Coty: the tall leader was firm, and tactful

Nasser became Head of State. As a counter-move King Feisal of Iraq and King Hussein of Jordan proclaimed the union of their Kingdoms in the 'Arab Federation' with King Feisal as Head of State and his cousin as deputy. M. Pflimlin's Paris government seemed to be both helpless and divided. This was General de Gaulle's hour; after twelve years' patient waiting, he announced that he was ready to 'assume the powers of the Republic'. The vacillating government introduced special emergency powers in metropolitan France for three months (Algerian terrorists were claiming an increasing number of policemen and 'innocent bystanders' as victims) and renewed the special powers in Algeria. Two weeks later M. Pflimlin resigned and General de Gaulle accepted President Coty's invitation to form 'a Government of National Union', was given a vote of confidence and special powers for six months to deal with the grave situation. There was much talk of dictatorship but the tall leader of the Free French showed just as much firmness as tact.

In April King Baudouin opened the Brussels World Fair and the glittering symbol of the *Atomium* rose over the displays of almost a hundred nations, including the boldly contrasted American and Soviet pavilions.

At Brussels World Fair, among nearly a hundred pavilions, the U.S.S.R. (above) and the U.S.A. (below) contrasted

July opened with Sudanese-Egyptian dispute worsened by Sudan's diversion of the Nile waters for the first stage of a vast irrigation project. Nasser visited Tito and they issued a joint statement against 'Power blocs'.

U.S.S. 'Nautilus'—first ship to sail under the North Pole ice-cap

Early in July Eisenhower signed the Bill which permitted wider nuclear co-operation in the military field between the U.S. and her allies. Mr. Khrushchev's note to Eisenhower called for an agreement 'on measures to prevent possibility of surprise attack by one State on another'; this was referred to the Geneva meeting in October. Alaska became the forty-ninth State of the Union which broke the heart of Texans who could no longer claim to be the biggest State of the U.S. Explorer IV—to study radiation above 600 miles— was launched into orbit. *Nautilus*, the American atomic submarine, passed under the ice-cap of the North Pole: eight days later U.S.S. *Skate* repeated this remarkable feat. The International Geophysical Year's special committee agreed that co-operation should go on for another year. On August 27, a hydrogen bomb was exploded about 300 miles above the South Atlantic and two other 'nuclear devices' were tested within the next ten days.

In September Britain's first ballistic rocket, the Black Knight, was successfully tested at the Woomera range, Australia. In October the Soviet Union announced the resumption of nuclear tests; the U.S. multi-stage rocket, Pioneer, was fired at Cape Canaveral—after two days it descended, having failed to hit the target. Early in November Soviet scientists observed a volcanic eruption on the Moon; the American Atlas was successfully fired over its full range of about 6,300 miles. In December the Americans fired a monkey into space in the nose-cone of a Jupiter ballistic missile; it travelled 300 miles

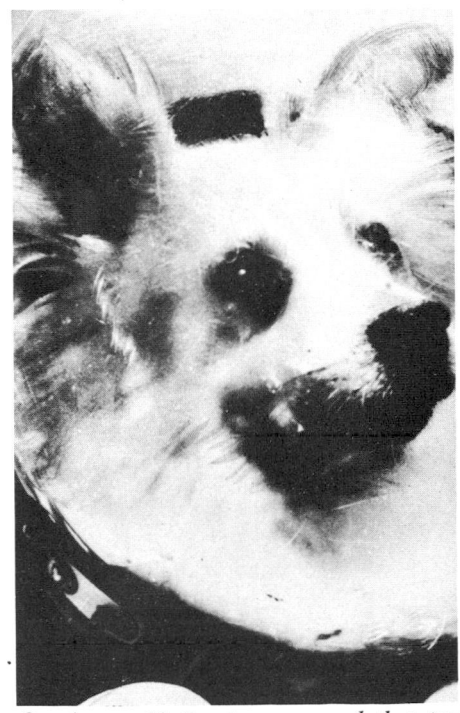

On August 29 Russia announced that two dogs, fired to a height of 279 miles, had been brought back safely to earth in the best of health

up and 1700 miles in distance before coming down in the South Atlantic. Six days before Christmas an artificial satellite, weighing $4\frac{1}{2}$ tons, was put into orbit; it circled the world, carrying appropriately a message of goodwill

G.I.s cheerfully withdraw from the Lebanon as a frustrated local exporter wistfully waves (a carpet) good-bye

recorded by the President, Greetings to all the World, which was variously impressed. Britain and Iceland had a 'fishing war'; in August the ancient Republic declared that if the Royal Navy tried to support the trawlers inside the twelve-mile limit, this would be regarded as an 'attack on Iceland'. The Foreign Office, in a brief statement, refuted this 'as tendentious and misleading'.

In Iraq, King Feisal, Prince Abdul Ilah and the members of the Royal household were murdered; next day General Nuri s-Said was killed. The British Embassy in Baghdad was ransacked and set on fire. Major-General Abdul Karim was appointed Prime Minister and Commander-in-Chief. King Hussein of Jordan immediately assumed power as head of the Arab Federation. President Eisenhower announced in a special message to Congress that he was sending U.S. forces to the Lebanon at the request of President Chamoun. The Muslim members of the Baghdad Pact (now robbed of its headquarters) met at Ankara and approved the American landings. The Security Council met in emergency session. The Americans asked for 'appropriate arrangements to protect the independence and territorial integrity of the Lebanon'; Russia called for the immediate withdrawal of the American forces. Two days after the Iraq revolution, King Hussein asked Britain and America for military aid. British parachute troops landed the next day in Jordan.

Khrushchev proposed a Geneva meeting to discuss the Middle East crisis. Jordan severed relations with Nasser's United Arab Republic. Mr. Macmillan and President Eisenhower refused the Geneva meeting and suggested a special meeting of the Security Council: De Gaulle agreed, with the proviso that if the U.N. discussions failed, a Summit meeting should be called. A day later Khrushchev announced that he was willing to have the conference within the Security Council meeting in New York. The Western leaders thought that five days' notice was too short for this and proposed August 12; De Gaulle plumped for a meeting at Geneva on the 18th. In the meantime Khrushchev visited Peking for talks with Mao; their joint statement demanded an end of the nuclear tests, abolition of all military bases overseas, the withdrawal of the Anglo-American forces from the Middle East and an immediate Summit Conference.

On August 1 King Hussein of Jordan abolished the Arab Federation by decree. Khrushchev now withdrew his support for the Security Council meeting on the Middle East and threatened to ask the General Assembly for

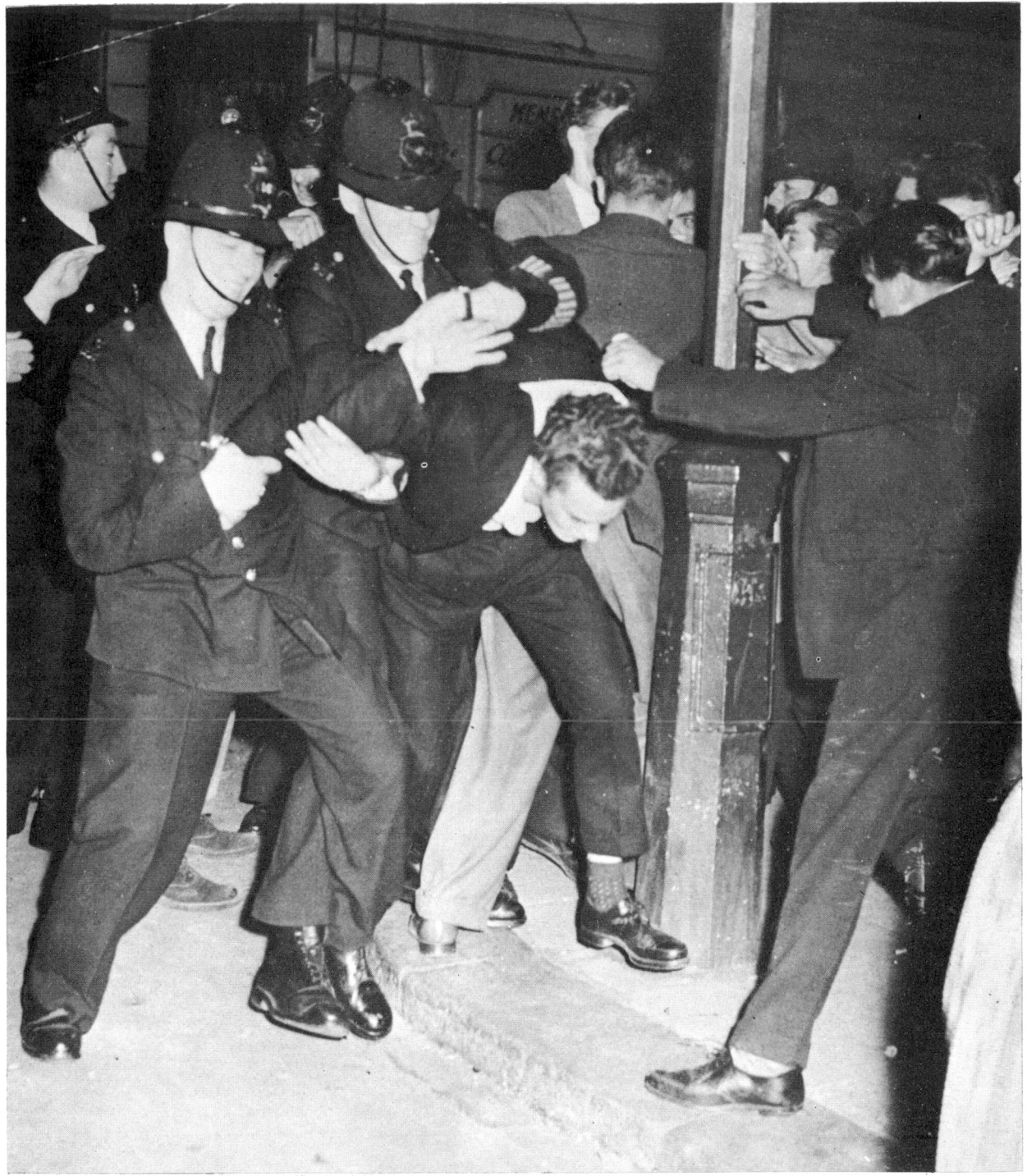

In Notting Hill Gate—short shrift for London race rioters

a condemnation of Anglo-American 'aggression'. When the General Assembly met, it adjourned until August 13. All this talk did not lead to very much; the Arab resolution on the Middle East was adopted unanimously at the emergency session—which put the responsibility on the Secretary-General to make 'such practical arrangements as would adequately help in upholding the principles and purposes of the Charter in relation to Lebanon and Jordan'. This meant anything or nothing; the American forces withdrew from Lebanon by October 25, the British from Jordan by November 2. There is no doubt that the prompt action of the two governments prevented the pro-Communist Iraqi revolt from spreading to the neighbouring countries. In December the U.A.R. and the Soviet Union signed an agreement on Russian co-operation in the first stage of the High Dam project. Four days later—perhaps to show his impartiality—Nasser ordered the arrest of about one hundred Communists in a wide-spread police action against Egyptian and Syrian 'anti-government subversives'.

Mr. Strijdom, the South African Prime Minister, died and was succeeded by Dr. Verwoerd, firmly determined to continue the apartheid policy.

Ugly racial riots broke out in Nottingham and London's Notting Hill where the large influx of West Indians, coming to Britain in search of work, had created many problems.

Early in September the East German government proposed the setting up of a Four-Power commission to discuss peace terms with Germany; also a commission of East and West Germany 'to work out a common German attitude'. The three Western Powers did not reply. Later that month the U.S.S.R. backed up the East German proposals. Britain, France and the U.S. answered that German reunification must be discussed before a peace treaty could be considered.

The constitution of the Fifth Republic was endorsed by a national referendum throughout France, Algeria and Overseas France—except Guinea. In December General De Gaulle was elected President of the Republic. The franc was devalued by 17·55 per cent and made convertible to non-resident holders. The new budget cut subsidies by £200 million and introduced new taxes to the same amount. De Gaulle was beginning his long and difficult battle to solve the seemingly insoluble Algerian problem and to restore his country to the status of a world Power.

On October 9, Pope Pius XII died at Castel Gandolfo; a beloved though somewhat remote Pontiff, he was buried in St. Peter's. After a protracted conclave, Cardinal Roncalli of Venice was elected Pope and crowned on November 4 in St. Peter's as Pope John XXIII.

U Nu, the Prime Minister of Burma resigned for the second time and became a monk; General Ne Win formed a 'non-political' government, promising to put the country into order and then hand it back to the politicians.

There was martial law in Pakistan where President Iskander Mirza abolished political parties, abrogated the Constitution and dismissed the Central and Provincial governments and assemblies.

Three Russian scientists—Professors Cherenkov, Frank and Tamm—won the Nobel Prize for Physics: Dr. Frederick Sanger of Cambridge the Prize for Chemistry. The centenary of the presentation of the theory of evolution by natural selection was commemorated by many meetings and exhibitions honouring the great work of Charles Darwin.

In Burma: the Prime Minister became a monk

257

London saw Chekhov's 'The Cherry Orchard' played magnificently by the Moscow Arts Theatre

In November Mr. Khrushchev, addressing a Polish delegation to Moscow, started another crisis by suggesting that the U.S.S.R. would hand over its share in the control of Berlin to the East German Government and calling on the Western Powers to do the same. West Germany immediately replied that this would mean a one-sided denunciation of international agreements and would increase world tension. The East German Embassy in Moscow delivered Notes to sixty countries, asking recognition of the East German Republic and accused the Western Powers of using Berlin as a centre of espionage. The November elections in Eastern Germany brought the usual 99·87 per cent vote for the single list of the National Front candidates. On December 14 the Allied and West German Foreign Ministers met in Paris to discuss the Berlin situation. They rejected the Soviet proposals of which nothing more was heard until the end of the year though Russia complained of the Western Powers' 'habitual failure to describe the East German régime as the German Democratic Republic'.

The day after the Christmas holidays the British Treasury announced the non-resident convertibility of sterling. The European Payments Union ended automatically and the Monetary Agreement was brought into force as most European countries in the West followed the British example.

The new Greenwich Observatory at Herstmonceaux Castle was completed; a great United Nations Conference on the peaceful uses of atomic energy was held at Geneva. Comet IV proved the faith of De Havilland's, establishing a new west-east record of 6 hours 28 minutes by crossing the Atlantic as a passenger aircraft. An R.A.F. Vulcan made an appearance at *two* air shows—one in Britain and one in Canada—on the same day. The Fairey Rotodyne, the world's first vertical take-off airliner was shown to the public for the first time in June.

Rome: John XXIII, the smiling Pope, blessed the city and the world

'West Side Story' from America: a singing Romeo and Juliet of mean streets

Lehar's *Merry Widow* saved Sadler's Wells from bankruptcy—it was so successful that arrangements were made for a regular operetta season by the Company; the L.C.C. and I.T.A. also came to the aid of British opera. The centenary of Covent Garden Opera House was celebrated with a superb performance of Verdi's *Don Carlos*. There were four new British operas, by Richard Arnell, Joan Sharp, Humphrey Searle and Benjamin Britten, though these were comparatively modest efforts. In the theatre Agatha Christie's *The Mousetrap* broke the record of *Chu Chin Chow* as the longest consecutive run in history, entering its seventh year. *My Fair Lady* came to Drury Lane. *Auntie Mame* and *West Side Story* were other successful musical imports from America. Peter Shaffer's *Five Finger Exercise* was the most exciting play by a newcomer. Harold Pinter's *The Birthday Party* and N. F. Simpson's *A Resounding Tickle* transposed (and partly parodied) the somewhat obscure art of Ionesco. Graham Greene's *The Potting Shed*, John Osborne's *Epitaph for George Dillon* were serious essays in drama but not as successful as the two playwrights' earlier work. T. S. Eliot's *The Elder Statesman* was a

'*The Inn of Sixth Happiness*' (*Kurt Jürgens and Ingrid Bergman*)—*an English spinster sets out to save China single-handed*

distinguished achievement. The Moscow Arts Theatre company came to London and *Expresso Bongo* (Wolf Mankowitz) set a new style in a rowdy, funny and, in spots, even touching musical.

In their third year the Commercial TV companies made huge profits but were still under fire both for the lack of quality and the American domination of their programmes. However, something like a native school of British TV drama began to emerge and the documentary and news programmes were of a consistently high level. F.I.D.O. (an organization to buy up feature films and keep them from the TV screens) was set up. Among British films *Ice Cold in Alex*, *Orders to Kill* and *Dunkirk* showed that the last war was still providing striking subjects. *The Naked Truth*, *The Key*, *The Man Upstairs*, *A Cry from the Streets*, *The Inn of Sixth Happiness* were also successful. *The Sheriff of Fractured Jaw* combined the widely divergent talents of Kenneth More and Jayne Mansfield in the first 'Western' made in a tongue-in-cheek Europe.

A jubilant crowd flaunts a hangman's noose, and a Batista officer awaits death

January 1959; Fidel Castro's bearded men had swept down from the hills of Cuba and President Batista's régime disintegrated like a rotten piece of sugar-cane. Batista fled to Dominica where his fellow-dictator Trujillo received him with sympathy. There were mass executions in Havana; bulldozers dug huge graves for the dead.

The Russians launched another satellite, the largest they ever got into space. Malta was given a new constitution (somewhat less democratic than the previous one) and Mr. Mintoff, the island's fiery leader, protested angrily. Mr. Mikoyan visited America where he was given V.I.P. treatment; in Hollywood he kissed an actor and in Washington he declared: 'In Russia we believe in freedom *from* hoodlums.' Britain shivered in fog and frost; heavy snowfalls created traffic chaos. Russia proposed a thirty-one-nation peace conference on the future of

Fidel Castro speaks

Germany, with the same agenda which had been rejected by the West both in 1952 and 1954. In Cairo the Anglo-Egyptian financial negotiations approached a successful conclusion.

When Mikoyan left the States (after having a private argument with the State Department which he made public) his plane developed engine trouble over the Atlantic; luckily, it made a safe emergency landing in Newfoundland. Parliament reassembled and Mr. Macmillan expressed his willingness to meet the Russians.

The total H.P. debt of Britain increased by £100 million. At the Twenty-first Congress of the Soviet Communist Party Mr. Khrushchev, in a six-hour speech, promised the abolition of income tax, denounced Marshal Tito, the United Arab Republic and capitalism. Sir Robert Watson-Watt made many people shiver when he described botulinic toxin, a substance of which half a pound would be sufficient to kill everybody in the world.

Mr. Macmillan in Moscow—the white fur hat made news

Mr. Brandt: no taste for Soviet 'Freedom'

Mr. Dulles came to London in February. There was a general strike in Malta; plans were announced to help the Lancashire cotton industry, and for penal reform. Six of the Aden Protectorate States agreed to form a federation. In Paris the 'Ballet Rose' scandal exploded, involving very young girls and a former Speaker of the Chamber. In Zürich the Greek and Turkish Foreign Ministers reached agreement over Cyprus, without *enosis* or partition but full independence. The Defence Bill in Britain rose by £20 million. The Blue Streak rocket was to replace V-bombers. Unemployment stood at 2·8 per cent. After visiting Bonn, Mr. Dulles went into hospital for a hernia operation: his duties were taken over by Messrs. Herter and Dillon.

When Mr. Menderes, the Turkish Premier, flew to London, his plane crashed but he escaped with minor injuries. The talks about Cyprus started at Lancaster House; the negotiations were slow and difficult with Archbishop Makarios only half-satisfied with the Zürich agreement. There were violent demonstrations in Belgium where the miners went on strike against the rationalization of the mines. Signor Segni formed a new Cabinet in Italy. Influenza swept Europe and took its toll in Britain. The operation on Mr. Dulles revealed the tragic fact that he was suffering from cancer. Some students at Reading University hoaxed *The Times* with a fake diamond strike in the Thames valley. The Americans launched another satellite which was to report on the world's weather—which continued to be uniformly bad.

Late in February Mr. Macmillan went to Moscow and the greatest sensation about his trip—at least according to some journalists—was the white fur hat, twelve inches high, which he sported. The talks went well until Mr. Khrushchev developed a not-so-diplomatic toothache, which, however, did not quite immobilise him.

Mr. Khrushchev proposed to turn West Berlin into a free city—an idea the West Berliners, with their doughty Ober-Bürgermeister, Herr Willy Brandt at their head, didn't like at all. The British Medical Association withdrew a booklet called *Getting Married* under fire; some said it was 'immoral'. Jewellery, worth £150,000, the property of Lady Docker, was stolen from her Rolls-Royce.

After his Moscow visit Mr. Macmillan flew to Paris and Washington. Colonel Grivas returned to Athens in triumph. President Nasser denounced Communism (especially in Iraq). Khrushchev returned the compliment by saying hard things about Nasser. There were more riots and deaths in Nyasaland; Sir Roy Welensky's policies met strong criticism in Southern Rhodesia. The railwaymen decided to demand higher pay and the printing unions and employers reached deadlock in their negotiations. Another Communist was elected as General Secretary of the National Union of Mineworkers. Mr. Justice Devlin headed a commission of inquiry into the events in Nyasaland and the alleged massacre plot against Europeans. The Tibetans revolted against Chinese oppression; the Dalai Lama was reported to be safe. Mr. Suslov, described as the 'third most powerful man in the Soviet Union' visited London and Manchester.

In Cyprus many people were freed: Makarios was given permission to return and a temporary agreement was reached to solve this vexing and long-outstanding problem. There was trouble in Nyasaland, Kenya and Rhodesia. President Eisenhower visited Mexico. An unofficial strike at Dagenham by 300 men made 27,000 idle. Britain and Denmark agreed on a six-mile limit for fishing off the Faroes. Colonel Grivas was promoted to General and agreed to return to Greece.

In March there was an abortive revolt in Iraq against the anti-British regime; Colonel Shawaf, its leader, was captured and killed. The trouble in Africa worsened with many killed and wounded in Nyasaland.

Sir Roy Welensky: controversial policies

Fifteen thousand people marched from Aldermaston to Trafalgar Square in protest against nuclear weapons

Violence exploded in Algeria where six people were killed and sixty injured during the elections. The Dalai Lama reached India and the Chinese denied in advance that he was speaking the truth about the Tibetan tragedy. In the South African treason trial two-thirds of the accused had the indictment against them squashed. Christian Herter was confirmed as the successor to Mr. Dulles. The Mayor of Berlin visited London and the Bolshoi Ballet arrived in New York. There was an Anglo-American dispute about the right of B.O.A.C. to fly from San Francisco to Tokyo; Britain wouldn't allow the K.L.M. to fly to Singapore.

Khrushchev rejected the American proposal for a gradual reduction of nuclear tests. The radio-active fall-out by rainfall doubled within a year in Britain. Field-Marshal Montgomery arrived in Moscow and was met by Marshal Sokolovsky. The cotton industry was offered £30 million for reorganization and re-equipment.

The confused news from Tibet was of desperate and hopeless resistance to the Chinese; the Dalai Lama was on his way to India, a refugee. Tibet appealed to Nehru for help but he could or would do little, Tibet disappeared into Red China

Lord Beaverbrook, seen here with Sir Winston Churchill, celebrated his eightieth birthday

Steven Rockefeller, son of the Governor of New York, married Anne Marie Rasmussen, a maidservant in his father's house

Labour lost 322 seats in the local elections and the control of about ten councils, including St. Pancras. Britain was willing to supply arms to Iraq and West Germany. A team of British heart specialists flew to Moscow and operated successfully on a Russian child. Ronald Marwood was hanged for the murder of a policeman; the agitation for the abolition of the death penalty was given a new impetus. Progress was imperceptible at Geneva. South Africa moved to abolish the representation of Africans in her Parliament and ordered a million pounds worth of armoured cars for the police. A hundred Africans went on hunger-strike at Hola Camp, Kenya.

Late in May John Foster Dulles died, mourned by his President. The Anglo-Russian trade treaty was signed. Buganda was declared a 'disturbed area'. Alabama banned a children's book in which a black rabbit married a white one. Dr. Verwoerd forecast a white South African Republic with 'a white army and a white fleet'. Lord Beaverbrook celebrated his eightieth birthday with warm congratulations from his world-wide circle of friends. The Singapore elections were won by the Left-wing People's Action Party. An Icelandic gunboat fired at a British trawler. The last British soldiers left the Habbaniyah R.A.F. base. 'Able' and 'Baker', two female monkeys returned alive in the nose cone of a Jupiter missile from a height of 300 miles and gave a Press Conference. Liberace, the pianist, sued the *Daily Mirror* for libel and was adjudged considerable damages. The British Trade Fair opened in Lisbon.

De Gaulle declined to have American atom-bombers based on French soil. Teachers in Britain threatened to strike for a minimum salary of £600 per year. Mail from an American submarine was delivered by guided missile. Tshekedi Khama died in London. Dr.

Mr. Eisenhower, on a visit to Europe, visited the Queen in Scotland

Adenauer decided to remain Chancellor instead of running for President; this caused much distress to his would-be successors. British exports rose to a record level. Britain gave a home to the base-less U.S. bombers from France. Michael Redgrave and Stanley Spencer were knighted in the Birthday Honours. Eleven people died in Kerala, India's only Communist State, when a crowd demonstrated against the government.

Printers went on strike. Eamon De Valera was elected President of the Irish Republic. The Labour Party was torn by dissension over the hydrogen bombs. The Japanese Prime Minister visited Britain. To commemorate Bleriot's flight, the *Daily Mail* staged an Arch (Marble) to Arc (de Triomphe) air race. A series of bomb hoaxes upset the even pace of life in Harrod's and Selfridge's. Violent controversy surrounded the Gunther Podola 'affair'; this German-born blackmailer killed a young detective while resisting arrest; he was alleged to have been treated somewhat roughly by the police afterwards, and there were ugly rumours before he was brought to

Jacob Epstein: the man who carved biblical splendour in stone died and was mourned

trial, found fit to plead and sentenced to death. General Franco was finding the opposition to his régime more and more vocal—and by no means restricted to the Left-wing. The Report of the Devlin Committee on Nyasaland was, according to the Opposition, a severe indictment of the government; the government, on the other hand, was looking 'forward to the restoration of normal conditions'. The 'Black Diaries' of Roger Casement were made available to researchers in the Public Record Office. The Geneva Conference dragged on its weary way with a Summit meeting still far in the future. Mr. Carleton Greene was appointed head of the B.B.C. in succession to Sir Ian Jacob. There were increasing criticisms of the I.T.A. for breaches of the Television Act. Mr. Nixon visited Moscow and was a considerable success even though he had one or two acrimonious debates with Mr. Khrushchev—in public, too. Lord Birkett's patience and wisdom helped to bring the printing dispute to an end at last. The new Obscenity Act received the Royal Assent after five years of hard fighting to make writers' (and publishers') lives easier. An announcement from Buckingham Palace told the nation that Her Majesty was expecting her third child; the royal visit to Ghana was postponed.

The flashpoint of the Far East was Laos where Communist rebels reinforced by Vietminh 'volunteers' created trouble; the reports were completely confusing, some speaking of heavy fighting and some denying the very existence of a civil war. Preparations for an exchange of visits between President Eisenhower and Nikita Khrushchev continued. In August Jordan and the United Arab Republic made up their quarrel. There were severe riots in South Africa where the arrest of a number of women led to an explosion of pent-up feeling. Princess Alexandra toured Australia. Mr. Hugh Fraser acquired Harrods.

Chief Constable Athelstan Popkess of Nottingham became involved in a vehement dispute with the Labour Councillors of the city.

India and China discovered that a frontier dispute could spoil the most beautiful friendship; Nehru declared that India would defend Bhutan and Sikkim against all comers. The South African riots continued. The Labour and Conservative Parties published new policy statements for the autumn election. A new fuel cell, producing its own electricity, was demonstrated by its inventor, Mr. Francis Bacon, at Cambridge and promised to revolutionize transport.

Mr. Macmillan and President Eisenhower appeared together on television and Labour supporters thought that the President's warm praise of Mr. Macmillan was electioneering. As the Indian-Chinese relations worsened, Pakistan and India willy-nilly drew closer together. Krishna Menon, the chief Indian champion of co-existence, resigned. The T.U.C. was waging desultory war on the Communists in the Electrical Trades Union. The Thirteenth Edinburgh Festival opened—with the number omitted from the posters lest it dismay the superstitious.

The General Election was set for October 8. Eisenhower and De Gaulle reached agreement in Paris. U.N. sent a sub-committee to Laos in spite of Soviet objections. The Big Four announced a new disarmament committee to meet early in 1960 in Geneva. Lord Monckton was appointed chairman of a commission to report on the Rhodesian Federation. Ireland decided to start a television service with Mr. Eamonn Andrews as its chairman. Films lost two fine artists in Edmund Gwenn (who died at eighty-one) and Kay Kendall (Mrs. Rex Harrison) who died of leukemia at thirty-two.

Two days before Mr. Khrushchev and his family arrived in Washington, the Russians hit the moon—a bull's eye of propaganda, perfectly timed. He received a subdued and polite welcome. In Hollywood he was shocked at the American idea of a Can-Can.

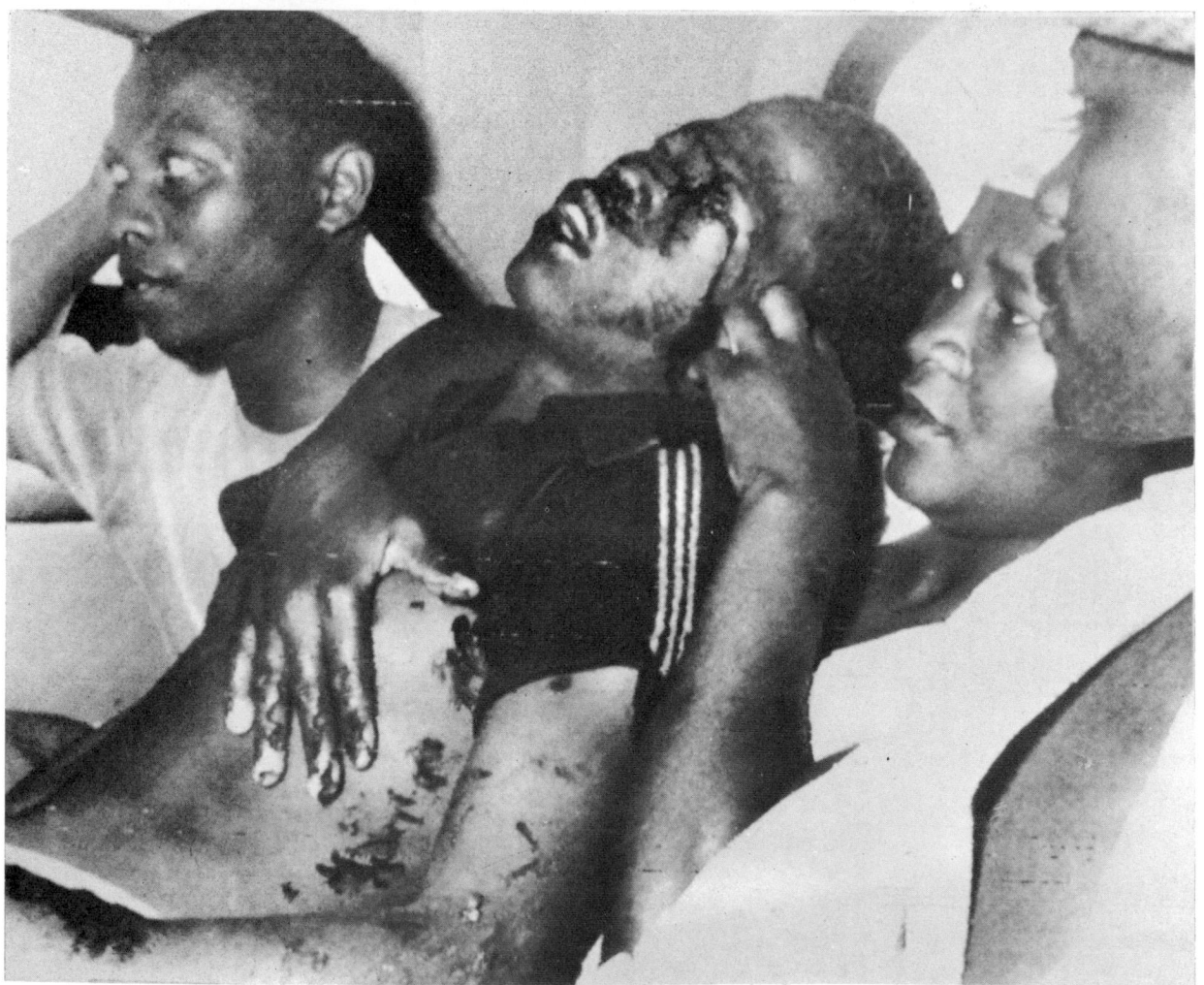

South Africa: apartheid continued with race riots and the restoration of order by the Nationalist Police

Donald Brian Hume, perhaps the most original murderer in Britain, was sentenced to life imprisonment in a Swiss court

Archbishop Makarios and General Grivas, having won their campaign for the independence of Cyprus, proceeded to fight each other. De Gaulle announced that a peaceful Algeria would be able to decide its own future. During his American tour, Khrushchev proposed a four-year programme of total disarmament and a couple of Summit meetings a year. His temper was changeable but he managed to keep it in face of some anti-Communist provocation. The British Parliament was dissolved and Mr. Herbert Morrison accepted a peerage. Public opinion polls were under fire because four newspapers were all getting their data from the same firm under different names. Rain came to London for the first time in forty days. In Baghdad seventeen people were executed for taking part in the revolt against the Kassem régime. James Swinburn, the Englishman whom Nasser had put into prison for 'espionage', was released; but his fellow-prisoner, James Zarb, remained in jail.

The London Stock Exchange suspended dealings in the shares of fifteen companies controlled by Mr. O. Jasper, one of the take-over tycoons. Two English schoolboys, aged twelve and eight, climbed the 12,000 feet high Wetterhorn.
Early in October Eisenhower and Khrushchev agreed on an early Summit meeting; both praised each other though in different terms and for different reasons. From Washington Khrushchev went on to Peking; the

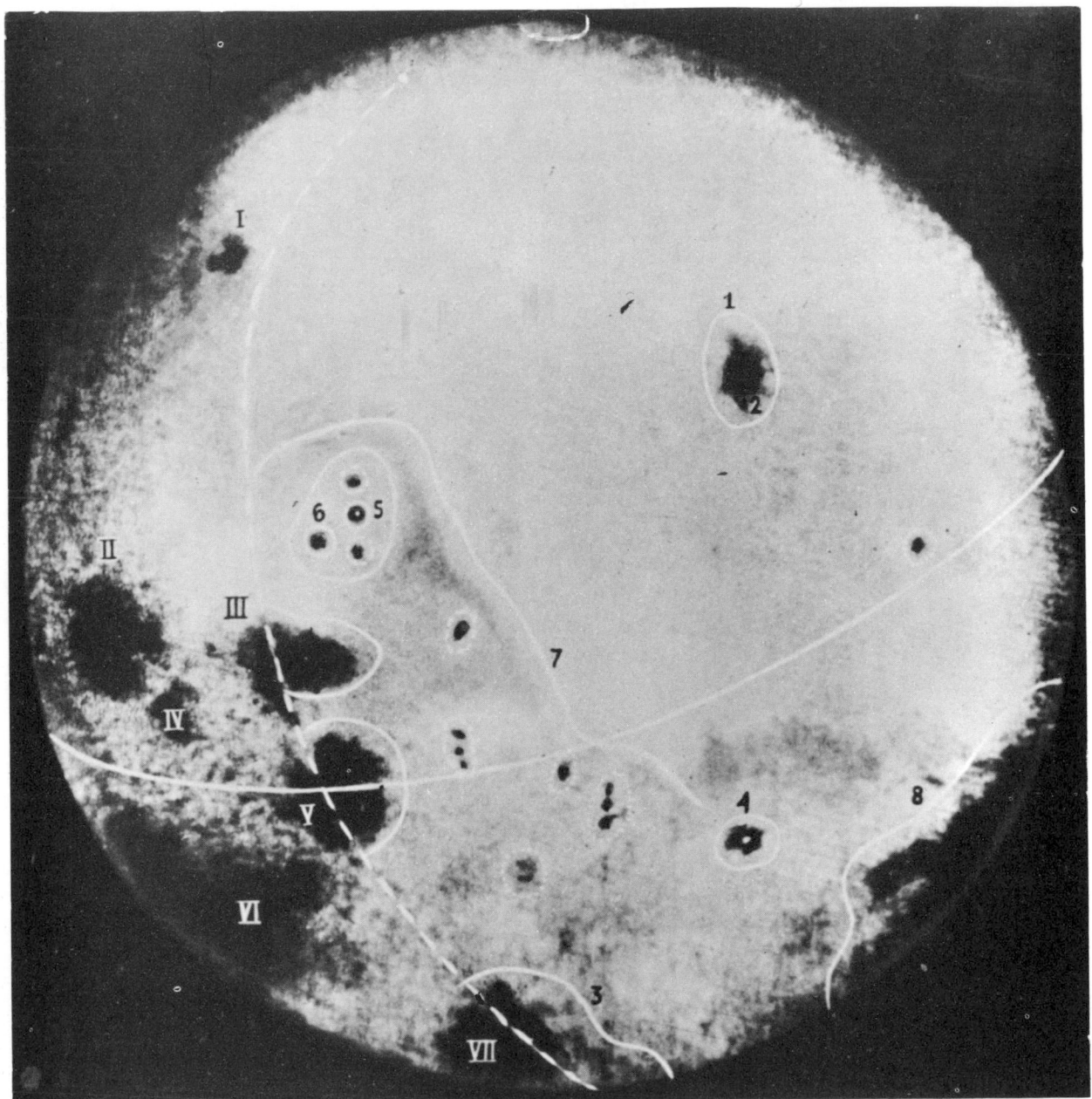

A Soviet rocket brought back pictures of the reverse side of the Moon, which turned out to be remarkably like the light side

Chinese were in a far less peaceable mood, a foreshadowing perhaps, of further historic crises in history. There was to be an inquiry into the affairs of H. Jasper & Co. Oxygen workers went on an unofficial strike. The Algerian rebels reacted coolly to De Gaulle's proposals. A million people lost their homes in Japan as a typhoon swept the country—the worst in history. Princess Alexandra visited Thailand.

The General Election brought back the Conservatives with a much increased majority, which proved that people believed the slogan: *You never had it so good.* The Liberal vote increased considerably but not the number of Liberal seats. America was rocked by the TV quiz scandals; it turned out that even geniuses like Mr. Charles Van Doren needed prompting in naming the U.S. Secretary of Treasury in 1878. Lord Hailsham became Minister of Science. Mr. Macleod Colonial Secretary; Sir David Eccles took over the Board of Education. Restrictions on foreign travel were abolished. The Labour Party began a long and painful inquest over the causes of its defeat. Fares went up and the Motor Show made London traffic a snare and a snarl. A Right-wing plot was discovered in France. Africans demonstrated in Nairobi against the restrictions under which Jomo Kenyatta was still living. An American diplomat was expelled from Moscow for alleged espionage. The rights of Tibet were debated by the United Nations but the Chinese had no intention of relaxing their grip. Churchill College, Cambridge, was inaugurated by Sir Winston himself, an advance in British scientific education.

London-Birmingham Motorway: cracks on the new highway

The new London-Birmingham motor-way was opened and, soon afterwards closed, when the surface cracked in several stretches. The new Betting Bill was published, proposing betting shops and legal gambling parties. The King of Laos died.

There was still more violence in South Africa; a white couple who adopted a coloured baby were expelled from the Union. The U.N. General Assembly condemned apartheid by sixty-seven votes to three. Belgium, too weak to cope with Congo unrest, promised constitutional reforms. Mr. Philip Noel-Baker won the Nobel Peace Prize. The Duke of Norfolk decided to move out of Arundel Castle as the upkeep was too high. A Dutch beauty

In Fréjus: 300 were drowned when a dam burst

Sahara: from beneath the sand Frenchmen drew oil

was elected Miss World. Salvatore Quasimodo, a Left-wing Italian poet won the Nobel Prize for literature. In November Dr. Adenauer visited London to bring about an Anglo-German *entente*—realistic if not necessarily *cordiale*. Prince Philip visited Ghana. The Algerian Provisional Government offered to negotiate with the French; the delegates they appointed were all in a French jail. The Outer Seven came into being and suggested collaboration with the European Common Market. America and Russia signed an agreement on cultural exchanges; two dozen books were withdrawn from a British exhibition in Moscow because Soviet officials objected to them. Lord Montgomery spoke up for apartheid and the Archbishop of Canterbury against adultery. The Shah of Persia found a new bride. The Labour Party Conference at Blackpool was less gloomy than was expected.
Signor Segni, the Italian Prime Minister, came to Britain; Dr. Adenauer visited Paris. Mr. Marples introduced a 'Pink Zone' in London, where no parking was permitted. Diplomatic relations were restored between Britain and Egypt. The Egyptians, showing little tact, announced that the house in which Lieutenant Moorhouse, an officer kidnapped at the time of the Suez landings, was killed, would be turned into a museum. President Eisenhower visited Italy, Greece, Turkey, Pakistan, Afghanistan and several other countries, showing remarkable stamina. Oil began to flow from the Saharan wells to the North African sea-shore. There was a terrible dam burst at Fréjus in the South of France in which over three hundred people were drowned. The NATO Council met, with Mr. Macmillan, President Eisenhower and Dr. Adenauer gathering in Paris. Archbishop Makarios was proclaimed President-Elect of Cyprus but there was still much argument about the size of the British bases on the island. Lord Harewood was appointed Artistic Director of the Edinburgh Festival. BEA and BOAC pilots began to negotiate for higher rates of pay to bring their status into line with other employees.

'Room at the Top': *Laurence Harvey in Britain's Oscar winning film, based on John Braine's novel*

Mr. Khrushchev was invited to a Summit meeting in April. The Geneva talks on nuclear weapons were again adjourned. Madagascar and Dahomey asked France for independence. King Baudouin visited the Congo; some of his subjects had to be dispersed by tear-gas as they expressed their wish not to be his subjects any longer. Parliament adjourned. There were violent protests against a proposed tall building in Piccadilly with a large crane on top and advertisements covering the front.

Dr. Barbara Moore, walking from Land's End to John o' Groats, proved that one should never underestimate a woman.

There was an unusually rich feast for cinemagoers in 1959. Unusual, experimental films like *The Savage Eye*, *Anna Lucasta*, *A Matter of Dignity* (from Greece), *Eve Wants to Sleep* and *Ashes and Diamonds* (from Poland),

276

'*The Mouse That Roared*': the protean Peter Sellers with Jean Serberg, in an Anglo-American H-bomb satire

Les Cousins and Jacques Tati's delightful *Mon Oncle* (from France) or Dr. Paul Czinner's ballet-film, *The Sleeping Beauty*: comedies like the vastly entertaining *I'm All Right, Jack, The Captain's Table*, *Upstairs and Downstairs, Too Many Crooks, Carlton-Browne of the F.O., Left, Right and Centre, The Mouse that Roared* and *The Tunnel of Love*; thrillers like Hitchcock's taut *North by Northwest*, the remake of *The 39 Steps, Compulsion, Sapphire*, which was several cuts above the usual murder story; big 'spectaculars' like the fabulous *Ben Hur* (third version), *Solomon and Sheba*; musicals like the delightful *Gigi*, the British *Expresso Bongo* (frank and rowdy), *The Five Pennies*, Britain could be proud of *Room at the Top, The Horse's Mouth, Libel, No Trees in the Street, The Doctor's Dilemma, Look Back in Anger*, and *Blind Date*. Hollywood proved its continuing vigour by *The Roots of Heaven, Separate Tables, The Journey, Anatomy of a Murder, The Diary of Anna Frank* and *The Nun's Story*. Certainly there was at least one film each week worth looking at.

'*Expresso Bongo*': *Wolf Mankowitz's rowdily, ironic tragi-comical musical, set in London's Soho, was a film of the year*

After many years in the U.S., Charles Laughton returned to England and at Stratford played 'Lear'.

Christmas spending was fabulous and a decade ended with the world uneasy but still undestroyed and just as bewildered as Sam the Space Monkey.

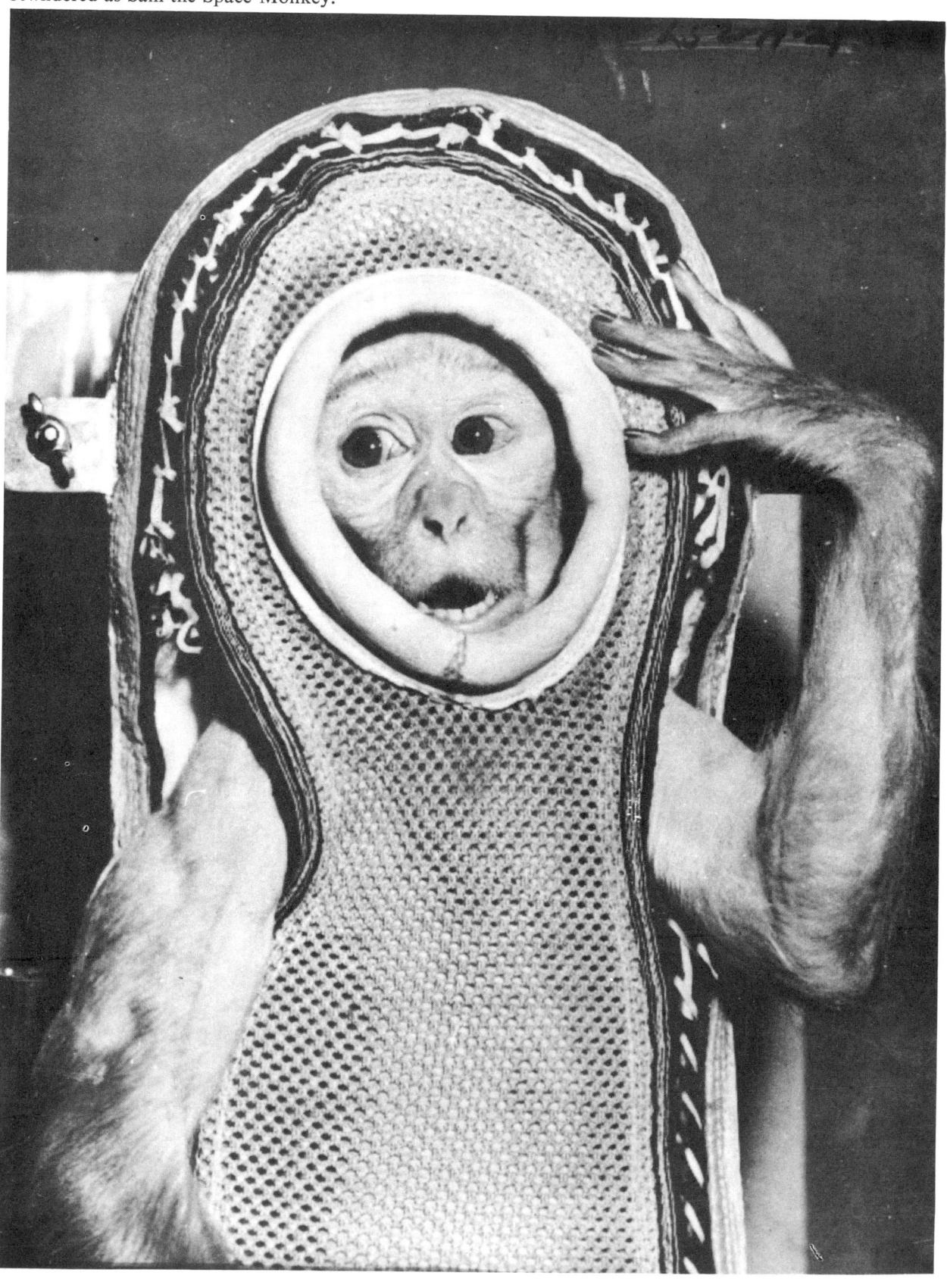

Randolph Churchill wrote the controversial 'The Rise and Fall of Sir Anthony Eden'

They said in 1959

We are very concerned with peace. We will even support the Pope if he is for peace.

FROL KOZLOV, FIRST DEPUTY PREMIER, U.S.S.R.

I do not have the power or the authority to change the shape of the world.

NEHRU

I get a little weary of talking about presidential prestige. I am thinking of the human race.

PRESIDENT EISENHOWER

We are not the kind of people we have been pictured. We do not gobble up babies.

KHRUSHCHEV

It is no good for man to seek escape in luniks and rocketry and to leave his soul morally earthbound among the television sets and expresso bars.

PRINCESS MARGARET

John Braine's long-awaited second novel, 'The Vodi', divided the critics

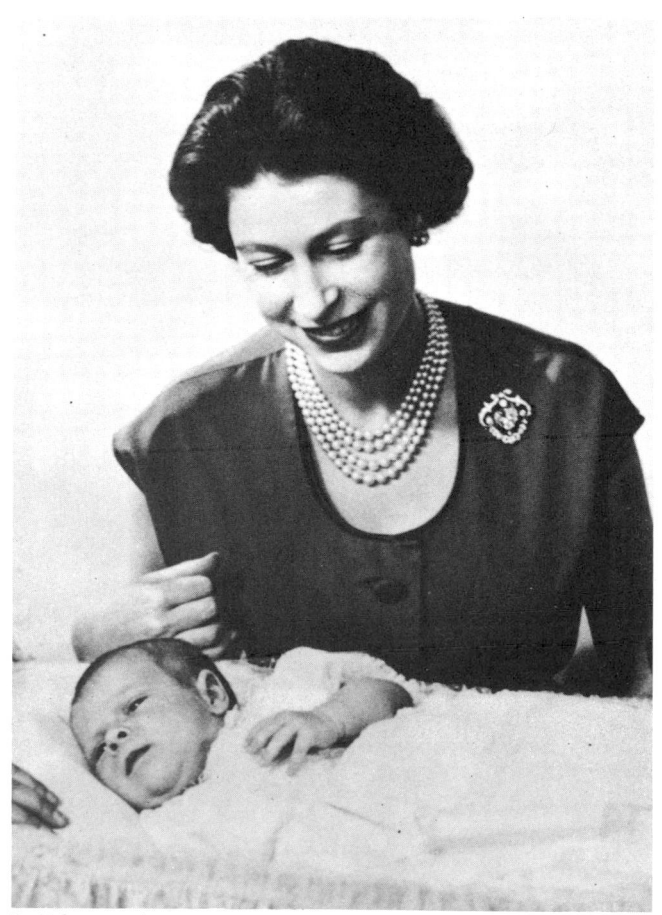

In May, Princess Margaret was married to Mr. Armstrong-Jones in Westminster Abbey

In February the Queen gave birth to a son, Prince Andrew

As the literally fearful fifties faded away, Mr. Macmillan left on an African tour, a continent that was producing a new trouble-spot almost every week. In Europe anti-Semitism was bent on proving that it was far from being dead by daubing swastikas and anti-Jewish slogans on the walls of a dozen cities. The French cut two noughts off their francs which thereby became New. Albert Camus, the Nobel Prize-winning great conscience of non-conformist literature was killed in a car-crash. Three leading British aircraft companies merged; the British banks announced a 22 per cent average profit and three company directors were arrested for fraud.

Talks on Cyprus began in London with independence only five weeks away. Mr. Macmillan visited Ghana, Nigeria and Rhodesia. Khrushchev announced a one-third cut in the conventional forces of the U.S.S.R., and agreed to give another £400 million to Egypt to finish the Aswan High Dam. In Algeria paratroops and French colonists rebelled against De Gaulle but the revolt collapsed quickly, mainly through the President's patient, masterly inactivity. Mr. Macmillan spoke out against apartheid in South Africa and the European police lost their heads during his visit to Blantyre, breaking a good many black ones.

In April President De Gaulle of France came to England on a State visit, was welcomed by the Queen and the London people, and spoke to members of both Houses of Parliament in Westminster Hall praising the public spirit of the British

A Russian scientist suggested that space-ships must have landed on earth thousands of years ago. Prince Andrew the third royal baby, was born in February. The French exploded their first atom bomb; the Ghana government froze all French assets. Mr. Macmillan returned from Africa and agreement was reached on the future of Kenya with some dissentient voices from the white settlers' side. Thousands of dockers went on strike and the Electrical Trades Union insisted on its right to run elections in its own special way. The West German Government asked for military bases in Spain but nobody else thought this a good idea.

Princess Margaret became engaged to Mr. Antony Armstrong-Jones, a brilliant society photographer who had never figured among the nominees of the gossip columnists. The Princess became a May bride. The internecine war in the Labour Party became even more vocal.

The Prime Minister was elected Chancellor of Oxford University. Certain oil-heaters were declared to be dangerous. A ten-nation disarmament conference opened in Geneva, prepared to go on for a year or longer. The leading British banks offered £1,000 reward to anybody helping to foil a bank-raid; the next day four men got away with nineteen times the reward in a hold-up. In South Africa demonstrators were mowed down at Vereeniging where they gathered to protest against the pass-laws. In the Harrow and Brighouse by-elections, the Conservatives held the first seat and gained the second from Labour.

The sky darkened in Africa, from the Cape to the Congo. Mr. Macmillan flew to Washington to discuss the suspension of minor nuclear tests. Mr. Khrushchev had an enjoyable time in France—where his security was ensured by giving hundreds of anti-Communists an enforced holiday on Corsica.

The Budget increased the tax on profits and closed a few loop-holes for evaders; cigarettes became dearer and champagne and beer cheaper. Apartheid was discussed in the United Nations where France and Britain abstained in the Security Council voting which went against South Africa.

Mr. Khruschev made threatening noises about Berlin. De Gaulle had a triumphal tour of New York and Washington; the Channel Tunnel scheme was revived but many Britishers did not like to be linked *that* close to France.

Caryl Chessman was executed after twelve years legal wrangling in San Quentin Prison. Riots started in Istanbul. Lord Morrison of Lambeth became President of the Board of Film Censors. Early in May the U-2

After twelve years legal wrangling Caryl Chessman was executed in San Quentin Prison, California, a cause of international controversy until the end.

In the Argentine, Israeli security agents kidnapped Alfred Eichmann, Gestapo chief responsible for the murder of six million Jews, and brought him to Israel for trial

incident began when Soviet anti-aircraft units shot down an American 'spy-plane'. The pilot, Lieut. Powers, survived and was arrested. The incident revealed the wide organization of such flights and led to the wrecking of the Paris Summit meeting where Mr. Khrushchev demanded an apology from Mr. Eisenhower and failed to get one. Powers was later tried and sentenced to ten years imprisonment.

Menderes and his government were overthrown by the joint action of students and the army in Turkey. *Triton*, the American nuclear submarine travelled 41,000 miles underwater around the world.

President Eisenhower was abused with equal heat by Mr. Khrushchev and anti-American Japanese; his firmly-scheduled visit to Tokyo was finally cancelled. Katanga, a rich province of the Belgian Congo announced its decision to secede from the not-yet-born Congo Republic. Mr. Lumumba, a former post-office clerk, was asked to form the first independent Congo government; his defeated rival, Kasavubu, was offered the Presidency.

The Congo became independent and started on its long agony; tribal jealousies, transposed to international scale, brought arrests, murders, indignities and chaos in which whites and blacks suffered equally and in which U.N. faced the hardest test since the Korean War.

Mr. Aneurin Bevan, for so long the stormy petrel of British politics, beloved and execrated in almost equal measure died; a great man who missed the solid achievements of greatness. Britain and Cyprus agreed on the size of the British base in the island. The relations of Cuba and the United States deteriorated rapidly. The House of Lords came out against chimes on ice-cream barrows. Mr. Macmillan came out for Lord Hume as Foreign Secretary; Mr. Heathcoat Amory and Mr. Lennox-Boyd became peers and Mr. Selwyn Lloyd Chancellor of the Exchequer. The Congo bloodshed inspired riots and reprisals in Kenya and Southern Rhodesia.

Over seventy people were killed on the roads at the August Bank holidays—and five new roads were to be built for more people to be killed on. There was a mysterious *coup d'état* in Laos and an invasion by Communists which was not quite a figment of somebody's imagination. The first radio satellite was launched by the United States; an American pilot reached the greatest height, 131,000 feet, ever reached in a plane; another

Patrice Lumumba, a former post-office clerk, was asked to form the first independent Congo government: his defeated rival, Kasavubu, was offered the Presidency

Mgr. Laurian Rugambwa was made the first African cardinal of the Roman Catholic Church. Here Cardinal Rugambwa takes possession of his titular church in Rome

parachuted sixteen miles from a balloon. Two Russian dogs and an assortment of mice and flies returned alive from a flight in outer space. *Lady Chatterley's Lover* was hauled into court and acquitted with the enthusiastic support of writers and clergymen while others were less enthusiastic.

A bomb, intended for King Hussein, killed the Jordan Premier and a number of his officials. The last Belgian troops left the Congo and the United Nation troops had the impossible task of keeping the peace—especially as some of the governments that had sent them were more interested in making political capital of tribal war. Mr. Khrushchev announced that he would lead the Russian delegation to the U.N. General Assembly and bring quite a party with him—including Messrs. Gomulka and Kadar. The Americans decided to confine him to Manhattan; but he managed to give several Press conferences from a balcony. This was considerably less devastating than the effect of a hurricane called Donna which hit New York. Fidel Castro also attended the General Assemply; and his retinue caused the manager of their hotel to develop bleeding ulcers. Thirteen new African States were admitted but no one could decide who should represent the Congo which had by now three heads of government. Dr. Hammarskjöld was given a unanimous vote of confidence. King Baudouin of Belgium became engaged to a charming Spanish girl who wrote fairy-tales.

Sir Roy Welensky made a strong stand against the British Government's plans on the future of the Rhodesian Federation. Floods in the West of England cut off Cornwall from the rest of the country. Nigeria became independent. General De Gaulle was making overtures to the Algerian rebels. Asanuma, the leader of the Japanese Socialist Party was stabbed to death in front of a large audience. Two liberal newspapers, the *News Chronicle* and *The Star* died, being swallowed by Associated Newspapers. The arguments within the Labour Party became more virulent with Mr. Anthony Greenwood's resignation from the Shadow Cabinet.

Loch Hell was offered to the Americans as an anchorage for nuclear submarines. Mr. Randolph Churchill won a slander case. Fidel Castro mobilized his militia against 1400 American Marines; but as they were only on shore leave, he had no chance to fight.

In New York, in September–October, Mr. Khrushchev, in and out of the U.N. General Assembly, proclaimed the superiority of the Communist system. Inset: Boris Pasternak, Russian Nobel Prize winner, author of 'Dr. Zhivago', died in May

Mr. Kennedy was elected American President in one of the closest contests for many years; eight years of Republican ascendancy ended and America had the prettiest First Lady in any man's memory.

Ford's (America) decided to take over Ford's (Britain). President Diem foiled another sort of take-over bid in South Vietnam. Michael Foot was elected M.P. for Ebbw Vale as a successor of Aneurin Bevan. Peking and Moscow started to argue publicly whether war between Communism and Capitalism was inevitable or not. The Archbishop of Canterbury visited the Pope.

In November, Mr. John F. Kennedy was elected President of the U.S.A. He spoke of 'new frontiers' and promised an adventurous policy. Inset: *Lt. Powers, the American U-2 pilot, sentenced in Moscow for aerial espionage*

Instead of snow, rain and floods came to herald Christmas. The conference on the future of the Central African Federation started with little promise of agreement. De Gaulle visited Algeria where he found himself less popular than he expected. Mr. Dean Rusk, the new American Secretary of State was given Mr. Chester Bowles as his Under-Secretary. Adlai Stevenson became the new U.S. Ambassador to U.N.O. A revolt against Haile Selassie collapsed in Ethiopia. As the year ended, our comfort was that we had weathered many storms and still had hope of survival and faith in progress which, next year, led to a unique frontier.

On April 12, 1961, Major Yuri Alexeyvich Gagarin (*above*) was launched into outer space in a four-and-half ton Soviet space ship that orbited the earth once and safely landed 108 minutes later. The voyager, hailed as 'the Columbus of Space', had opened awe-inspiring vistas to politically-divided mankind.
On May 5, Cdr. Alan Shepard was the first American to enter space.